CRISSCROSSING THE GLOBE FOR FREE

Memoirs of a Charter Flight Attendant

Cynthia Swensen McAlister

CRISSCROSSING THE GLOBE FOR FREE:
Memoirs of a Charter Flight Attendant

All Rights Reserved ©2002 by Cynthia Swensen McAlister

No part of this book may be reproduced, stored in a retrieval system, or transmitted by any means, electronic, mechanical, photocopying, recording, or otherwise, without written permission from the author.

For information contact:
McAlister, Inc.
926 East Fremont Ave.
Sunnyvale, CA 94087
planeanxiety@aol.com

ISBN:
0-9727534-0-0
0-9727534-1-9

Printed in the United States of America

CONTENTS

	Dedications	vii
	Foreword	ix
CHAPTER 1	THE JOURNEY BEGINS	
	The Interview	2
	Training	4
	Onward And Upward	10
	Does Anyone Know Where We're Going?	15
CHAPTER 2	MY ROOKIE YEAR 1972-1973	
	I've Never Heard Of You Either	18
	The Feared Telex	21
	Horrendous Trips	28
	Keep On Trucking	31
	Stowaways	33
	Stoke-on-Trent	39
CHAPTER 3	LAYOVERS AND MORE	
	Santa Claus Is Flying On TIA	45
	Where Did Everyone Go?	51
	Italy and England	54
	A Senior Flight Attendant Or Not	58
	X Marks The Spot	63
CHAPTER 4	HONG KONG OR KOWLOON?	
	Shop Until You Drop	68
	The New Territories	78
	The Passengers Are Here	83
	Home Sweet Home	87
	Wedding Plans June 1975	91
CHAPTER 5	VIETNAM, WAR ZONES & AIRLIFTS	
	Drifting Over Yugoslavia 1974	96
	Cyprus Invasion July 1974	99

	Vietnam	100
	Tan Son Nhut in April 1975	105
	Angola Airlift 1975-76	110
	Iranian Revolution 1978	111
	Vietnamese Refugee Flights	112
	Cuban Airlift 1980	122
CHAPTER 6	THE PHILIPPINES	
	Military Flights	126
	The Maharaja & Oasis	129
	The Harvest In Cavite	140
	Mad Marcos In Baguio	144
	Muslim Gold In Olongapo	145
	Manila Bay	148
CHAPTER 7	DC-10'S, JAPAN AND STRIKES	
	McDonnell Douglas DC-10's	152
	Situations In Flight	157
	Japanese Adventures	162
	Trans International Strikes	168
	The Black Bird	175
CHAPTER 8	ALHAJJ AND SAUDI ARABIA	
	Nigerian Pilgrims	182
	Jeddah, The Twilight Zone	196
	Hello Muddeh, Hello Fadduh	198
	Ouagadougou and More	201
	Aramco Charters to Dhahran	204
CHAPTER 9	KOREA, 747's, AND WHERE IS DIEGO GARCIA?	
	The Iditarod	214
	Seoul, Korea	217
	Panmunjom, DMZ	225
	Diego Garcia	230

CHAPTER 10	SOUTH AFRICA	
	Are We There Yet?	236
	Kruger Park	240
	Being Black In South Africa	244
	For Whites Only	247
CHAPTER 11	HEY! HOW COME THEY GET STEAK WHEN ALL WE GET IS CHICKEN?	
	Snippets	254
	Where Did The Glamour Go?	263
	The Boeing 747 Aircraft	268
	Mule Milk Cousins	271
	Ding, Ding, Ding	278
	Just Give It To Me	287
	Why Didn't You Tell Us?	298
	Delays and Dilemmas	301
CHAPTER 12	SOUTH AMERICA: FROM HERE TO MATERNITY	
	The Road Less Traveled	306
	Who Would Guess?	311
	The Galapagos On Tame Airlines	313
	The Local Chamas Indians	320
	Zig Zaging To Machu Picchu	324
CHAPTER 13	YOU NAME IT; I'VE BEEN THERE	
	Fijian Idiosyncrasies	331
	Seven Days In Tahiti	336
	Kuala Lumpur, Malaysia	343
	U.S.A. Adventures	346
	The End Of An Era	359

*This book is dedicated to my husband
Bill McAlister, and our children
Teri Cherie, and William Robert
for their love and support.*

*Also to those who are the backbone of the airline industry,
and ambassadors to the world;*

*And to those who mix with all cultures, nationalities, and
religions, and keep the lines of communication open.*

FOREWORD

It was the seventies. People bought pet rocks in little paper cages with "how to care for" instructions and round canary yellow happy faces. Bell-bottom pants and mini skirts worn with see through blouses, with and without bras, were popular. Some uninhibited individuals stripped off their clothes and dashed through public events and airplanes full of passengers. We discoed to John Travolta's Stayin' Alive and Bring the Boy's Home, by Freda Payne played on the radio.

In 1972, the number of hijacking attempts of United States aircraft grew to thirty-one. President Nixon issued an emergency order in December 1972 that required the nation's airlines to inspect all carry-on luggage and electronically search all passengers for weapons, along with positioning of an armed officer at each boarding gate.

Also, in December 1972, the International Air Transport Association announced airlines would be able to set their own rates on transatlantic routes beginning in February 1973 which began the airline deregulation process.

To further complicate the situation, the federal government mandatory fuel allocation program went into effect in November 1973. Airlines were to reduce their fuel consumption ten to fifteen percent within seventy days. Flights were cancelled to meet this goal. The uncertainty of the energy crisis, fuel shortage reductions, and the airline fare wars made it difficult for airlines to survive.

This was a time when twenty-one year old women were called girls. A time when females were taught to smile, look pretty and accept the world of discrimination and sexual harassment. I was a young adult who wanted to increase my horizons and travel. Ultimately, I found that if I worked as a stewardess for an airline this goal would be attained. I'd made the decision to live in California, where my boyfriend was living. He later became my husband and joined me on numerous occasions at various locations around the world. This was a possibility since he worked for his father who considered world travel a worthwhile diversion.

I had called various commercial airlines and none of them said new hires would be based in San Francisco, Oakland, or San Jose. These bases were popular and only stewardesses who'd been with the airlines for years were awarded them. The only other option would be to fly for one of the charter airlines. My first choice was Universal Airlines, for no other reason than they were hiring. Braniff Airlines handled Universal's training. Their headquarters was Dallas, Texas. I was hired in 1972 and flew to Dallas for training.

On the last day of training, just after graduation, the nineteen trainees were led into a conference room to hear an announcement. Apparently, Universal was having financial difficulty. We the joyful graduates of an hour before were told the airline was going bankrupt. I flew home to Los Altos, California that afternoon disappointed and unemployed.

Two weeks later, I received a letter asking if I would like to join the Trans International team (TIA). They had gotten my name from Universal. The letter read, "CHARTER IS SMARTER." I decided to 'try it again,' and was hired.

Not one of my trips with TIA in the following fourteen years I was employed was without incident. I suppose I must have been a little crazy flying into areas that were in political turmoil, underdeveloped third world countries, transporting refugees, religious groups, and others who were unfamiliar with air travel. What else could possibly happen did occasionally cross my mind. Maybe air travel was safer than driving a car, but what were the odds if you put in over sixty-five flight hours a month for fourteen years? I didn't particularly want to be in some situations, but my desire for adventure was greater than my apprehensions. At this time, the question of my mortality wasn't of major concern to me and it wouldn't be until I became pregnant with my first child. Although I felt concern in some situations, I thought I was invincible.

Crisscrossing the Globe For Free: Memoirs of a Charter Flight Attendant, details the exploits of a Trans International charter flight attendant from 1972 to 1986. A number of flights were routine, but most were out of the ordinary. Like the time my hut mates and I served dinner to our guards Neishi and Kumba in a grass hut in Kano, Nigeria.

I might mention to family and friends that I had just returned home after taking two hundred and twenty-four eighteen-year-old military men, into Tan Son Nhut Airport in Saigon or that the crew needed rations to survive in Africa on a twenty-four day stay while transporting pilgrims to Jeddah. It sounded peculiar even to me.

Who would guess that a South American army tank would follow us to our hotel in Lima since we were out after curfew due to a flat tire or that while flying over Slavic airspace we'd be circled by military jets and ordered to land. How bizarre.

I might mention that TIA was contracted to transport refugees from Cuba, Angola, Saigon, and other places and I was scheduled to work those trips. These were complex situations where the history of the country and the political background needed to be addressed along with the in-flight experience to explain the situation adequately.

We, the Trans International flight attendants, were young Americans. We expected to be treated with respect while traveling abroad. After all, we lived in a country where we had freedoms, privacy rights, the right to free speech, the right to gather, the right to worship and the right to know the charges against us if arrested. Outside the cocoon of the United States of America, life was different.

I kept a journal of my fourteen years with TIA, who changed their name to Transamerica Airlines until they went bankrupt in 1986. To avoid confusion, and since Transamerica Airlines and Trans International were both owned by Transamerica Corporation I use the name Trans International (TIA) throughout my book, *Crisscrossing The Globe For Free: Memoirs Of A Charter Flight Attendant.*

CHAPTER 1

THE JOURNEY BEGINS

1
THE INTERVIEW

My journey began in June of 1972 when I entered the Trans International business office in Oakland, California. A woman brown from the sun and about twenty years older than myself motioned me to sit before a large oak desk by the front window.

"Good morning, my name is Kathy. I'll be doing your interview. Why do you want to be a Trans International stewardess?"

"I heard that Trans International is a financially stable airline that flies all over the world and their one base is in Oakland, California," I replied. "Also, my love of travel and adventure might be genetic. My father was a Naval Officer and both my grandfathers were military. Grandfather Lyman Knute Swenson was a graduate of the Naval Academy and the captain of the Juneau during World War II. My maternal grandfather at West Point was in Eisenhower's class. He was selected for the first Foreign Service class and later stationed in Toronto, Alexandria and Casablanca." I was pulling out all the stops. She didn't react to my flood of information.

"What do you do in your spare time?"

"I enjoy reading and skiing."

"Do you live with your parents?" she asked.

"Yes."

"Do you have a boyfriend?"

"Yes."

Being married was a big no-no in 1972. Prospective stewardesses no longer were required to take an oath in which they would not marry nor have children as they did before WWII but being married was still not accepted.

"What other languages do you speak?"

"French," I replied.

"It says here you are five feet two inches tall. Did you know you're supposed to be at least five feet three inches? Well, stand on your tip toes when they measure you," she said. "You'll have one more interview. Make sure you are confident about your second language. The next language test is Friday. Please go through that door on your left and wait with the others."

An hour later, the receptionist called my name. My second interviewer wore a white suit with a hot pink blouse. Her short curly hair was pushed back on the right side and held with a tortoise shell clip.

"Would you mind being away for two or three weeks at a time?" she asked.

"No."

"Does it bother you to stay up all night?"

"No."

"Can you be back here on Monday at eight o'clock to begin training?"

"Yes."

"Step over here so I can measure you." I did as suggested and stood on my tiptoes to reach the required 5'3" red line on the tape measure.

She wrote something down, handed me some papers, and told me to return on Monday, for the first day of training. I wouldn't be required to take the language test on Friday unless I wanted to start in a later class. I was relieved since my French language skills were marginal. I'd only taken two years of French at Los Altos High School.

I was instructed to be at training at nine o'clock and not one minute later or else I'd have to stay after class for one hour. I was not to wear pants to class, my hair had to be done in an attractive manner and failure on two examinations meant dismissal.

I had gone through Universal's training program only weeks ago and passed, so I wasn't worried about passing Trans International's. Been there done that, I thought.

2
TRAINING

Nine o'clock Monday, thirty-six trainees gathered in a classroom two blocks from the Oakland Airport, for the first day of training.

When I entered the room Bobbie, our instructor, handed me a powder blue instruction manual. A cartoon drawing of a woman wearing a mini skirt and three inch high heals festooned it's cover. The cartoon stewardess sat on a suitcase plastered with location stickers. She held in her hand an extra long cigarette holder with a lit cigarette on the end; and above her head was the word Stewardess, in capital letters.

Bobbie gave the class a preview about what she'd be discussing during the next three weeks: crashes of other airlines and the reasons they happened according to the Federal Aviation Administration (FAA) reports. How to perform Cardiac Pulmonary resuscitation (CPR), what commands to yell after an emergency landing, and where the emergency equipment was.

"We will inflate an example of one of the DC-8 rafts in the water at a local hotel. Firefighters will demonstrate how to put out fires with the equipment on Trans International Airlines aircraft. Trainees will also be required to pull slide inflation handles on the fuselage next to the doors then slide down the slide. Your first lecture will be on aerodynamics and you'll be tested on aerodynamics first thing tomorrow morning," the instructor said.

The lecture on aerodynamics lasted four hours. I took notes on the basics and thought the rest of the information was just information that the instructor thought we might be interested in, but didn't really need to know.

The next morning, Bobbie handed out the test on aerodynamics. I put my name on top of the test and started reading the questions. I had no idea what the answer was for the first question so guessed and put a small pencil mark by it. This was a timed test and I hoped I'd have enough time to return to that question. Everything the instructor had discussed yesterday was on this test. Damn, I started thinking I might fail.

After I finished question twenty, I counted the pencil marks I'd put by the answers I didn't feel confident about. I already had five pencil marks. There were forty questions. I knew that I had to get at least an 85% to pass. I finished, but now I counted ten pencil marks by questions I wasn't sure of. All but three trainees had turned in their tests. I started going over those questions. The other two turned in their tests so now everyone was waiting for me to finish. I brought my test forward and Bobbie put it on top of the stack.

I failed the first test even though I'd gotten 84% correct. This experience shook my confidence. I knew that if I failed one more test I'd no longer be in this class. Each night I studied. This class was nothing like the training for Universal Airlines. Universal had told the trainees what the questions were on the few tests given.

The second lecture and test was on company policy and specific rules and regulations. The third test was on first aid. The fourth test was on emergency procedures. Each plane was different and each door could be different, so the stewardesses needed to be trained and proficient at each door. The instructor sat us in a mock up of an aircraft then told us what plane we were in and at what door. She might add something like a fire situation to the list and then say, "go." The trainee strapped into the jump seat by the door would yell her commands, open the door, inflate the slide, and yell "Come this way," or "Go that way" if there was an obstruction.

The next test was on emergency equipment, where it was located, and how to get it down and use it. Trans International Airlines carried CO_2 (carbon dioxide) extinguishers, H_2O (water) extinguishers, first aid kits, an ax, O_2 (oxygen) bottles, megaphones, and radios. Before every flight, these items were checked by one of the stewardesses. I was trained on the 727 and DC-8 stretch aircrafts. Three stewardesses were on the 727 and six or seven on the DC-8 stretch. The first 727's were built in 1964. This three engine jet aircraft had low speed landing and takeoff performance, which made it ideal for landing at small airports with short runways. The DC-8 stretch was a four engine aircraft and was ideal for long flights.

We learned The FAA (Federal Aviation Administration) had a book of regulations that they called FARs (Federal Aviation Regulations). These included rules concerning hand-carried luggage, refusal of transportation, carrying prisoners, and weapons, locking the cockpit door, amount of emergency equipment necessary and required number of stewardesses on board before the aircraft could takeoff. Trans International required stewardesses to go through a three-day recurrent training program once a year and complete a home study package before attending or risk two weeks suspension. The military airlift command (MAC) also had a set of rules and regulations.

When the stewardesses first boarded the aircraft; they performed their specific preflight duties. Some of the duties were stocking the bathrooms, leaning over and specifically touching each and every life vest under every seat, visually checking the emergency equipment and inspecting the galleys to make certain there were enough meals and supplies to feed our passengers. There were usually 254 passengers on the DC-8 stretch aircraft, three seats on the left side of the aircraft and three seats on the right, all one cabin with no dividers.

Trans International, a charter, flew full. A company or individual bought all the seats on the aircraft. Each stewardess had a specific place she had to stand during boarding according to her number. After boarding, we had a specific area to do the pre-flight briefing and we had a specific place to sit on takeoff according to our number. After takeoff, we had specific duties to perform according to that number also.

The senior stewardess in charge gave the other stewardesses a pre-flight briefing (review of emergency procedures). She chose what to discuss. She might choose ditching (landing on water) out of the window exits on the DC-8. This briefing would be done as if it were an emergency, but we wouldn't get the rafts down, or open the windows; we would talk it through. The stewardess responsible for briefing the over wing exits on the DC-8 in a ditching would be number six. She would do the explaining for that briefing. We were taught to choose three able-bodied persons for each exit.

"Quite often" the instructor said, "stewardesses will be called out with only a few hours notice. You will encounter many delays and once out on the line (away from home), could be turned around, and sent elsewhere at a moments notice. Also, you can't refuse a trip for any reason, even if you're getting married."

Last of all, we learned how to serve meals on a mock up (the shell of an airplane) used for training purposes. We were shown where everything was located and how to secure the galley. This took a couple of hours.

After taking a test on the emergency evacuation procedures on the DC-8, Bobbie announced that someone failed the test and then released us for lunch. I asked her if it was me and she said she thought it was. I went back to the class anyway, but didn't take my seat since I'd already failed one test. I stood next to the door and held my breath. The instructor called out the name of the person who failed the test. It wasn't me. If the announcement had taken seconds longer, I might have passed out. I was relieved.

Graduation day arrived. I was instructed to get my visas and shots ASAP. I would need a Korean visa, Philippine visa, and Japanese visa at this time, and was told to visit each embassy in San Francisco to speed up the process. Some visas were good for sixty months; others were only good for six months. I also needed to be vaccinated against cholera, yellow fever, small pox, tetanus, and typhoid.

I had the choice of yellow and white or blue and white uniforms to wear for the class picture. I chose blue. All trainees wore short white gloves and white plastic boots that came almost to the knees. Our skirts were shorter than our arms were long. Our hair was pulled back and clipped with a tortoise shell clip or up in a bun. In addition, we had our blue and silver flight wings pinned to the left side of the uniform dress.

After pictures were taken, we were given our first trip destination. I was going to Bangor, Maine and my six-month probation period was about to begin.

Donna & I in uniform, 1972.

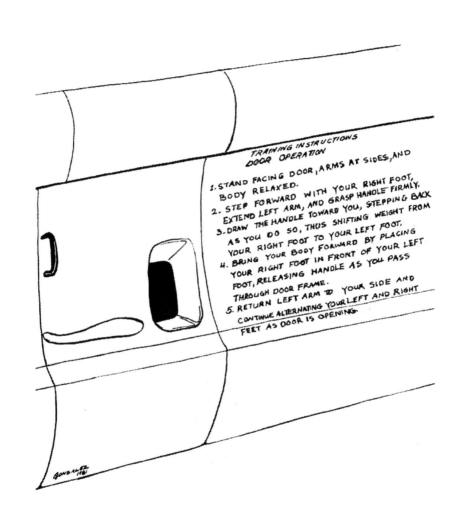

3
ONWARD AND UPWARD

At five o'clock on July 14th, 1972, I awoke in San Jose, Calif., to David Gates of Bread singing Diary. I reached over, hit the top of the radio with my palm, and rolled out of bed, ready for my first flight.

I'd left my uniform dress draped over the desk chair. I reached for it and slipped it over my head, glanced at the clock, then zipped up the back. I slid into my long white plastic boots, grabbed for my plastic uniform purse, and headed for the Oakland International Airport for my first flight to Bangor, Maine.

Two hours later, two hundred fifty-four Portuguese Californian farmers boarded the Trans International DC-8 on their way to the Azores by way of Bangor, Maine. We departed. A passenger informed me that his seat didn't recline so I wrote a note for maintenance.

An hour out a passenger call light illuminated. I responded. A middle-aged woman clutched her left side. "My side is hurting and I've a history of heart problems," she said. "I took one of my heart pills a few minutes ago but it still hurts." The woman, middle aged and a little over weight was traveling with her granddaughter who became hysterical. We moved the granddaughter away as soon as possible. The senior stewardess reached for the PA system and asked, "Is there a doctor on board?"

I stuck a pen in the hole next to the stewardess call button. The four masks in that row of seats dropped, but not completely down. Another stewardess went to the aft galley of the DC-8 and activated the built in oxygen system. I reached over, grasped the yellow mask with my right hand, and pulled further down to start the O_2. Bending the clear tube in half I listened closely for the hissing sound of oxygen, since the bag didn't inflate and only 1/2 liter of O_2 was traveling through the line.

I placed the elastic strap over the silver haired woman. Very little oxygen came out of the yellow rubber masks unless there was decompression, but she seemed to be relieved. Nobody answered the call for a doctor. The senior stewardess asked the captain to have an ambulance meet the aircraft. We were a few hundred miles from Bangor, Maine.

When we arrived at Bangor the ambulance was waiting nearby with lights flashing on the active runway. Once the aircraft was stopped and the blocks were placed under the tires, four paramedics ascended the stairs carrying a metallic stretcher. All passengers were asked to remain in their seats. The four paramedics moved down the aisle to where the woman was seated. The granddaughter who was reseated by the forward galley was informed of the situation.

"I want to go with my grandmother," she said. A crewmember walked the granddaughter over to her grandmother. "How are your feeling?" the granddaughter asked.

The woman eyed the stretcher, "I'm ok now."

"You must lie down on the stretcher and let us carry you," one paramedic replied.

Reluctantly, she scooted back and lay flat on the milk white sheets. Straps were placed around her and they made their way slowly through the narrow aisles, descended the stairs on their way to the ambulance. They departed lights flashing but no sirens. The passengers and crew then deplaned. I was exhausted and relieved that my first flight was over.

I was later to learn that something usually went wrong. Sometimes it was a minor inconvenience such as a schedule change or a lack of hotel rooms. Whatever the case, it was always a very different unexpected situation.

We had no time for fun here in Bangor, Maine—we barely had enough time to sleep. We had arrived in the evening and would leave for California in the morning. I was told it was unusual to return home so quickly. I was also told about a Trans International DC-8 ferry flight (no passengers) that crashed during takeoff at John F. Kennedy International Airport on September 8th, 1970. The National Transportation Safety Board determined the cause of this accident was due to pieces of asphalt and rocks that lodged themselves between the leading edge of the right elevator on the wing. The airplane couldn't level off due to this debris. The aircraft went almost straight up and then down, killing all twelve crewmembers. The report concluded that the new large jet aircraft caused erosion on the runways. The products of this erosion, pieces of asphalt and rock were being blown onto taxiways, ramps, and runways.

When we arrived back at the airport on July 15th, I asked about the woman on yesterday's flight. Our representative said she had an anxiety attack. That afternoon, July 14th, the woman and her granddaughter departed on another flight to the Azores.

A man had a radio playing on the ground. He said he'd tried to play it in the air but it didn't work well. I told him that playing it in the air wasn't a good idea since it interfered with the cockpit ground communications and we might end up back in Portugal if he did. He laughed.

The passengers on our return trip were Portuguese farmers also. These passengers were annoyed with the prior stewardesses since the officials at the Bangor Airport told them that they had to deplane in Bangor, even though the tour agent had told them it wasn't necessary.

Seat 20C's tray table was broken, the rim was torn off and pen marks covered it. "I'll be back shortly," I said to the passenger.

Once back in the galley I placed masking tape in my in-flight apron pocket to tape the tray table up. There were three basic options in-flight that stewardesses had to repair items that were not co-operating: tape it closed, kick it in place or if all else failed call the engineer. Walking back through the cabin, I noticed a child putting gum on an armrest. Reaching into the child's seat pocket, I removed the small white plastic lined bag. I glanced inside to make certain it was not already used and handed the bag to the mother. "Please have your child put her gum in here," I said.

Bulging out from under the seats and being caught under the wheels of the food and beverage carts were passengers carry on luggage. I nudged them back with the inside of my shoe. No heavy items were allowed in the overhead racks of the stretch DC-8 since it was one open compartment. Only light items such as coats, pillows, and blankets could be placed up there.

Me being new to this, some of the jargon used was strange. For example deadheading, I thought a deadhead was a follower of the Grateful Dead rock band.

However, in airline jargon it was, I learned, a crewmember riding as a passenger on the airline they worked for. Sometimes the crewmember was in uniform and sitting on the crew jump seats if no other seats were available.

"Why are you not working?" a passenger asked a uniformed crewmember deadheading back to Oakland, California.

"I'm deadheading," she replied. "That means I'm positioning for a flight on my airline, or going to my domicile (home)."

"Why do they use the word dead?" the passenger asked.

"I've no idea," she replied. "I don't understand why they call the airports 'terminals,' either. I'd heard in my training class that once after a lengthy delay, Trans International gave out coupons to the delayed passengers and said over the public address system that the coupons could only be used in the terminal restaurant. The passengers were already distressed and now they were told they could only eat in the 'terminal' restaurant." The passenger laughed.

The passengers this day had one annoying custom. If they wanted attention, they made the noise "pssst" which was a local Portuguese custom I later learned.

"Pssst."

I turned and saw a man holding up a coffee cup. The stewardesses were becoming pissst.

Sometime during the night, the fire warning light illuminated on the cockpit panel, but no fire was apparent. Some in-op red lights in the cockpit were ignored since they were not critical to the safety of the flight. A red light along with bells, clicks, voice, or physical feedback such as a stick shaker would announce a serious malfunction. An engine warning light was never ignored.

Later I learned that engine #1 had a short in its system. (The DC-8 aircraft had four engines, two on each wing.)

At 0800, we arrived at Oakland's crew scheduling where all trips began and ended for Trans International airlines crews. Even if the crew was scheduled to commercial out of San Francisco, the crew first had to check into crew scheduling in Oakland.

We greeted the crew taking the aircraft out from Oakland to Hawaii to Guam this night. They were delayed due to the engine problem.

My first trip was over. I felt this was probably an unusually difficult trip even though my fellow crewmembers said it wasn't. At Oakland crew scheduling, I checked to see if I had a pre-alert. I did. I was flying to Rome, Italy, the twenty second of July. The problems during my prior flight faded from my memory and I was elated to be going to Rome.

4
DOES ANYONE KNOW WHERE WE'RE GOING?

July 22, 1972, five days after my first flight, I showed in Oakland to commercial (take a commercial airline) to New York to commercial to Rome, and then crew rest. Three days later, we'd depart from Rome at 0945.

We flew to Rome stayed the three days at the Universal Hotel then showed in the hotel lobby at 0745, to board the limo set up for us by TIA, to take us to the airport.

We climbed into our hotels limo and arrived at Rome's airport. After a hectic search for our Trans International aircraft, we found it hadn't landed yet. As I lugged my luggage back and forth in the July heat perspiration dripped from my forehead and I stopped for a moment and tugged at my polyester dress to release it from my body.

We saw our plane land, and as it hit the ground, a tire popped. The thick rubber tire looked like tissue paper flapping in the wind. Smoke from the extra friction billowed up under the plane. Even from where I stood the smell of burning rubber was distinct. Though we were scheduled to leave at 0940, we didn't depart until 0140 the following day.

In the evening, when we arrived in New York we found that we were not going home, but to San Bernardino, then Anchorage. This information was sent by telex to the Trans International representative, who met the flight on arrival. Our Trans International representative was uncertain about this change so we were asked to stand-by.

This sort of schedule change was the norm when flying for charter airlines. Commercial airlines had set routes and aircraft that could be substituted if a mechanical delay occurred. We were given an itinerary at Oakland's crew scheduling department before each trip, but schedule changes were common and quite often we learned where we were going only after we'd completed the flight the day before.

I'd heard about another Trans International crew that received a schedule change; they were scheduled to work New York, Philadelphia,

Bermuda, Baltimore, and Boston with a layover in the latter. When they boarded the passengers in Bermuda and the senior began her announcements, she said their arrival time in Baltimore would be one o'clock. Immediately the stewardesses heard chattering.

"Bill, this plane is going to Baltimore," a passenger said to her husband. "We're on the wrong plane."

The crew was told by the Oakland scheduling department that they were flying to Baltimore. They were supposed to fly to Connecticut—at least that's where the passengers were going. A new flight plan was filed.

Apparently, Trans International found another crew to work the San Bernardino, Anchorage flight since we commercialed home as planned.

Upon arrival at Oakland crew scheduling I passed a class of prospective flight attendant's touring the Oakland facilities, only some were males. Apparently, males were fighting to gain positions as stewards in the early seventies. Antidiscrimination suits were filed citing the Civil Rights Act and Equal Rights Act. After a time of confusion about what to call the men, all airlines changed to the non-gender specific flight attendant instead of stewardess.

CHAPTER 2

MY ROOKIE YEAR 1972-1973

1
I'VE NEVER HEARD OF YOU EITHER

Once we arrived at any destination, there were problems. Off we'd go to baggage claim hopeful the luggage handlers remembered to open the crew cargo hold first. If our big red suitcases appeared, we checked for damage. One flight attendant had her bag completely smashed in. Mine had been only one-half smashed. It had always amazed me that a suitcase that traveled from the ticket counter to the aircraft can be so abused. Our suitcases, American Tourister, were the ones that were thrown out of planes and tossed around by monkeys in advertisements on TV. Baggage handlers should be filmed tossing the bags into the cargo hold instead of monkeys.

Next, we waited for transportation. Trans International traveled all over the world and had no regular routes. This caused problems with hotels and transportation. If the flight attendant didn't know she was going to Malaga, how was the transportation and the hotel supposed to know? The hotels and taxis on most occasions had never heard of Trans International Airlines. Someone, usually the senior, trekked over to a limo with the hope that this one would take us to the hotel. We'd know the name of the hotel because on live (passenger) flights, our representative handed the senior a sheet of paper that had our hotel name on it, then he promptly disappeared. This disappearing act wasn't out of disregard for the flight attendants, but regard for our passengers, for whom he's responsible. Trans International did attempt to make reservations but quite often, we were delayed and the reservations canceled or there were circumstances beyond our control.

My next scheduled trip with Trans International was a commercial to Mexico City, and then work home the following day. No need to sleep before a trip like this, I thought. I arrived in Oakland crew scheduling and deciphered the itinerary. The commercial flight departed at 0200 from San Francisco. Then we were to change planes in Texas after two hours on the ground, then go somewhere else in Texas, change planes again, this time with three hours on the ground. Next stop Mexico City, a place none of the crew had ever been before, so we didn't know the hotel and transportation procedures. No representative meets commercial or ferry flight so no company personnel was around to inform us.

We arrived in Mexico City and our senior flight attendant located a bus that took us to the Siesta Hotel after she convinced them that our Trans International Airline credit was good. The driver had not heard of Trans International Airlines. Upon arrival at the Siesta Hotel, we were informed that our reservations were cancelled. There was a convention in Mexico City and the Siesta had given our rooms to guests who didn't receive a discount. So here we were—up since yesterday morning. It was now 1500 in Mexico City and still no hotel. Our senior flight attendant staggered over to the pay phone and called Oakland crew scheduling again and was assigned another hotel. We dragged our suitcases out the door and sat and waited for our senior to begin her convincing speech, "Yes we are an airline, and no we aren't TWA," so he would accept our Trans International Airline billing. We piled in once again and headed for the newly assigned hotel.

When we arrived, to our horror, the walls were filthy, the floors had hair on them and we had our doubts that the sheets had been changed, but what could we do? All the other hotels were booked with convention people. We were supposed to stay in first class hotels, but sometimes that wasn't possible. In fact, half the time that wasn't possible. We had a hotel committee but by the time we returned to Oakland, the harm had been done, and it might be years before we returned to the offending location. The following day we flew passengers back to Oakland.

Since we weren't full paying guests hotels didn't give Trans International flight attendants the prime rooms unless it was off-season. We were assigned the rooms close to the elevators that go ding, ding, ding all night or next to the ice machines that go clunk, clunk, clunk. If construction was scheduled, you could bet the flight attendants rooms would be in that area. We also got the joy of toilets that didn't flush, TV's that didn't work, and balcony doors that didn't lock.

Another problem we encountered on layovers was that the hotels were not accustomed to the extra electricity we needed for our hairdryers, heating coils, electric curlers, and irons. We tended to blow fuses. This didn't make us popular with the hotel personnel. The maids saw the hairdryers, electric irons, heating coils and irons resting on the bathroom counters cooling off. They knew who did it.

Still, this didn't annoy us too much since we had our thoughts set on the terrific, exotic cities.

2
THE FEARED TELEX

Oakland crew scheduling telexed only bad news. News we were not to go home as planned, news a passenger had a complaint, or news we were fired. After working two months with Trans International, I received my first telex. We had finished our second Atlantic crossing (over and back twice) in seven days and were scheduled to go home. Our Trans International representative greeted us upon our arrival in Bangor, Maine with the feared telex. "Could you please take this trip scheduled to Frankfurt, Germany in eight hours?" our representative pleaded. Since we wouldn't have our fourteen hours rest, block-to-block we could refuse it. The crew agreed to go as long as Trans International would promise to schedule us home after the third Atlantic roundtrip in nine days.

We departed that night. Upon arrival in Frankfurt, Trans International booked us single rooms at the Park Hotel. I entered my room and promptly lay down exhausted on the fluffy down comforter. Not meaning to, I feel asleep and awoke to the sound of a bird chirping. I turned my head and glanced at the phone, it was doing the chirping and I lifted the receiver. This was my hour alert to fly to Charleston, South Carolina. I glanced at my watch and realized I had been in the hotel only six hours. Still in my uniform, I washed my face, redid my makeup, and worked the flight back to the United States.

Upon arrival in Charleston, our senior gave us more bad news. Trans International had broken their promise. We were to work to London, England after crew resting in Charleston. This amounted to seventy-five flight hours in twelve days.

I broke out in tears. Some crewmembers talked of quitting. When I finally arrived home a few days later, I slept for two days, so tired the walk to my mailbox was too much of an achievement for my exhausted self.

After some time at home, I received a call from the manager of flight services. He wanted to know why I was upset.

"I'd just flown seventy-five flight hours in twelve days with less than minimum rest in two locations," I replied.

"You got fourteen hours rest at all layover's but Frankfurt," he replied obviously annoyed at my behavior.

"True," I replied. "But the only reason we had minimum rest in Bangor, Maine was because the flight was delayed. We received our wake up and sat in the hotel lobby for four hours waiting," (Crew rest begins when blocks were placed under the airplanes wheels upon arrival and end when the blocks were removed upon push back). He repeated that I had my fourteen hours rest. Had someone called the FAA about this horrendous trip? Why so much concern about me being upset? I felt this call unusual. Finally I agreed that I'd gotten my fourteen hours rest in all locations but Frankfurt, but mentioned that we did the company a favor by taking the Frankfurt trip and that the company had promised to send us home upon our return in the United States.

"I had agreed to take the trip, and Trans International did not make those kinds of promises," he said. This ended our conversation.

Another example of disregard for F/A's during my rookie year happened in Toronto, Canada. We ferried in, gathered our belongings, and headed for the terminal. It was unusually dark, and we had a difficult time finding our way through the terminal. This was strange and we began to worry. No people were around, but at 0200, few were. We trekked to the other side of the terminal and reporters met us. The airport had been evacuated since fumes from an electrical plant next to the airport were considered toxic. The cockpit crew knew this and a car had driven them around the terminal, but the F/A's were not informed. Symptoms of inhalation of these fumes were stomachache, headache, and nausea and one of the F/A's experienced this. The following day our names were in the *Toronto* newspaper since we walked through the airport after it had been evacuated. Scary.

During my first year, there was a major turnover in rookie F/A's. Most would arrive home so exhausted they'd wake up thinking this was all a bad dream. I kept my sanity by keeping a journal. I felt if I hung in there things would improve and I so wanted to see the world. Due to the turnover rate of Trans International F/A's, we needed only a few years seniority to become a Pacific Queen. Pacific Queens flew mostly military routes that left at a scheduled time and returned at a scheduled time. Rooms were blocked off for us and the shopping in the Pacific was excellent. If I could hold off that long, I'd have more control over my life, or so I thought. And where were some of those beautiful exciting places I visited during my rookie year? — well, read on.

The hotel where we stayed in Milan, Italy was on Lake Maggiore. This was an ideal spot for a honeymoon. The lake was crisp and clear and an island in the center housed a castle. Across the water, one could see the Swiss Alps. The hotel itself was no less breathtaking. It was an old mansion with chandeliers, sweeping staircases, high ceilings, and the loveliest French provincial furniture kept up to perfection.

The only problem we had was lugging our suitcases up to the fourth floor. If the trek up the stairs hadn't taken my breath away, the view once I arrived at the top certainly would have. Later that evening we discovered another problem—central heating. The rooms in the center of the hotel were warm and toasty- almost too warm. The further out from the center of the hotel, the cooler the rooms. My roommate and I had a corner room. It had a terrific view of the lake but it was terribly cold. We slept all night bundled up in our socks, sweaters and hats with our coats over us for extra warmth.

The following day we took the train into Milan to see the Milan cathedral and check out a male statue that we heard was good luck if we touched a certain part of it. I loved being in Milan. The memory of Milan keep me going when situations arose that were not pleasant.

Another interesting layover during my rookie year was in Geneva, Switzerland. We were scheduled to stay for six days. Geneva was extremely expensive. A basic meal cost the equivalent of twenty dollars U.S. in the early seventies and for that reason we could only afford one meal a day. We trekked to the supermarket for snacks and wine.

During our stay, one crewmember asked the reception desk what we might do for entertainment.

"A prince from Saudi Arabia is in town and he might like to have the crew visit him and stay for dinner," the receptionist replied.

She got the crew together feeling a little apprehensive about what was in store for us. A chauffeur drove us to the prince's hotel. He had an entire floor to himself and greeted us at the door dressed in traditional Arab garb with the flowing white robe. He sported a beard and looked fifty years old. The room was ornately decorated with French provincial furniture and oil paintings. We sipped our beverages both alcoholic and non alcoholic and talked with him and his entourage about places we'd been and countries we hoped to visit.

"I have a little game to play," the prince said as he motioned to one of his entourage. Each of us picked a number from one to six (there were six F/A's). Each number had a corresponding present. I received a fourteen karat gold watch with onyx and tiger eye inlay. One flight attendant received a black velvet gown with silk lining and gold filigree. At ten o'clock, the prince ordered dinner. A variety of dishes hot and cold were rolled in. After dinner, the chauffeur drove us back to our hotel. This prince owned the new Hilton Hotel near the airport in Jeddah, Saudi Arabia.

This experience became another of my happy thoughts. It was a remarkable evening.

In 1973, Caracas, Venezuela had a lot of charisma with its lush foliage and rolling hills. This was an oil rich country but the oil had so much sulfur in it that it would cost too much to refine.

My roommate and I took the local bus through the countryside going nowhere in particular. We noticed that before the bus stopped someone would clap his hands. Apparently, that was the signal to stop and let the passenger off. Once we arrived at an interesting location, we clapped our hands, and it worked—the bus stopped. We leisurely toured the area by bus the three days we stayed in Caracas, and had a terrific time.

Also, during my rookie year, we worked to Spain, Malaga to be exact, where we stayed for seven days. While there we took a bus to Algerciras, where the Rock of Gibraltar was visible. We entertained the thought of catching a ferry to Gibraltar then Morocco. Our hotel informed us that the white slave trade was a problem for women in Morocco and they particularly liked blonde-haired women like us. "In 1970 two Pan Am F/A's took the trip and were never heard from again," he said.

This had us worried but not discouraged. We departed on our adventure after writing a short note on hotel stationary stating our plans just in case we disappeared.

It was a lovely ride to Algeciras with the Mediterranean Sea on one side and the hills on the other. The houses were white, with flat roofs. Few people were on the streets this morning. The only women we saw wore black clothing with black veils. We arrived at the harbor at 0900 to find the ferry left daily for Morocco at 0830. The ferry did not stop in Gibraltar due to bad relations between the Spanish and the British. Disappointed, we toured the Algeciras area instead. I hoped I would return someday and complete the journey. My Grandfather Fletcher was consul general of Gibraltar in 1944.

Early in 1973, we flew passengers into Trinidad where I met a girl (Brenda) about my age on the local bus. We talked and she invited me to her home for tea. It was a two-story house with wood shutters. Wooden stairs led to the second floor on the outside of the house. When I entered, I noticed this was not only the living room, but also the dining room, bedroom, and laundry room all rolled into one. The room was small, about the size of my living room in California. A table, a chair, and a bed were the only furniture. On the wall, there was a calendar and nothing else. Tea was made and we sat outside and drank with her grandmother, grandfather, mother, and father along with the children. I asked if they would like me to take a picture of their family. The children were thrilled with the idea but couldn't understand why they couldn't see the pictures immediately. Once home I developed and enlarged the family photo and sent it along with others to Brenda in Trinidad. I received a thank you letter and we corresponded on a couple more occasions.

Venturing away from the comfort and safety of the hotel to meet local people and others, visiting in the vicinity made my travels memorable.

The children of Trinidad.

The Algeciras harbor and fish market.

3
HORRENDOUS TRIPS

I learned during my rookie year that I should attempt to sleep before every flight so I was prepared for the unexpected, since one half of my trips were horrendous.

My first year with Trans International (TIA), I showed in Oakland for a one and one half hour flight to Los Angeles with a crew rest scheduled in Los Angeles. What an easy day, I thought.

The descent into Los Angeles International was smooth, but we landed so hard that all the passenger-reading lights flashed on and off.

A telex awaited us from Trans International. We were no longer to go to the Hacienda Hotel on Sepulveda Blvd. Instead, we were instructed to commercial directly to Cleveland, Ohio on United Airlines. That United flight was scheduled to arrive in Cleveland the following morning. Our easy day turned into an all night flight.

One of the United flight attendants gave me free headsets, a bottle of wine and after dinner drinks. She had been a F/A with United for two years and said she made three thousand dollars a month. I told her I had been working with Trans International less than a year and made eight hundred dollars a month.

When the crew arrived at the Cleveland Sheraton, no rooms were available. We were not expected until tomorrow, and the crew waited two hours for rooms. We had minimal ground time in Cleveland, fourteen hours block to block. With the two hours it took to deplane the passengers, and arrive at the hotel, along with the two-hour wait for the room, four hours had already been used of our fourteen hours rest. Not only that, but it was TIA's policy to get the crew to the airport two hours before departure. Therefore, we had eight hours in the hotel room. Departure would be at 2100 local.

Eight hours later, we were off to the airport. We boarded the limo that took us to Ohio Air (that's where the TIA aircraft was parked). This night we would ferry (no passengers), to Cherry Point, North Carolina.

Once at Cherry Point, we'd board passengers and take them to Panama.

During the ferry flight, our engineer came to the back of the aircraft to check the lavatories. He had complained about an in-op lavatory for two months. Then on one of his flights he was called to the back because smoke came from one of the unoccupied lavatories. The passengers had boarded. The engineer told the F/A's to evacuate the aircraft in case of fire, which they did. The engineer found out later that the air circulation motor in the lavatory had shorted out. TIA was less than pleased at his call to evacuate and reprimanded him. The Trans International cockpit crews and F/A's were extra safety conscious and I was thankful they were.

From Cherry Point to Panama, we had a full load of marines dressed in green fatigues and carrying rifles. The rifles had the pins taken out and were placed on the floor under the marines' legs. The majority of the men looked to be nineteen years old. They were scheduled to stay in Panama for twenty-one days to learn how to survive in the jungle. After the marines deplaned, the crew ferried to Cleveland for the night. This additional leg of the trip caused the crew to go one hour over duty. The crew was on duty for sixteen hours and working over fifteen hours block to block would be an over duty day. It was a horrendous workday.

I always carried emergency food in my suitcases for when I arrived too late, or was too tired, to get a bite to eat. I pulled out a can of tuna, plastic fork, napkin and paper cup, and set them out on the round wood table. I opened the can with my can opener, poured the oil down the toilet, and opened the curtains so I could see the bright lights of Cleveland.

The next evening we departed for Frankfurt, West Germany.

Evening arrived and we boarded a group of almost exclusively German-speaking passengers. Trans International had ordered a movie in German, which pleased the German passengers but annoyed the English-speaking passengers. Trans International had also ordered extra cases of beer. All the passengers appreciated the beer. These passengers were permanent residents of the United States, but most hadn't learned

English. They lived in a small community with all German-speaking people.

We arrived with our Germans in the afternoon and had twenty-four hours at the Canadian Pacific Plaza in Frankfurt. My roommate and I walked a mile away from the hotel to an area with narrow cobblestone streets off Elizabethan Avenue. This was where the discos and bars were located. We sat and drank wine out of green goblets until the sun started to set, then walked back to the hotel to sleep before our flight to Sea-Tac International in Seattle, in the morning.

The final leg of the trip was to "commercial" to San Francisco and I looked forward to seeing my fiancé, Bill.

An inbound TIA crewmember that brought us the aircraft that we were to take out of Frankfurt, informed me that I had been scheduled on their crew, except that I had sick leave by my name on the sign in sheet in Oakland. I wondered what my fiancé thought when Oakland crew scheduling called to give me my final alert and I had already been gone for two days?

Once home I asked my fiancé if he was upset to hear from Oakland crew scheduling after my departure. He said he wasn't concerned since he had dropped me off in Oakland. I never found out who put me on sick leave that day in 1973.

4
KEEP ON TRUCKING

After the required five days off after the previous ten-day trip, crew scheduling called.

"Tomorrow show in Oakland at 0800 to commercial to New York and later on to Greece."

I was elated. I'd never been to Greece.

Our DC-8 crew of ten left Oakland crew scheduling at 0800 and arrived in San Francisco at 0900 to board a non-stop United Airlines flight to New York. United didn't serve meals on this coast-to-coast flight; instead they set out a buffet. Thirty minutes in-flight, I picked up a piece of soft Swedish rye bread and piled it high with turkey, provolone cheese, lettuce, and tomatoes. The buffet was tasty; not like the hot chicken and beef entrees, I'd served for almost a year now.

The Salem Limo Company greeted the crew at John F. Kennedy Airport and delivered us to the Hotel Commodore. Yellow taxis were everywhere and honked their horns and moved inches from the car in front, then honked again as if that car could move out of the bumper-to-bumper traffic. They looked like a hive of angry wasps.

We arrived at the Hotel Commodore and checked in at the front desk. A crewmember was assigned by the senior flight attendant to watch the crew luggage. Crew luggage and purses had been stolen in the past, and the TIA supervisors stated the crew must continue the trip with or without their luggage.

The Commodore was a massive old concrete building located at Grand Central on 42nd Street. It had numerous tiny elevators and brass revolving doors that connected it to Grand Central Station. The rooms were small, cold and smelled musty. I walked over to the radiator and turned the knob. It made a hissing then a clunking sound before it started to warm the room. Then I went to my topside (the bag that crewmembers carry on the aircraft) and took out my yogurt. I opened the window, looked out, and saw nothing but a wall and an alley below.

Yogurt in hand I placed it on the platform outside the window (to keep it cold) and closed the window. I then swung my purse over my shoulder and headed for Times Square, which turned out to be crowded, noisy and fun.

My roommate and I found the place that sold half price tickets and stood in line for two hours. During that time, we were approached by locals who offered us special discounts for tickets they couldn't use, asked if we'd like to be on two different game shows, and were offered free tickets to an off Broadway production. We chose to go to the free off Broadway production.

Morning came and it was off to the airport again. When we arrived at the airport the incoming crew said that TIA had contracted with Disney to take Snow White and the seven dwarfs to Shannon, for a promotional tour of Ireland. During the Disney characters stay, they were to visit the Quinnsworth supermarkets to promote a film that was to be released in Ireland. I wasn't on this flight but a friend said they were in full costume ready for the camera crew that was to meet them in Shannon.

Our crew worked to Shannon, stayed for two days, then ferried to Bangor, Maine where we were scheduled to pick up passengers on their way to Athens, Greece. The crew was scheduled to stay in Athens for six full days. I had researched what to do in Athens beforehand so I could get as much sightseeing in as possible.

5
STOWAWAYS

We departed Bangor, Maine for Athens, Greece fifteen minutes late. One hour into the flight, after the beverage and meal service was completed, I walked up to the cockpit, tapped the engineer on the shoulder, and asked him what the fifteen-minute delay was about. He turned and said there was a knocking sound under the galley floor and the flight attendant in the front of the aircraft thought this unusual so called the cockpit to report the sound.

"Maybe there was a stowaway in the wheel well who wants to get out," the captain replied jokingly.

As it turned out, it was a valve, involving cabin pressurization, which was trying to open but was stuck. The engineer took care of the problem.

The captain's joke about the stowaway brought on a discussion among the crew since it seemed everyone had had a stowaway at one time during their career. A crewmember mentioned that once when she worked the aft galley she noticed a man who entered a lavatory but didn't come out. They were about to depart and there were no extra seats in the cabin. The flight attendant knocked on the bathroom door and he opened it. He was unaware he had snuck onto a charter airline and that charters usually fly full. He was taken off the plane when he couldn't produce a ticket.

Another flight attendant chimed in that once in Africa, she heard a crying sound coming from the baggage area. They were in the process of taking pilgrims from Kano, Nigeria to Jeddah, Saudi Arabia. The crewmember thought one of the passengers had placed their baby in with their luggage so she informed the senior. The baggage handlers opened the baggage door, hunted down the sound, and opened the bag the sound was emanating from. A Chatty Cathy doll was in the bag. I wondered what the Nigerian passengers were doing taking a Chatty Cathy doll to Mecca.

The flight to Athens went smoothly and the passengers clapped when we landed. The crew caught the limo to the Apollin Palace Hotel and we checked in. Afterwards, I stayed in the lobby to talk to the receptionist.

"This is my first time in Greece. What do you suggest I do?" I asked.

"Well, this is Saturday and the firework display is only on Saturday so I would suggest you go to the Acropolis to see the show."

I changed out of my airline uniform and headed for the Acropolis. The Apollin Palace, located far from town, made it necessary to travel by bus to the train station, then by train into Athens, then by bus to the Acropolis. Once there, I had my picture taken by a Greek photographer who took pictures of tourists. It was to early for the fireworks so I wandered into town where the shopkeepers offered me ouzo in small shot glasses. Then at dusk I started becoming concerned about how to return to the hotel. Anxious, I pulled the Apollin Palace matchbook out of my purse and showed it to a Greek in a white sailor outfit who spoke no English, but recognized the name of the hotel. Being alone at the time I chose not to stay and watch the fireworks as planned. My Greek sailor was sweet enough to take me back to my hotel by bus, then train, then bus. I offered him dinner on our arrival. Meals were included and he accepted. I walked into the restaurant with my Greek sailor friend to the chagrin of my fellow crewmembers. We joined them and motioned to the waiter. After dinner, my friend thanked me for dinner and headed out into the warm night.

The following day the crew rented a van, packed a picnic lunch, and drove to the Poseidon Temple to watch the sunset.

The ride to the temple was spectacular. I looked out the window and saw a group of slender tanned anglers who tossed out nets that unfolded over the turquoise water.

We drove by milk white homes with red roofs nestled into the hillside and clustered by the Aegean Sea. The morning was cool and the skies were blue. We bounced along in the rented van with the bad shocks for hours until we saw five massive pillars on a hill overlooking the Aegean Sea, and what looked like the base of a once majestic structure. The crew sat in a shady spot under an olive tree, ate our picnic lunch, then relaxed and wandered for hours. We looked for the location where the nineteenth century poet Lord Byron carved his initials into the stone and chatted with other tourists. The immense canary yellow sun started to make its way down to the sea and the sky exploded in color as the sun neared the horizon.

Later that evening the crew ate at a restaurant where they not only had food but also Greek dancers. A group of young men dressed in short skirts and puffy white shirts walked through the diners and bowed to the women. They held their hand out for us to take and brought us up to the dance floor. The music that played was "Zorba the Greek," and the young men guided us first in a circle dance then another traditional dance. It was great fun for my second to last night in Athens. As the crew watched and enjoyed the wine, a belly dancer stepped onto our dinner table and shook her hips for the men.

That night I discovered another Trans International crew was registered at our hotel. I asked the front desk if my friend Debbie was registered. She was and I called her. Debbie had arrived from Dakar, Senegal two days previously. A male crewmember on her crew had become sick in Dakar and a doctor diagnosed him with malaria. His roommate wanted a single room.

"He could get a single room if his roommate had a contagious disease, but he would have to prove that it was contagious," the TIA representative replied.

The male crewmember thought that was insane, moved to another room, and billed it to Trans International. TIA sent a telex to the crewmember, which said he was fired and responsible for his flight home. The crewmember called our Union (Teamsters) and they replied he'd have his job back in a week. He gave it half a moments thought and hopped on Air France, headed in the direction of Oakland. A certain amount of F/A's were required for a certain amount of seats on the aircraft. Seats were removed in the cabin and placed in the belly and the flight departed.

The following day I set my alarm clock for 6am. No matter how tired, I was determined to take a boat ride to an island my last full day in Greece. I heard that Aegina was the closest island, about an hour out of Piraeus. I slipped the map I purchased in California into my purse and headed for the elevator all by myself. I planned to take a bus to the port of Piraeus, only the bus wouldn't stop at the bus stop. A woman who spoke English said I had to wave at it. I waved and it still went by. The next time I saw the bus that was supposed to go to Piraeus, I jumped up and down, waved my arms, and yelled for it to stop. I looked silly but at least the bus stopped. I boarded and the people were helpful and friendly when I asked about the harbor.

I arrived at Piraeus and looked at the schedule that was posted at the ticket booth. Aegina was spelled slightly differently on my California map so I asked the man in the booth if it was the same island. It was and I purchased my ticket for very little drachma and boarded the ferryboat with the locals. I walked to the bow of the ferry, pulled up a chair close to the wood railing, kicked my shoes off, and put my feet up. Leaning back in the comfortable deck chair, I closed my eyes, breathed in the fresh clean sea air, and fell asleep.

I awoke when the ferry bumped up against the dock and looked at my watch. It was already noon. The ferry docked at a little port that was green with foliage. I disembarked and headed for a quaint restaurant by the dock. The locals were interested in why I had chosen their island to visit. They thought I was in the 1972 Olympics in Munich, since I wore a turquoise blue sleeveless pantsuit. Turquoise blue was apparently the olympic color that year.

After lunch, I boarded a bus to a temple a local resident mentioned. The bus was packed and it was impossible to lift your arm and scratch your nose if you wanted to. We passed by donkeys with packs on their backs led by their owners and the hilly scenery was spectacular. I felt I had stepped back to the nineteenth century. Tourists rarely visited

Aegina, a small fishing village, since the large cruise ships don't dock there. The homes were all one or two story white buildings with red roofs. At sunset, I arrived back at the hotel.

A few years later, I had another long layover in Greece. This layover some friends and I decided to go to Corinth. The taxi ride from Athens to the bus station at Kifissou normally took twenty-five minutes, (if you get into a cab that knows where he's going). Ours didn't so it took forty-five minutes and cost twice as much. The bus station was gray and dirty. No clean tables whatsoever and no one cleaning them. This killed our appetite and we walked out to the busses and matched our ticket letters with the Greek letters on the bus and boarded. The bus was full of local people. It was clean and had curtains, air vents, lights and Greek music playing. The bus also had a television set located in the top of the front window. The countryside was lovely and dotted with little concrete square houses about three or four stories high. Each level had a balcony going all around the structure. Most of the homes were white, some pink, and some green. We passed a group of nomads who were camping alongside the road in old gray tents. There were approximately twelve tents in all of a good size. These men were digging for water along the dried out riverbed. I know because I asked the Greek man who sat next to me. It looked as if they had found some since water was spurting up about three feet into the air.

We crossed a bridge over the Corinthian Canal. The canal was four miles in length and 247 feet wide. This was where ships passed between the Adriatic and the Aegean Seas. Minutes later, we arrived in Corinth and walked to St. Paul's Church located by the water. It was a little church and ornate. Paintings of the apostles and stories of the New Testament filled the dome. The sunlight shone through the different colored glass in the dome causing the sunlight to filter in, in different colors. There were chairs to sit on during the service but the Greek Orthodox people stand except for the old and disabled.

Next, we took a taxi to the Temple of Apollo, a fifteen-minute ride from St. Paul's. The driver waited for my roommate and I, and charged only 250 drachma (eight dollars U.S.) for the roundtrip. We drove through an old part of Corinth—one story stone houses with flat roofs lined the street on the way to the temple.

The Temple of Apollo was situated on a hill covered with wild daisies, poppies, both red and yellow, and small purple flowers. A small Greek Orthodox Church was in the foreground. Behind the temple was a mountain with a castle on top. A museum was located nearby that contained surgical instruments, dolls, jewelry, pottery, and sculpture from before the time of Christ. Totally satisfied with the day we headed back to Athens at dusk.

The next morning I was asleep when the phone rang. The call was our wakeup for our flight to Manchester, England. This would be my first trip to Manchester.

Greek dancing in Athens.

6
STOKE-on-TRENT

We arrived at 1000 in Manchester, England, on a commercial airline and headed to the Portland Hotel. Exhausted from the day before, I slept. Awakened by a loud buzzing noise, I walked to the window, looked out, and saw no one. I went to the door and opened it; others looked out also.

This sounds like a fire alarm, I thought. I grabbed my coat, purse, and jewelry and left the room without my shoes and in my pajamas. I headed for the emergency exit sign at the end of the hall and tried to open the door. It wouldn't open. I headed for the stairs at the other end of the hall and started my trek down the six flights. Since it was noon, everyone in the lobby was dressed except for the crewmembers. One had a facial mask on her face and no coat over her pajamas. Another had on a pink silk robe.

Apparently, there had been a minor fire in the coffee shop. It was quickly put out and my roommate and I returned to our room and slept for twelve more hours.

Later I asked why the fire exit didn't open.

"It should have opened automatically when the fire alarm sounded," the maid replied.

I reported the malfunction to the desk.

At 0300, my roommate Christina and I were wide-awake and hungry. We made a meal of the wheat thins, sardines and grape nut cereal we had in our suitcases.

Yesterday morning, I had asked the front desk about the highlights of Manchester and they had told me to go to Stoke-on-Trent, in Staffordshire, about one and one half hours south of Manchester by bus. It was where the stoneware and chinaware factories were located.

We boarded the bus at 0700 in front of the Roma Pizzeria for two pounds and started our journey.

The Royal Doulton warehouse was huge. Stoneware and chinaware were stacked to the ceiling and I was amazed that I could get a service for eight of English stoneware for eighteen dollars.

While I waited for the china to be wrapped, one of the workers offered us a tour of the factory.

For the next hour, we watched clay being molded, cut, shaped, and finished with one of Doultons designs. The best values were for the seconds (china that had minor flaws).

After the tour, I returned to pick up my china. It was packed in two boxes.

"These boxes sure are heavy," I said lifting them slightly. "Could you carry them to the bus stop for us?" we asked the workers.

The workers carried our boxes the two blocks to the city bus and the bus driver lifted the boxes into the baggage compartment. As the bus started rolling past the Royal Doulton Factory, I started thinking that I might not be able to manage these boxes along with my luggage. Once we arrived back in Manchester, I needed to get them across the street and then I could store them in the baggage room next to the front desk. I was thankful that we were scheduled to commercial home after working to Bangor, Maine.

The following day I hired a porter to place my boxes of china on the crew bus headed for the airport. We departed for Bangor, Maine.

A telex message awaited the crew in Bangor. The representative said there was a problem with a DC-8 in Amsterdam and that they needed a crew ASAP. Damn, I thought. I couldn't leave the boxes in storage at the Twin Cities Motel in Bangor since we were not returning to Bangor, but going through New York and they were too heavy to mail.

The next morning we left for Amsterdam. I got up early to load the boxes onto the crew bus so as not to be obtrusive. I lugged the china up the ramp to the aircraft and placed them in the back of the closet. To do this I had to remove all the soda cases and other items in the closets first. It was quite a workout. Once we arrived in Amsterdam, I placed the china on my suitcase wheels. I usually used these for my big suitcase but that wasn't as heavy as the boxes of china.

At the Sonesta Hotel, I paid a porter to take my bags and boxes to my room on the third floor. There weren't any elevators in this section of the hotel and I climbed the stairs. Once inside I looked out the window to see the view. I was so tired I almost cried when I saw I was directly across the street from a burlesque nightclub called the 'Bronco Saloon.'

Fulfilling my fears, at 2200, I awoke to loud music. I dug my earplugs out of my suitcase, climbed back into bed and went back to sleep.

I had set an early wakeup call for the next morning. When the call came, I summoned the porter. I wanted to be certain he had sufficient time to load my luggage and boxes of china into the crew bus. The porter arrived and picked up my bags and boxes. I heard a commotion on my floor but didn't think much about it. I was engrossed in a movie.

An hour later, we were off to the airport headed for New York.

The catering this day was a problem. At least twenty passengers said they had asked for kosher meals and none could be found. Two other passengers said they asked for vegetarian meals. The crew placed the crew's rolls, salads, and desserts on the trays without entrees.

"We've paid for our meal and should get what we ordered." one woman replied. She was right. I didn't blame her for being angry.

The flight ended and I struggled with my boxes of china that I had once again placed in the closets behind the soft drinks.

Perspiration was running down my forehead. "I'm never going to purchase heavy stuff on a trip again," I said aloud to nobody in particular. "If Trans International turns us around for another crossing I'm going to sell my china on the streets of New York."

I tailed behind the others heading for customs stopping occasionally to rest my aching arms. I noticed that one of my boxes was rattling.

"Listen to this," I asked once I arrived at customs. I tipped the box on its side then tipped it on the other side. "Did you hear that? I think my china's broken. I wonder if that noise I heard outside my room in Amsterdam was a box of china falling down the stairs?" I handed my customs declaration to the official and he waved me through.

My next task was to open the boxes once at the Hotel Commodore. Each piece was carefully wrapped in brown paper. I unwrapped the first piece. It was broken. I continued to unwrap the china. Occasionally I had an unbroken piece. It appeared that my two boxes of china had fallen off the luggage cart in Amsterdam. I had been so careful. I always had a porter take my boxes to the room and had carried the boxes on board the aircraft myself. I was disappointed the porter hadn't told me what had happened. Sadly, I placed the two boxes of broken china outside my door, changed clothes for dinner, and looked forward to commercialing home tomorrow. This trip had taken me to New York, Greece, England, Maine, Amsterdam then back to New York. I was truly crisscrossing the globe for free and this was just the end of my rookie year.

CHAPTER 3

Layovers

1
SANTA CLAUS IS FLYING ON TIA

I traveled because it was exciting and different, and even though my layovers may not seem lovely, I cherish the memories. I was usually scheduled to go somewhere new and exciting and this made me smile. After the trip, I'd smile again and think how lucky I was to make it through the tough parts without losing my sanity. Any veteran traveler knows life's full of surprises and that includes vacations. Hotel rooms weren't always quiet and well maintained, the weather wasn't always what I desired, some roommates smoked or had habits that annoyed me, delayed flights were common and my luggage had been lost numerous times. Even after a disaster trip, most planned another. I was no different, only I was on a constant trip, with little time in between to catch my breath and then I pressed on to yet another destination.

After the required time off at home I received my next assignment which was to return two hundred fifty-four Japanese to Oahu, Hawaii from Oakland, California on December 7th, 1975. I studied the rest of my itinerary. It appeared to be a dream trip; just like all the other itineraries, I'd studied my rookie year.

As we deplaned at Honolulu International Airport, the trade winds propelled anything that wasn't tied down and ominous clouds promised to drop buckets full of rain.

A cockpit member offered my roommate, Shirley, and me his suite on the top floor of the Kuhio Hotel. We accepted not knowing that the cardboard panels in the ceiling of the top floor had a tendency to fill with water and fall during rainstorms. Although, the engineer didn't tell us at the time he offered the suite to us, that's why he gave us the suite. It had happened to him and now it happened to us. That night the hotels employees scooted around our suite, placed buckets under the drips, and removed the cardboard panels that fell in the closet, bathroom, living room and bedroom. It upset Shirley since she helped the hotel personal clean up, and pack our stuff. It didn't bother me since I slept through it all. Shirley told me the next morning that she thought I might have been knocked out by one of the falling panels only none were present on my bed. She entertained the thought of putting her makeup mirror to my mouth to see if I fogged it, but she was too busy cleaning up and making sure she had packed everything into both of our suitcases. Shirley also asked if I had taken anything to sleep.

"No," I replied. "I just had a extremely busy time at home and was completely exhausted."

No other rooms were available, so this scenario was repeated each night until the storm passed. To amuse myself I went to the library and studied palm reading.

Our five-day layover passed and the crew was called to take passengers to Columbia, South Carolina. I overheard one our representatives remark to another "There are two of them upstairs."

Two what I wondered, Ill or annoyed passengers, troublemakers, terrorists? I wanted to make sure I knew whom they were talking about and asked the representative.

"Only two cockpit members upstairs," he replied. "The captain and the co-pilot."

I laughed because they were supposed to be upstairs in the cockpit of the 747 aircraft preparing for the flight, while the engineer checked the outside of the aircraft (his walk-a- round).

The passengers boarded leisurely and vociferously. This was the first sunny day of their vacation. These merry travelers returned to South Carolina just as white as they left.

We departed and after the meal service, I noticed the galley water spigot faced the wall instead of downward which had happened to me once before. The water spigot would turn when used and spray on a passenger seated across from the galley. I'd adjust it and it would swing around again. That passenger appeared to be a food and beverage magnate. The gravy on the beef entrees would splash and the peas would roll off the meal trays when removed from the galley board and landed in his lap. I was so apologetic; so sincerely apologetic. Then a pea landed on his head and sat there. I looked at that pea and started giggling. First, I closed the galley curtain to compose myself. That didn't work so I ducked under the galley board and headed for the lavatory. Moments later I took a deep breath and returned to the galley, looked at him and said; "Excuse me sir something landed on your hair, can I remove it?" He reached up and knocked the pea off. I offered to fill out a passenger incident report so that TIA would pay for dry cleaning. He declined. I was as relieved as the passenger that the meal service was over.

We had one annoying passenger this day. He asked a F/A about the mile high club and said that he wanted to join. She ignored him.

We bounced into Columbia, South Carolina on the 13th day of December and began a four-day layover. My roommate Anne and I chose to use the four-day layover to tour South Carolina by bus, which rarely I might add arrived on time and was filthy. On one excursion, we rode out to the Richmond Mall for a clothing sale advertised in the local newspaper. We asked the bus driver to tell us when we were close.

"You can't miss it," he said.

We did miss it and attributed the mistake to the rainy weather and what the locals called a mall. We envisioned a huge covered mall. This mall consisted of only ten outdoor shops and D.B. Whites the department store. I came across a long red robe at D.B. Whites and decided to get into the Christmas spirit by making a Santa Claus outfit out of it. Anne and I purchased red thread, cotton balls, felt for the hat, pom-poms, and quilt filler to finish the hat along with glue. We laughed at our creativity.

The following day we pinned it together, but there was one problem. How were we to sew the nightgown into pant legs?

We entered a Singer sewing machine shop on Main Street the next morning. "I have an unusual request," I said. "We're staying at the Holiday Inn and won't be home until just before Christmas, so would you mind if we used one of your machines to sew up the legs of a Santa Claus suit that we're making?"

The salesperson looked at what we created, laughed and said, "Sure, no problem." She asked if we had any thread, which we did and the salesperson threaded the machine. I sat down and took only a couple minutes to sew up one side of the leg and down the other.

That evening we set off for a movie. An employee at the Holiday Inn offered to drive us and we were thankful until he informed us while he drove, that he had the flu.

Anne and I were the only patrons that evening at the movie. We supposed the locals had parties to attend and families to visit that close to Christmas. After the show, we rushed to the bus stop to catch the last bus of the night at 2130 back into town. It was blustery outside. I used some red poster paper I had purchased before the movie to shield my face from the wind. I had purchased the poster paper to create large 18-inch H's and O's to decorate our hotel room door with a HO! HO! HO! (We wanted to use the hotel lampshade for the outline of the O's and the phone book to make the H's.)

The 2130 bus didn't show. At 2215, we were cold, wet and worried. I asked a woman, who at first I thought was a man, if she knew if the city bus ran until eleven pm. She didn't know. Five minutes later, a bus pulled into the Veteran's Hospital parking lot, stopped, and turned off its lights. Anne and I discussed whether to forge our way through the wind and rain to the bus or wait where the bus stop awning sheltered us somewhat.

We chose to set off toward the bus, but to our dismay, a four-foot fence divided the bus from us. Rain dripping from our faces, we scaled the fence, jumped down the other side, and ran toward it. The bus was locked so we stood outside the entrance of the Veteran's Hospital and shivered from the cold, while we waited for the driver to return.

He returned five minutes later. We inquired if his route was our route. It was and we boarded the empty city bus and headed for the Holiday Inn. We arrived after midnight exhausted.

On December 17th, in Columbia, two limos waited in front of the Holiday Inn to transport the crew to the airport. The limos were jam packed with crew and luggage. The limo driver couldn't close the trunk. I rode shotgun and kept an eye on the open trunk in case anything, especially the Santa suit, should bounce out. Nothing did. We ferried (empty) to Nassau, a one and one half hour flight.

Since we hadn't any passengers, it was an opportune time for the crew to discuss union negotiations. Some of our grievances were:

1. Working twenty-four hour duty days.

2. Being turned around (sent out on another trip without more than fourteen hours of crew rest) at Oakland crew scheduling upon arrival when originally scheduled to end trip.

3. Lack of notification of schedule changes until arrival at airport.

4. Being taken off flight status (fired) for refusing to continue trip after working a sixteen-hour duty day.

We arrived in Nassau about 1800, one hour later than we were expected and found our limo had left. Apparently, our driver had gone to dinner. Upset, our captain demanded a limo, but he didn't command much authority since he was wearing forest green polyester slacks and a powder blue polyester shirt. He wore this outfit off the flight from Columbia to Nassau and not his official uniform. I thought this strange.

Once we arrived at our hotel, the Balmoral Beach, we moseyed up to the bar and ordered a "Goomba." It consisted of white rum, pineapple juice and coconut rum. The waitress told us they were $2.75 each but we were charged $3.75 when the check arrived.

We glanced at the prices on the menu at the fancy Balmoral Beach restaurant but ate at the coffee shop due to lack of sufficient funds. The next day, December 18th, we would have a 1500 pickup and work Nassau, to Atlanta, to Houston and then ferry the aircraft to San Francisco, before we ferried to Oakland across the bay.

When we checked out of the Balmora Beach Hotel in Nassau, rain poured down—five minutes earlier it had been bright and sunny. A limo drove us out to the aircraft, but we got soaked anyway. By the time the passengers arrived the rain had stopped. I supposed the baggage handlers didn't attempt to load the luggage during the rainstorm since it took them one hour after the passengers had been seated to accomplish that task.

This crew had the same old plane (67T) all trip. It sat and we sat. It had been a terrific trip—lots of rest and relaxation and little work. In-flight, I dressed in my Santa Claus outfit, slung a black garbage bag over my shoulder, with pillows inside, and walked quickly up the aisle. Passengers liked my version of streaking up the cabin and a few took pictures.

A seemingly endless line of passengers filed out when we landed. Many asked, how many passengers on the DC-8 and DC-10?

"We had 256 passengers on the DC-8 and 376 passengers on the DC-10," I replied.

After we landed in Houston and the passengers deplaned, we ferried the aircraft to San Francisco. I wondered why we ferried to San Francisco, then ferried to our base in Oakland on the other side of the bay, but decided it was another one of life's unanswerable questions. Then, after we landed in San Francisco, the baggage handlers loaded a Lotus car into the belly of our aircraft. That explained the San Francisco destination.

In the meantime, our flight engineer removed the crew's big red suitcases from the belly to the cabin even though we ferried to Oakland. I supposed the owner of the Lotus had paid for exclusive use of the cargo compartment. Our flight engineer mentioned to check the suitcases for water damage since they sat in the rainstorm in Nassau. I opened my suitcase and everything inside was soaked. The cockpit's crew bags were dry. I supposed the baggage handlers took theirs out of the rain. The following report explains:

ACCIDENT-ILLNESS-INCIDENT REPORT

'All cabin crew bags were left sitting in a three-inch deep puddle in torrential rain for at least thirty minutes outside the ground handler's office in Nassau. The first officer saw them being put onto a cart and said that a stream of water poured out of each suitcase when lifted. Upon examination, the contents were found to be water damaged.'

The good news was that this crew would be home for Christmas.

2
WHERE DID EVERYONE GO?

In 1976, after I worked a flight into Chicago the crew was given permission to go to the coffee shop for a two-hour layover. I had a phone call to make so I said I would join them later. After my call, I looked around and the crew wasn't there. I checked to see if there was another restaurant, but there wasn't. Then I checked in the employee cafeteria, but still no crew. I became worried. I called operations in Chicago and they put me on hold while they checked the information about the flight. About two minutes later, a woman came back on the phone. "I know everything about the TIA flight. What's your question?" she asked.

"Do you know where the TIA crew is that landed in Chicago thirty minutes ago?" I asked.

She went to check, returned to the phone and replied. "I'm sorry your flight has just taken off."

My heart started racing. I dropped the phone, ran back to the gate where we arrived and the plane was still there. I breathed a sigh of relief and boarded.

"Where were you?" The Trans International representative asked annoyed.

"Remember, you said we had two hours before takeoff," I replied out of breath.

"Since we had no passengers leaving from Chicago, the captain had decided to go early," he said.

Shaking and breathing heavily, I took my seat, the door was closed, and we departed.

Usually, the most common delays I encountered were the one to two hour varieties. It was when I had six hour delays and sat on the airplane with the annoyed passengers that I was most irritated. This happened so frequently that there was a special pay code on the TIA flight attendant gross pay calculations, RPAX (remain with passengers). After eight years of extremely long workdays, I decided to write the union and complain. I hadn't written any letters before this since I was fearful of being fired. I was still fearful but it was an important issue and needed to be addressed.

In October 1980, I wrote the union twice about over-duty days:

Glenda,

I'm addressing this letter to you since I feel that I have reason to be upset with the scheduling department.

My first grievance filed against Trans International with the Teamsters Union was concerning over duty days that appear on my itinerary as sixteen hour duty days when in fact they were over duty and constantly so. One of the trips that Trans International states was not over duty was the Yokoto, Elmendorf, Travis leg. I had enclosed a copy of my over duty form. I was hoping to layover (stay) in Alaska instead of coming all the way home to California, as this was an eighteen-hour duty day (without delays). I didn't get to stay in Anchorage.

Dear Glenda,

This letter is about a flight that is constantly over duty. Scheduling states it is not an over duty day, therefore we have to take the trip.

The flight I am referring to is OAK/SEA/FRA (Oakland/Seattle/Frankfurt).

The crew was told when we received our final alert that we would be showing at 1645 the 21st of October and crew rest in Seattle. Scheduling then proceeded to call everyone to tell us that the show time had changed to 0730Local October 22nd, and that we were working OAK/SEA/FRA.

Sincerely, all seven of the flight attendants

These letters were among many that the crews wrote concerning these extra long duty days. The F/A's were against the over-duty days that were planned by the company from the start of the trip. We realized that by TIA scheduling crew's in this way they were saving a good deal of money but at the crews expense and well-being. The crews could understand why we had to work over duty when there was a delay in departure since we couldn't abandon the passengers; but TIA constantly, from the get go, month after month scheduled us to work eighteen-hour days.

Sometime in the early eighties, the crews started staying in Anchorage instead of flying through to Travis. We no longer were expected to fly Oakland/Seattle/ Frankfurt either. Slowly, things they were a changing, as the Bob Dylan song goes.

3
ITALY AND ENGLAND

On July 7th, 1978, the flight to New York was two hours late and had the usual problems most of which were to numerous to mention. This day we had no communication with the F/A's in the back of the aircraft, since the PA was in-op. Once again, we did the announcements with the megaphone. The forward galley ceiling leaked also. Unfortunately, it dripped right on me when I served the meals. The air-conditioning was in-op too, and this aircraft had just come out of Oakland.

On July 8th, we were off to Rome, Italy aboard another TIA aircraft with another set of problems. This aircraft had no water, so no coffee, tea, or bathroom water. The passengers were from Rome, and spoke little English; they didn't complain, and just accepted it. I removed another little critter with legs out of the ice bucket without changing my expression. No one suspected a thing. Unfortunately, the lettuce in the coffee pot came out in someone's cup. I retrieved it quickly. How lettuce got in the pot, I'll never know.

July 1978, our last full day in Rome, Italy my roommate Sara talked me into traveling from Rome to Florence by train. I was concerned we might not be able to return for our flight the next morning since Florence was four hours away. Last month in Venice, the canal transportation workers decided to strike for a few hours after I had crossed the canal. The ticket taker spoke to me in Italian but I couldn't understand what he said so I smiled and said, "no thank you." I ended up stuck on the opposite side of the canal with a view of our hotel, but no way to return. The only mode of transportation back was by boat; therefore, the only way to return was to swim.

Sara was certain we'd return in time for our flight tomorrow, so I departed for Florence with her.

We rode through Rome on our way to Florence, and I saw worn down houses with red pipe roofs. Most needed a new paint job. Every balcony had flowers and plants on it. I noticed that many locals had grape vines in their yards. I hadn't seen any vegetables yet, only grapes.

We traveled north through the country past rolling hills. The foliage outside of Rome was lush with trees and bushes. We passed farms partially hidden by the 6am fog. Forty- five minutes out of Rome, cornfields appeared and fields of sunflowers.

We chugged by a green murky lake lined with ferns and other bushes. As we neared the Tuscany Region, the terrain became flatter and soon the hills were behind us. We approached the Apennines Mountains and passed fields of grapes. As we neared the city, I was amazed at the amount of tunnels we traveled through in our already dimly lit train car. By late morning, we pulled into the Florence Train Station. Many five and six story, cream-colored houses with red piped roofs dotted the city.

We raced all over Florence, visiting the Baptistery of San Giovanni, which faced the Florence Cathedral and whose gilded bronze doors depicted scenes from the Old Testament. We also ran through the Cathedral of Santa Maria del Fiore, known as the Florence Cathedral. The Franciscan Church of Santa Croce where Michelangelo's tomb was located along with the tombs of the statesman Machiavelli, the poet Conte Vittorio Alfreii, and operatic composer Rossini. We had heard of the underground labyrinths but had no time to investigate.

We only stopped once to get something to drink and paid the waiter upon ordering. It was about 1740 and the train was scheduled to leave for Rome at 1745. We started to drink our drinks then discussed whether we could make it to the train terminal in five minutes. Remembering we hadn't purchased our tickets yet, and without finishing our drinks, we stood and ran all the way to the terminal. The train had started to move down the tracks when we jumped on. The conductor only fined us the equivalent of one dollar each for not purchasing tickets beforehand. The four-hour train ride back to our hotel the Universo was a relaxing break from the exciting but hectic self guided tour of Florence.

At breakfast the next morning, a fellow crewmember, Kathy, said a mouse woke her up by running across her face. She planned to write the hotel committee to complain and shivered as she spoke of the eerie feeling of those four little feet scampering over her.

Also, in 1978, the crew went to see the musical 'Chorus Line' in London. The taxicab we climbed into after the show spied a taxicab ahead of him that he said was stolen. The taxicab driver turned to us and asked if we minded following the stolen cab until he could get in touch with a Bobbie to handle it. The four of us in the cab thought this diversion might be interesting so off we went following the alleged stolen taxicab. The man in the alleged stolen taxicab wasn't driving fast so neither were we. Within five minutes, we saw an equestrian Bobbie clip clopping down the road. Our taxicab driver rolled down his right window, pointed to the taxicab in front of him, and said calmly, I believe that taxicab was stolen. The Bobbie mounted his horse and started after the stolen taxicab. We followed. The man in the alleged stolen taxicab pulled to the side of the road and climbed out. The Bobbie chatted with him. They appeared to be having a polite conversation. Then a patrol car arrived. The man voluntarily climbed into the back seat of the patrol car without handcuffs and without having to lean against the car and be patted down for weapons. It looked as if they knew each other. Then they drove off.

Our cab driver gave us a free ride to the train station since he felt he had inconvenienced us, which he hadn't. We had found the diversion exciting.

It reminded me of the time when I was in London for the fourth of July. One of the male crewmembers packed some one-inch sound making firecrackers before he left the United States. The crew met in a room that overlooked the roof of the hotel restaurant in London, lit the firecrackers one by one and tossed them onto the roof one or two stories below. Not long after the firecrackers were tossed, we heard a tap, tap, tap on the door. A Bobbie in full uniform stood outside.

"You're disturbing the patrons in the restaurant," he said.

We explained we'd been celebrating the Fourth of July and assured him we wouldn't toss any more firecrackers and he excused himself.

We boarded the train to return to Gatwick after 'Chorus Line' and chatted, not paying attention to the stations, we passed.

"This is Gatwick!" my roommate said with conviction as the train started up again. We grabbed our purses and jumped off the train. Then discovered it wasn't. The angry conductor reprimanded us for causing him to stop the train and we apologized. Embarrassed we climbed back aboard.

I arrived home a few days later and was informed I would be in a senior upgrading class after five days off. I can't say I was thrilled to attend the class but it gave me an extra week at home with my fiancé Bill.

Feeding the pigeons in Venice, Italy.

4
A SENIOR FLIGHT ATTENDANT OR NOT

In May 1979, I had decided to become a senior F/A. I attended the necessary training in Oakland and headed out to work my first trip as a senior accompanied by a check senior F/A. This was the first of two senior check rides. Connie, my check ride supervisor wrote my overall performance was very good and that I was well prepared. I was complimented on my announcements, on my composure and how well I handled a nasty situation with the meal carts. During my first meal service three carts stuck in the DC-10, lifts at various times; the entire meal service had to be changed.

"Cindy handled it beautifully and never once showed signs of anger or anxiety as I know many others would. The nicest compliment I can give Cindy is that five of the other crew members came up to me and told me what a great job they thought she was doing," Connie wrote. "I feel Cindy will make a fine senior F/A."

That was my first senior check ride. My second was quite different. This time I was called into the supervisor's office in Oakland to explain upon my return.

On August 16th, at 1230, I received a call from crew scheduling, they had a trip for me that evening. I was to commercial on PSA (Pacific Southwest Airlines) from San Francisco to Los Angeles. Show time at Oakland crew scheduling was 2000.

Crew scheduling had blundered. The flight I was to take to Los Angeles departed at 2000. The scheduler had given me the departure time in San Francisco, not the show time in Oakland. Crew scheduling booked me on a PSA flight from San Francisco at 2100 only now I wouldn't have my fourteen hours block to block necessary crew rest.

It was 2000 when the taxi arrived in Oakland. "My flight leaves at 2100," I said to the driver. "Can you get me to San Francisco in time?" "Yes, get in," the driver replied. He slid through stop signs and raced through traffic lights before entering the freeway. We dashed around cars and sped by trucks at what seemed like ninety miles per hour on our way to San Francisco. I held on.

"I think PSA leaves every hour for Los Angeles until midnight," I said white knuckling it.

"Don't worry, I was paid to get you there on time," he replied.

After forty minutes of fear and anxiety, we arrived at San Francisco International Airport. I checked in at ticketing and boarded the flight. I was more thankful to be alive then to have made the flight.

Upon arrival in Los Angeles, I called Oakland. They rescheduled me for another senior's trip, and she was to take mine so I would get my fourteen hours block-to-block rest I was to inform the other senior of the change only she didn't answer her phone. Apparently, she was visiting a relative in the Los Angeles area. My check senior attempted to call me, but the phone lines were crossed. Every time she called room number 206, she got room number 208. My check senior asked the fellow in 208 to knock on my door and tell me my phone was in-op, which he did.

August 18th, I showed in the lobby of the Hyatt Hotel on Sepulveda Blvd., for my second senior check ride to Oakland, California then on to Bangor, Maine. The crew consisted of New York based new hires. I knew none of them. I later learned that they were unaware this was my rookie senior check ride. They thought I was a senior already. The Hyatt Hotel limo drove us to the airport.

Once we arrived at the aircraft, I waited for my passenger manifest, which showed up thirty minutes late. This delayed our departure, which angered everyone. I checked the passenger count and the manifest number and they differed. I informed our TIA representative and the captain. The captain chose to depart anyway and not delay the flight any longer. That's when the galley girl informed me we weren't catered with crew meals. In-flight, I asked the captain to radio ahead to Oakland to make sure catering knew of the problem.

There was another TIA aircraft on the ground in Los Angeles, a DC-10, along with our DC-8, 67T. The passengers all spoke German.

We had a F/A on board who spoke German and she made the announcements after I finished my English version. Before the F/A who spoke German could finish the announcement in German, the captain overrode the flight attendant's PA.

"Flight attendants take your seats for takeoff," our captain said.

The German speaking F/A had just gotten to the portion of the announcement where she was instructing the passengers about the life rafts. She hung up the PA and headed for her seat at the forward jet escape. I hadn't told the captain that the cabin was secure and the announcements were completed. We had already begun to pick up speed for takeoff. I buckled in.

We served all the canned orange juice on the Los Angeles, Oakland leg of the trip since the individual orange juices were frozen. The TIA representative in Oakland was upset that we asked for more orange juice and crew meals and motioned check senior Gloria over for a discussion. We were catered our orange juice but not our crew meals. He said we should have eaten at the hotel in Los Angeles. I overheard him saying he didn't care if we had crew meals. All he cared about was an on time departure. The hotel coffee shop in Los Angeles was closed since it was under construction and show time was 0600, too early to go elsewhere. Nothing was re-catered for the Oakland, Bangor leg. The F/A's and the senior check F/A went hungry.

My crew arrived in Bangor, Maine famished and two passengers short. Apparently, two of our German-speaking passengers boarded the wrong aircraft in Los Angeles. I wondered where that Trans International DC-10 was going? What a surprise for them. I pointed out the discrepancy in the manifest before we left Los Angeles. I also informed the representative in Oakland upon arrival but I still received a telex from the supervisor's office stating they wanted to speak to me immediately upon my return to Oakland, California. I suppose they had to blame someone and that someone was I.

The 19th of August 1979, we were to work from Bangor to Berlin, Germany then ferry to Hamburg. This day I wasn't in top form. My check senior wanted me to run through a pre flight briefing, for a ditching over the wing. I was to brief twelve imaginary able bodied men to take life rafts out the four over-wing exits. It seemed to take forever. I even bored myself. Everyone wanted to get on with their pre flight duties. I had to pay attention to all details since this was my senior check ride. I found this out when I tried to skip some details such as lift the arm rests up and roll the window onto the seat. Of course I would roll it onto the seats. What did she expect me to do-carry it back to the aft lavatories? I was annoyed.

After the above briefing, I checked the passenger manifest. The passenger count was correct but an R (return flight) was located next to the flight number and this was an originating flight. I began my announcements and blanked out. I couldn't think of what to say after, "Good morning ladies, and gentlemen." I was so embarrassed. Gloria helped me along. Once I got started, it came easily again. It seemed that all the crewmembers were a little stressed out this day. The PA worked on the ground but was low on volume in the air. The passengers could barely hear me.

Everything else went well on the flight except the liquor paperwork was all screwed up. There were three metal bins stuffed with seventy cans of beer located in the aft of the aircraft. We needed to count that beer before the liquor service. After the service, we were twenty-three dollars short. It took an hour and a half to get the liquor paperwork in order.

The passengers deplaned in Berlin, and the crew flew on to Hamburg. Our representative had set up the hotel, but not the transportation to the hotel. I called the local transportation number given me and it was incorrect. I called an unauthorized transportation number and asked them to call London Operations for payment. London refused to authorize payment since no crews had stayed in Hamburg before. I was thankful when I saw our representative's smiling face at Hamburg Airport. He isn't paid to meet ferry flights. All went well once we arrived at the Canadian Pacific Hotel.

August 22nd, we worked Hamburg/Keplavick/Detroit, nine hours of flight time, then commercial to Oakland to end trip. Upon arrival in Oakland, I went to the F/A supervisor's office to clarify what had transpired August 16th, thru 24th. I wasn't fired, but I wasn't to become a senior F/A either. Later I concluded that the few dollars a month more wasn't worth the aggravation. Bad luck, bad day, bad week, bad trip. Things were bound to get better.

5
X MARKS THE SPOT

Tenerife Airport in the Canary Islands off the coast of Morocco, West Africa had flaws. The person who mapped out the airport site died before the building plans were completed. The people who worked with him had chosen to finish the project with his plans. They located the map he used and on the map were little xxx's. His assistant thought that these xxx's were the places considered for the airport location, so he picked one of these locations marked with an x as the new airport site. As it turned out, the xxx's indicated the most hazardous areas and was in fact the worst places to build an airport. They built the airport and only then did they realize their mistake.

This day in 1979, after working into Tenerife Island just west of Las Palmas Island in the Canary Archipelago, a few crewmembers rode by city bus to an area where locals charged tourists a fee to ride camels.

The camel man motioned me over and waved his hand in the hot island air. The camel bent its white bony legs and lay down when the camel man hit it with a stick behind the knees. The saddle was wide with a blanket over it and camel man helped me swing my leg over the tan leather seat.

He held a thick rope that tied around the camel's jaw, which I hoped would prevent the camel from spitting, but it didn't. The camel turned his head toward me and opened his mouth. I thought it was going to bite me and I wanted off. The camel man thought this funny and refused to let me off until my ride was over. He led me around the dirt streets of Tenerife; I rocked back and forth and passed white clay homes and palm trees while I clenched my teeth. Although I was pleased that I rode a camel, the rest of the day, I smelled like that beast.

Later we went on a tour of a banana plantation. I mentioned to our guide that I had heard tarantulas lived near banana plants. He said they liked to, but now there was a repellant on the bananas to kill them. I kept an eye peeled for them anyway.

A month later, on a layover in Las Palmas, Canary Islands our representative called my room and told me that since my roommate was on sick leave he had located another F/A to replace her. My roommate was in the room at the time and I asked her if she had called to go on sick leave.

"No," she said.

I told the representative this and he said the other flight attendant was waiting for them at the airport so it was too late to cancel her. Besides, she had just commercialed in and he would feel silly if he asked her to commercial back. Therefore, we worked with one extra F/A.

On another occasion in Las Palmas, there was a schedule change.

"You have fifteen minutes to get dressed," the captain said after he tapped on my door.

According to our contract, we were supposed to get one hour. When possible, I dressed in less than the one hour if I'm told to do so. I had just given myself a pedicure and my toenails were bright red. I dressed and put my stocking on last.

Once on the aircraft, I felt a tugging sensation around my toes. I walked into the bathroom, took off my shoes, and pulled my nylons away from my toenails. The almost dry nail polish had more sticking power than the krazy glue I used to repair my broken nail.

Years ago I would not have imagined that I'd have the opportunity to visit such fascinating places. My layovers kept me on the go and enthusiastic about future destinations.

My camel ride in Tenerife, Canary Islands.

CHAPTER 4

HONG KONG OR KOWLOON?

1
SHOP UNTIL YOU DROP

In the early 1800's, Hong Kong, meaning 'Fragrant Harbor,' when written in Chinese characters, was a fishing village and an English gateway to Asia. Chinese green tea became popular among Europeans along with silk and porcelain. The Chinese needed almost nothing the west had to offer. The British set up a third-party trade to remedy this problem. The Brits first exchanged merchandise in India and Southeast Asia for cotton and opium then traveled to China. Instead of the English trading the usual silver for desired merchandise, they traded opium to the Chinese. The Chinese government banned the use of opium and sank two English ships that carried 20,000 chests of it (2.5 million pounds) into China. The British considered this an act of war, battled China, and won. In 1842, China ceded Hong Kong Island to the British and the treaty Nan King was signed. This didn't stop the fighting however and in 1860, China ceded Kowloon and the New Territories to Britain. In 1898 Britain signed a ninety-nine year lease for Hong Kong, Kowloon, and the New Territories.

On December 7th, 1941, six hours after the Japanese attacked Pearl Harbor they attacked the British Crown Colony of Hong Kong. After eighteen days of battle, the British Colony fell to the Japanese on Christmas Day 1941 and Hong Kong didn't return to the British until the end of WWII. By the time I started flying in 1972, Kowloon and Hong Kong had become real tourist attractions.

I'd flown two years, six months when scheduled to work a trip to Anchorage, Alaska then on to Kai Taik Airport in Kowloon. This was not the first time I'd been there. Some people didn't realize that when they booked a trip to Hong Kong they actually stayed in Kowloon and not the island of Hong Kong.

We approached Kowloon over the water and strategically flew through the skyscrapers of the British Colony. Glancing out the window after checking seatbelts for landing, I saw skyscrapers that looked so close; I thought I might be able to see people in their apartments. The no smoking sign went on, (The F/A's signal to sit down and buckle in). I buckled my seatbelt and concentrated on my emergency procedures. The aircraft touched down at Kai Taik Airport at 0700 local, 1500 California time. The F/A in the forward cabin opened her door and a smelly sulfuric odor filled the cabin, which came from the polluted water adjacent to the airport. A passenger inquired if I was flying immediately back to Anchorage. To most that would be a stupid question but a F/A had gone on sick leave in Hong Kong and one on our crew was to replace her and fly back in two hours. I had to reply, "sometimes".

We retrieved our suitcases at baggage claim and boarded the bus to the Holiday Inn. I was given a single room since a F/A on another flight had come down with food poisoning and one on our crew had been rescheduled to replace her. This left an odd member of junior flight attendants, and I as the most senior junior, received a single room at the Holiday Inn.

My fiancé and I had planned to marry June 29, 1975 and I needed a wedding gown. I'd been awake for twenty-four hours, but was determined not to sleep the day away. I inquired at the Holiday Inn about a tailor and they suggested one two blocks away. I walked the two blocks mesmerized by the animation of Kowloon (or lack of sleep) and entered a twelve by fifteen foot establishment. "Do you make wedding gowns?" I asked.

"Yes," the tailor replied. For twenty minutes, I thumbed through two books.

"I like this one best," I said pointing to a full-length fitted gown with long lace sleeves. "I'd like to make one change though. Could you change the collar to sit up on my neck?"

"That shouldn't be a problem," the tailor replied.

"How much would it cost?" I asked.

"This one's made with French lace. I need to calculate how much the material is per yard." He pulled out a pad of paper and started calculating the cost and handed me the slip of paper. The total cost of my wedding gown was seventy-six dollars.

"How long will it take to finish it?" I asked.

"One week," the tailor replied.

"Could you make that six days?" I asked. "I've only six days before my flight leaves."

"It can be made in six days," he replied. "There will be three fittings."

I took out my wallet and handed twenty U.S. dollars to the tailor as a down payment, he wrote up a receipt, and measurements were taken. Exhausted, I went back to the hotel to sleep.

The next morning I awoke at 0800 and lay there thinking. What had I done yesterday? Did I really choose a wedding gown? I was fearful I had blundered in ordering so hastily. Noticing a newspaper under my door, I reached for it. It was the Sunday paper. The tailor's hours of business were: Monday thru Friday 10 to 6, Saturday 10 to 7, Sunday closed. Powerless at this time to deal with the problem I turned the TV on to the Holiday Inn information channel. There was a piece on Victoria Peak. I lay there until my stomach growled, then walked over to my suitcase, gathered my Grape Nut cereal, Sanka, sugar, cup, spoon and heating coil. After breakfast, I called the conceriege.

"I want to visit Victoria Peak. How do I get there?" I asked.

"Grab a red taxicab," the conceriege said. "The Star Ferry and the taxi ride shouldn't cost more than seven Hong Kong dollars (one dollar fifty cents U.S.).

Ten minutes later, I'd exchanged money and met up with Trisha, Kathy, and Carmel with whom I'd planned to sightsee. We departed for Victoria Peak on foot. Outside the hotel, throngs of people flowed down the sidewalks like water down a hill. They pushed us along. I thought of stopping to see if the people would flow around me like a rock in a stream or nudge me as they passed. Everyone seemed to be in a state of urgency, constantly moving. We arrived at the Star Ferry and cued up for the fifteen- minute ride. Going with the flow, we sat in the first available seats. The ferry drifted away from the dock and I gazed back at

Kowloon's tightly packed concrete skyscrapers, which looked like giant fingers that gathered up the people that arrived. There was a ferry in front of ours, and a couple others returning to Kowloon in a constant parade. The sky near the horizon was a yellowish color and the water murky, but it didn't smell bad as it had when we landed. I glanced at the locals. Some read the Hong Kong paper and some slept before we bumped up to the dock on our way to Victoria Peak. Numerous taxicabs lined the exit to the ferry. Taxis for some unknown reason didn't have any identification on them. They were identified only by their color, red. We chose one, piled in, and made our way through the cramped streets of Hong Kong. We pointed out numerous shops we wanted to stop at on our return to the ferry (none of which we could locate later).

The taxicab stopped by an ornate restaurant gleaming in gold and Chinese red with a tiger painted on the entrance to ward off harm. The driver pointed in the direction of a cable car and said that was as far as he could take us. We purchased tickets and boarded the cable car to head up the mountain to Victoria Peak.

Later on the peak, we entered a restaurant with red and white-checkered tablecloths, drank English tea, and ate while we appreciated the magnificent view of the city. Victoria Peak was peaceful, quiet, and high above the madness of Hong Kong, the total opposite of the crowded streets below. I enjoyed both the journey to Victoria Peak and the solitude once we arrived.

Over lunch, we decided to visit Tiger Balm Gardens, a park that displayed effigies from Chinese mythology. I had learned from a pharmacist in Kowloon that Tiger Balm was an ointment that smelled like Vicks vapor rub, and was used for sore muscles, colds, and other ailments. After I clicked a few pictures we decided to shop.

A short while later a taxicab stopped and we four climbed in. Off we went to the flea market. Tables, shaded by awnings, were located on both sides of the flea market's lengthy alleyway. Locals and tourists shopped for leather goods, snuff bottles, jade, ivory, porcelains, wood-carvings, trinkets, toys, ornaments, embroidered jackets, and copies of

American products. Many of the designer labels were glued on, not sewn on.

With the arrival of dusk, we decided we should catch a taxicab to the Star Ferry. We waved at the red taxicabs that passed by, but none acknowledged us. Frustrated and exhausted we devised a plan, and waited for the next red Datsun, which was the same make and model of the other taxicabs to stop by the traffic light. We jumped in. "Take us to the Star Ferry," we said in our determined New York voice.

The driver who said not a word, stepped on the accelerator and drove to the Star Ferry. When we arrived, I handed him what I thought was the appropriate fare.

"I'm not a taxi driver," he said in perfect English. He just happened to have a red Datsun, which was the commonplace taxi.

After we thanked him profusely, we cued up with the others who waited to board the Star Ferry. "I bet that was the first time he got hijacked by flight attendants," I remarked.

Once back in Kowloon, the four of us walked into the Red Chinese Store. Chinese herb medicines, regional food products, furniture, and clothing were displayed. They also carried art objects, mink and leopard-skin coats, laces, brocades, silks, ivory and toggles (Chinese buttons). Hong Kong also had numerous antique shops that were crammed with artifacts. Even the cabinets for sale were full of stuff.

That evening I started to worry about my wedding gown. My first fitting was at ten o'clock Monday.

The next morning I awoke to the sound of the phone ringing. I lifted the receiver. "Hello," I said.

"This is your nine o'clock wakeup."

"Thank you," I replied. I lay there a minute trying to orient myself, then rolled out of bed and looked in the mirror. It was midnight in California, no wonder I felt so awful. I dressed in my Gloria Vanderbilt jeans and yellow shirt, then slipped out the door to visit the tailor.

I arrived at the tailors and recognized the man inside as the one I'd talked to on Saturday.

"Good morning," he said.

"I have a problem," I said. "I came in on Saturday afternoon and picked a wedding gown. The problem is I had just flown in from the United States and was exhausted. I think I might have made a mistake." I showed him my receipt.

"Your first fitting was scheduled for ten o'clock today, but the gown isn't here yet. I'll make a call and see how far along they are." He spoke into a phone, and then came back to me. "I'm sorry, the order can't be cancelled. They purchased the material on Saturday and started immediately. You did say you wanted it in six days didn't you?"

"Yes," I said. "I was just too hasty in ordering."

"If you had waited until today, we couldn't have finished it before your flight home. In fact, the gown should be here by noon for your first fitting. After today's fitting, you'll have another at ten o'clock on Wednesday and the final fitting on Thursday at four o'clock. What time do you leave on Friday?"

"I leave at noon on Friday," I replied. I reminded him that I wanted the collar up around my neck and he said not to worry.

I returned at noon for my first fitting. The gown was pinned to fit exactly. When the tailor stopped pinning, I carefully stepped off the wood platform and walked gingerly to the dressing room. Carefully I slipped the dress off my shoulders, redressed, and stepped out.

After my fitting, I joined my friends and we four wandered down Temple Street and Jordan Ave where the hawkers were. Hawkers were local people who had items to sell but no shops to sell them in and no licenses. Sometimes these items were purchased in China and black marketed in Hong Kong. The hawkers wheeled wooden carts around the streets of Hong Kong and Kowloon. A canvas covered the merchandise. When the city officials weren't present, the hawkers removed the canvas. Each hawker had one type of product. For instance, one cart would be filled with belts or blouses or ski jackets. At first the items looked cheap since they were jumbled together, but then I noticed the designer labels. Local people and tourists flocked to these carts. Where else can you buy a sweater with a designer label for two dollars U.S. and a designer belt for a buck? I brought an envelope of one-dollar bills to expedite purchases. However, the buyer had to be quick to purchase because if a city official came near to the hawker, he would throw the canvas cover over his goods and take off running, wheeling his wheelbarrow type cart at lightning speed. Sometimes they left you holding their goods, but the man who watched out for the city officials collected them later. The hawker rarely stayed in one place for more than five minutes.

Because Hong Kong was such a wonderful place to shop, I had been requested to buy items for friends and relatives. They'd all say, "Don't worry, I'm sure I'll like whatever you like," before the purchase. On this occasion I was to purchase a Seiko watch with a red second hand, day and date, blue face and an expandable watchband. I looked for hours for this watch. I discovered I would need to change the watchband and had the store paint the second hand red. This was done and I returned with what I thought was a perfect purchase. As it turned out the watch had all these qualities except that the numbers were too small for my relative to read without glasses so she sold the watch to someone else. I was disappointed.

The evenings were as busy as the days. Some shops stayed open late, sometimes until ten o'clock depending on the area. Families owned most of these shops and quite often lived behind their store. That evening, my roommate, and I decided to be adventurous and visit a tattoo parlor. An entire street consisted of these parlors, which weren't in the better part of the city, but it was well populated so we weren't concerned. We entered one dimly lit building that had spider webs and filthy "white" walls with trash in the corners. We entered this one since those on the street were closed. We climbed the narrow staircase careful not to touch the walls. Bare light bulbs hung from the wires at the landings. Trash littered the concrete floor and the hallway was filled with a fishy aroma. We peered in thru the side window and saw a gray couch with a white sheet draped over it. Next to the couch was a table with small glass containers and some paraphernalia.

The wooden door had an eight-inch peephole, just like the ones in 1920 movies about prohibition. We rung the bell and a man opened the peephole and asked what we wanted.

"We're interested in getting a tattoo," we said.

"I'm open at eleven o'clock," he replied.

We headed back down the stairwell and onto the street. The bright sunlight made us squint. I reached into my purse for my sunglasses and we turned toward the hotel.

When we returned to the tattoo parlor at eleven o'clock, the street wasn't as busy and being dark, the bare light bulbs on the ceiling made scary figures on the wall. The inside of the room was as dingy as the outside. The only pictures on the wall were of people with tattoos; one picture was of a man covered with tattoos from head to toe. Mom and a heart with an arrow through it seemed to be the most popular for men; the women had butterflies and flowers tattooed on their bottoms. We spoke to the tattoo man for a while and asked him about the needles used and the dyes. The needles sat on a desk-like table covered with papers and knick-knacks. These needles were in uncovered jars filled with yellow alcohol. The dyes were clumped on an artist's pallet. The tattoo'er dipped the needle in the dye then punctured the skin. The tattoo'e may lie down on a cot or sit upright in a chair. The tattoo parlor was popular this night with military personnel who docked in Hong Kong Harbor. However, my friend and I decided against getting the tattoo and headed back to the hotel

The next day, Tuesday, I met some friends and we decided to eat brunch at the Peninsula Hotel. We arrived at the magnificent building decorated in the European style. The entrance was grand and we ascended a sweeping red-carpeted staircase that looked to be fifteen feet wide. At the top of the staircase was the dinning area. The tables were covered with white tablecloths and fresh flowers were placed on every table. This hotel was one of the finest in the world. It also had a spectacular view of the harbor. Below we saw double decker buses along with the trucks, taxicabs, and other vehicles.

The waiter brought over a basket of freshly baked warm rolls, jelly, and butter. "Are you ready to order?" he asked.

I unfolded the white cloth napkin that covered the rolls and peered in. "I think I'll just have these and some tea for now." The waiter left and returned with the tea. By that time, my friend and I were on our second roll. "Could you bring us more rolls?" I asked. This was all we wanted. We planned to take a ferry to Lantau Island this day.

My friends and I headed toward the ferry to go to Lantau Island, camera in hand. The weather was cool, perfect for an afternoon cruise. We cued up to board. Little cakes were served on the ferry, which were delicious. I'm not sure they were ours to take—they might have been for the large group of Chinese who traveled together in our section of the ferry.

Once underway, we passed numerous little islands that dotted the water along with dozens of small fishing boats. The ferry docked where people swam. I picked up my purse and cued up with the other passengers to disembark. Lantau was lush and rolling hills covered the island. We thought about basking on the beach instead of going to the monastery but boarded a bus and headed up the narrow winding road. It felt like the bus was inches from the edge of the cliff. The driver drove fast around sharp curves; we leaned to the left then leaned to the right. By the time we arrived, both of us felt ill.

After the frightening bus ride, we walked up what seemed like thousands of steps before we reached the monastery. It appeared deserted. The grounds of the monastery were well kept with lots of flowers and open temples. Not one leaf had dropped off the perfectly manicured trees. People who chose to stay overnight were fed at the monastery. Cots were set up to sleep on if they didn't care to sleep on the ground. We decided instead to return to the hotel and slept in comfort.

Wednesday I returned to the tailor for my ten o'clock fitting. I slipped on the gown and it fit exactly. I fussed with the collar. "Don't forget I want this up around my neck to frame my face." I said.

"I'll pin it up now so the seamstress knows what you want," the tailor replied.

He stopped pinning and I stepped off the wood platform and walked to the dressing room. Carefully I slipped the gown off my shoulders, redressed, and stepped out.

The following day, Thursday, I would have my final wedding gown fitting at four o'clock. Thursday was also our last full day in Kowloon, and then we four flight attendants planned a trip to the New Territories and Aberdeen.

2
THE NEW TERRITORIES

Thursday, our last day in Kowloon, the same three friends and I visited both the New Territories and Aberdeen. We met in the lobby at nine, piled into a taxi, and instructed him to go to the train station fifteen minutes away. Once on the road we saw numerous elder Chinese men and women that carried birdcages through a park.

"Why are so many people carrying bird cages?" I asked our taxi driver.

"It's an ancient Chinese custom to take birds for walks," he replied. "The young don't practice this custom though. Birds represent freedom to the Chinese and magpies are a symbol if happiness and good luck."

I recalled an incident that happened on a flight from Hong Kong. A passenger brought his parakeet with him to his seat on the aircraft in a small box. The F/A took his parakeet to the galley and it escaped in the aircraft.

"Free drinks for the person who captures the bird," a F/A said over the PA.

The passengers laughed. Some stood up and watched the little parakeet flutter by. It lighted on someone's hair and before it could lift off again the passenger in row ten seat C grabbed it. "Free drinks for the passenger in row ten seat C a F/A announced. I smiled. It became a diversion from the cramped boring flight. Upon arrival, agriculture was informed of the parakeet and they wanted to see its immigration papers. The owner didn't realize papers were required. I never found out what happened to that little bird.

The taxi neared the train station and I gathered my belongings (coat, purse, tourist book).

At 0945, we boarded the train and started on our adventure. The train stopped only at Kam Tin, the walled village constructed in 1600, which was inhabited exclusively by members of the Tang clan. Next, we passed by several refugee camps; villages of old gray houses with upturned eaves, water buffalo, rice patties, and land as far as the eye could see.

I pulled out my tourist book and read about the New Territories. "The British colony of Hong Kong trades with Red China through the New Territories and the New Territories contain the airport, reservoirs, farm areas, industrial complexes, and desalinization plant." I started reading aloud. "In ancient China, there were no straight lines. A man built his house according to the position of an ancestral pond, or the grouping of trees. Architecture was based on feeling." This sounded romantic to me.

When we arrived at the border of China, we faced barbed wire. The Chinese people hadn't the freedom to leave China if they chose to. We observed life going on within the Chinese villages, on the opposite side of the Shumchun River through telescopes at the Lok Ma Chau police station.

I clicked a few pictures of the scenery and of the young Chinese girls who posed for pictures. Some were barefoot. The last picture I snapped was of a ten year old Chinese girl who carried a ten-month-old baby in a backpack. She wore long brown pants and a short brown jacket with red trim and poised for the camera, her back arched to balance her heavy load. Her arms hung limply forward. It was apparent from the look on her face that she didn't want to do this. How different life was for young girls here. I handed her a Hong Kong dollar and said "Thank you."

By lunchtime it was time to catch the train back to Kowloon. We were ready to locate one of those inexpensive restaurants located above the bakeries or up stairwells where most might not imagine a restaurant to be. They always had tablecloths, usually somewhat soiled and only chopsticks.

We ate at one of these elusive Dim Sum restaurants decorated with red and gold dragons. Dragons not only warded off harm, but were also rain spirits. They had power over when it rained and the type of rain. We were the only Americans present, and the other customers stared at us.

Young Chinese girls pushed trolleys around the room and called out what foods they offered. We'd motion her over and peered into the individual bamboo bowls and made our selection. Finished with the last of the tea, we took the lid off the teapot. The Chinese girl who brought us the tea returned and picked up the empty pot to refill. The cost of the eight dishes we chose came to five U.S. dollars.

During a previous trip, a crewmember had had a friend in Hong Kong with a large boat and that time she invited me to cruise around Hong Kong Harbor with them. Her 'large boat' had turned out to be a beautiful yacht, with a lovely lower deck nicely decorated, a kitchen, bathrooms, and a large upper deck. It had been a peaceful respite from the hustle of the city. We'd floated by the junks through Aberdeen and away from the masses of people. We drunk and talked on deck until one of the workers brought out a table and set it with a linen tablecloth, silverware, glasses, and plates. Then we dined on seafood and local delicacies.

Later some had swum. The sun had sunk behind the green hills. In the moonlight, the phosphorus in the water made it glitter. I had rested in the bow of the yacht, had watched the lights flicker on the water, and thought about the people who had lived on the junks. They rarely went ashore. Food was brought to them and their wastes were dumped in the water. The children grew up not knowing any other way of life. The parents fished by day and played mahjong by night. I remembered having watched a vender sampan (small boat) hand the mahjong player's food.

After day dreaming about past trips, we decided to catch a taxi to the Holiday Inn. I hoped to take a hot bath but knew that Hong Kong rationed water. If too much water was used at the Holiday Inn, there would be no water out of the tap or so the placard in the bathroom stated.

We arrived at the hotel.

"Please let there be water," I said aloud. I entered my room and turned the water lever on. There was water. I soaked in the tub for almost an hour and then slept.

Friday morning at 0800, the day we were to leave, I woke and remembered I'd forgotten my fitting yesterday. I quickly dressed and packed my suitcase for the twelve o'clock show (meet) in the lobby for the two o' clock departure back to the states. I ran to the tailors. It was closed. I peered into the door. No one was there. I sat down on the sidewalk and waited. At eleven o'clock the tailor arrived.

"I'm sorry," I said. "I forgot my fitting yesterday."

"I have the dress in the back," the tailor replied. "You need to try it on one more time."

I looked at my watch. It was eleven fifteen.

"If something isn't right I don't have the time to get it fixed," I said. "I need to be back at the hotel at noon."

"We could mail it to you," the tailor replied.

"I'll try it on quickly," I decided. I went to the dressing room, pulled the curtain, and held the dress in front of me. I glanced at my watch again. Now it was eleven thirty. I slipped out of my uniform and into the wedding gown.

"I'm going to need help with the buttons," I said. "I don't have time to button them all, I just need to get an idea about the fit."

"It looks like it fits you perfectly," the tailor remarked. "The length is right also."

I looked at the collar and tried to stand it up around my neck. It flopped down.

"Aren't there any buttons on the collar to keep it up?" I asked.

"No," the tailor replied. "This is very fine French lace, the buttons would tear the lace."

"I don't like it this way," I said. "It gathers around my neck like a clown collar."

"You could leave it with us and we could see what we could do to fit it up around your neck."

"No, I want to take it with me," I said. I glanced at my watch again and noticed it was now quarter to twelve. "Please unbutton me quickly." I redressed while the tailor wrote up the receipt for the final payment. I grabbed for my checkbook.

I was thankful I'd the foresight to pack and put my airline uniform on before I left this morning. It was now five minutes to twelve. I grabbed my dress and ran to the Holiday Inn. Entering the lobby out of breath, I looked at my watch. It was noon exactly. With the dress over my arm, I climbed aboard the crew limo. We worked back to Anchorage, Alaska this day on the DC-10.

3
THE PASSENGERS ARE HERE

I slipped my wedding gown into my topside and carried it with me up the stairs and into the cabin of our flight to Anchorage, Alaska. I was thankful I could pick it up before the flight.

In-flight I reached into a floor level food bin and the snaps popped open on my apron and the bin didn't budge. I got down on my knees and reached in behind the bin and tried to rock it loose. It still wouldn't budge and I asked the engineer for help. He wedged a screwdriver in between the bin and rocked it loose.

The senior F/A picked up the microphone at the forward door and announced, "The passengers are here."

We had a light load of passengers this day. I looked at all those empty seats and thought what a treat this was going to be. Only one hundred forty-nine passengers to take care of.

It was an icy cold evening in Anchorage, Alaska when the aircraft touched down. Not at all like the pleasant weather in Hong Kong. I pulled my knit gloves and crocheted hat out of my topside. I remembered staring out the window at the frosty trees and water on my last trip here and wondered how long it took to become acclimated to these winter temperatures. The last time I had a layover in Anchorage in winter I tried to walk the two blocks to the library, which proved too much of a challenge. Five steps out the door and my face froze. This time, thank goodness we were scheduled to take the commercial airline back to our domicile in the morning.

All the crew bags were on the carousal when we arrived except mine. I glanced over to where the passengers waited for their luggage. I sighed.

My suitcase never appeared. Thank goodness, I had put my wedding gown into my topside and not Big Red (my suitcase). Without Big Red, I joined the crew that waited in the crew bus outside the customs area.

"I guess I'll commercial home in my uniform tomorrow," I said. I looked down at the coffee stain on the front of my uniform.

"Mine's been lost three times in three years," a crewmember said. "At least you're going home. I was scheduled back to Europe the last time Big Red was lost and I had to wear my uniform for three days in Paris."

I smiled and felt better.

Curious about my days off, I reached into my topside for my logbook and started counting the hours. We blocked out of Oakland at 0800 on Wednesday and were supposed to commercial back to Oakland, Friday at 1300. I'd have five days at home.

The crew checked in at the Anchorage Holiday Inn, and I went to my room and hung up my wedding gown. Then met in Barbara's room with a hotel water glass and tidbits that had flown half way around the world in my topside. Some brought diet cokes and others brought wine. Half eaten bags of chips, peanuts, cookies, carrots, and mustard were clustered on the round Formica table. What wasn't consumed at this point would be tossed in the trash. Others brought needlepoint items to work on while we conversed.

I plunked down on the chestnut rug cross-legged and flattened my back against the mini bar. I had brought my uniform apron to sew a button on the waistband since the snaps popped each time I bent over.

We chatted about babies who were placed on the multi colored airline rug to sleep. Once a baby was wrapped in a blanket on the floor and I almost stepped on her. I woke the parents to let them know that babies shouldn't be on the floor. The annoyed parents replied that the TIA representative had said he would give them an extra seat and a bassinet. That flight had no extra seat and no bassinets. I informed them, for the safety of the baby, it would be necessary to hold her. Exasperated, the mother picked up the child and held her for the remainder of the flight.

I nudged my roommate and glanced toward the right hand corner of the room by the curtains. She tilted her head and caught a glimpse of the co-pilot and another crewmember cuddling. "I heard they'd been asking scheduling for the longest time if they could fly together," I remarked.

The captain stood up, removed his uniform jacket, and unbuttoned his white uniform shirt. I wondered what he planned to do. Our captain then put his shirt back on with the open collar in the back, then donned his jacket with the lapels in the back and adjusted his white shirt collar across his Adams apple. We started to get the idea when he retrieved the Gideon bible from the nightstand between the two double beds and approached the couple gesturing for them to rise.

At that point, we knew what he was up to and smiled. Distracted, the couple rose and the captain pretended to marry them. Everyone chuckled and congratulated the happy couple.

Even though the crew party was entertaining, I was tired and had trouble keeping my eyes focused and finally set off toward my room. I toddled over to my bed, pulled down the orange and brown comforter, lay down, and expected to recoup some energy before I changed into my pajamas. I glanced at my telephone, hoping my message light would be on and my suitcase would be found. It wasn't.

I awoke the next morning to the sound of the telephone. It was my 0800 wakeup, for the 0900 pickup. I pulled my shampoo out of my topside and scurried toward the bathroom. TIA hadn't delivered my misplaced suitcase. I quickly washed my hair and the coffee stains off the front of my uniform. I had no hair dryer to dry my hair and sodden uniform, so pulled it over my head damp and stepped into my blue leather pumps.

There was five minutes left before I was to meet the crew in the hotel lobby. I collected my belongings and headed for the elevator. The crew transportation was outside the lobby door and I headed for it.

After a short ride to the airport, we boarded the Alaskan Airlines jet to commercial to San Francisco. I reached for a pillow and blanket from the open overhead rack and sat down in my seat by the window. Still tired, I fell asleep.

I awoke when I felt pressure on my eardrums. The plane was on descent into San Francisco Airport. I reached under the seat for my purse, removed my mirror, and noticed that a portion of my mascara had migrated south. I stood and attempted to straighten out the wrinkles that had amassed on my uniform dress and headed for the lavatory. It wasn't long before I heard a knock on the lavatory door.

"We're beginning our final descent, you'll have to return to your seat," the Alaskan Airline F/A declared.

"Ok" I reluctantly replied feeling the gravitational force on my body. I unlatched the lock, stepped out, and returned to my seat.

"I feel like crap, how do I look?" I asked a fellow crewmember.

"You look better than you feel," the crewmember replied.

I smiled, fastened my seat belt, and we landed in San Francisco minutes later. I was so pleased to be home with my wedding gown. I just hoped Big Red would arrive before my next flight.

4
HOME SWEET HOME

    This day the only item I had to unpack was my wedding gown. I removed it from my topside and hung it in my closet. As always, once home, I pulled out the trash container that was located under the sink and positioned it by the kitchen table. I carried the overflowing shoebox where the mail was kept to the Formica table, sat down on the yellow padded kitchen chair, picked up the first piece of mail, an ad, and tossed it in the trash. After I'd sorted all the items that were not interesting, I started to focus in on the important mail. I picked up an envelope with an IRS return address and opened it.

    After the initial greeting the letter read, "We have some questions about your 1973 tax return. Please call the IRS and make an appointment to discuss the matter."

    I walked over to the olive green wall phone and dialed. A receptionist answered.

    "Hi, my name is Cindy Swensen. I received a letter stating the IRS has some questions about my 1973 tax return."

    "When would it be convenient for you to come in for an appointment," the receptionist asked.

    "I can come in today," I replied.

    "I can fit you in at three o' clock with Mr. Johnson. Is that a good time for you?"

    "How long will the appointment be?" I asked.

    "It's hard to judge, it would depend on how complicated your return is."

    "Ok, I'll be in at three," I said.

    "Be sure to bring your receipts with you."

    I walked to the bedroom, kneeled down, reached under the bed for the manila envelope marked 1973 taxes. I opened the envelope and looked at my pay stubs. My pay was only a little over seven thousand dollars for the entire year. Thumbing through the handful of receipts I could see nothing the IRS would be interested in so put everything back in the manila envelope.

At three o'clock, I entered the large modern IRS building in San Jose. I walked up the stairs to the second floor and over to the receptionist.

"Good afternoon, my name is Cindy Swensen, I have an appointment with Mr. Johnson at three."

"Please take a seat and Mr. Johnson will be with you in a minute," the receptionist said.

I glanced over to the brown leather sofa and started toward it. Magazines were stacked on the glass table. I thumbed through the selection. Not interested in any of them, I sat and listened to the soft music that played. Two middle-aged men sat on my right and discussed something about a document one of the men had in his hands. From what I could decipher one of the men was being audited and the other one was a tax attorney. It looked like everyone was paired up except me. I couldn't help but wonder if I should have asked my fiancé to join me. Was I being naïve to think this was of no major concern?

"Miss. Swensen, Mr. Johnson can see you now," the receptionist said.

I picked up the flat manila envelope that sat on my lap, pushed myself forward, and stood up. Two men wearing suits were on their way out of the office that I headed for. They left the door open and I entered.

"Good afternoon, please sit down," a man in a black striped suit said. He didn't introduce himself.

I sat in front of a large oak desk and waited while Mr. Johnson scribbled something on a file folder.

"Miss. Swensen, do you have any idea why you were asked to come here?" Mr. Johnson asked.

"All I know is that you have a question about my 1973 taxes," I replied.

"Well, it looks like you have made deductions that the IRS doesn't allow."

"The only deductions I've made are uniform deductions," I stated.

"Exactly," Mr. Johnson said. "May I see your receipts?"

I reached into the manila envelope, pulled out three receipts, and handed them to him.

"Is this all you have?"

"I also have my pay stubs," I stated. "Trans International takes out six dollars a month for uniform expenses."

I handed the manila envelope to Mr. Johnson. He took the envelope and pulled out the pay stubs and studied them approvingly. "Why does Trans International deduct six dollars?

"The deduction is for my uniform dress and coat." I replied.

"This six dollar company deduction for your uniform dress and coat is a legitimate deduction. However what are these three receipts for?"

"The receipt for eighteen dollars is for my white plastic uniform boots. The receipt for six dollars is for my white cotton uniform gloves and the third, for fifteen dollars is for my white plastic uniform purse," I replied.

"The company you work for didn't supply you with these items?" Mr. Johnson asked, his deep voice resonating.

"No, I needed to purchase them," I replied.

"Well, I'm afraid that the IRS doesn't allow these deductions," Mr. Johnson stated emphatically.

Exasperated, I asked, "Why not?"

"You could use these items outside of your job."

"I'm not going to wear white cotton gloves, plastic boots and carry a white plastic purse except when I'm in uniform."

"I'm sorry, the IRS will not allow these deductions. You need to write a check for the thirty-nine dollars and make it out to the IRS."

"I used these items all year as part of my uniform. If I wore them with my street clothes my boots would have worn out."

"It clearly states in the IRS rules that items that can be worn as street clothes can't be deducted," Mr. Johnson stated firmly.

"Thirty-nine dollars is about one sixth of my net paycheck every two weeks," I said frustrated.

"I'm sorry, I don't make the rules."

I reached into my brown leather purse and pulled out my wallet and wrote a check for the thirty-nine dollars and handed it to him.

"Thank you," Mr. Johnson said.

Still exasperated, I got up and walked out of the office.

Even though I had to write a thirty-nine dollar check for uniform items, I supposed I'd survive. To me Hong Kong was a seven-day vacation and my wedding gown had made it back with me. What else could I possibly ask for except my big red suitcase?

5
WEDDING PLANS

After being home for ten days, I received my next itinerary. I was assigned another trip to Hong Kong that would return June 16th, 1975, thirteen days before I was to be married. The schedulers were accommodating in scheduling me home for my wedding and my lost suitcase was delivered to my home, so everything was going well.

I entertained the thought of bringing my wedding dress with me for final alterations, but the idea of stuffing it in my topside again was not appealing. I also felt uncomfortable about placing it in my suitcase, even though the odds of Big Red being lost twice in a row would be unusual.

We landed in Anchorage, Alaska on June 15th, 1975 after a five-day stay in Hong Kong and were greeted by our airline representative with the feared telex in his hand. The crew anxiously gathered around the forward passenger door to hear the news. Apparently, TIA needed our crew to make another crossing. We were scheduled to fly to Hong Kong again, in thirty-six hours. I started breathing so quickly I thought I might hyperventilate. I was to get married June 29th in California in fourteen days. I called home that evening with the news. Family came to the decision that if I didn't arrive home in time for the wedding I could still get married over the phone by proxy and the party would go on. After I heard about this crossing, I wished we'd planned a small wedding that could be rescheduled.

The crew went to the Holiday Inn and then to the Monkey Bar for drinks and I told them what was going on. There was hope that I'd be home the 29th. I returned to my room and noticed my message light was on. I immediately called the message center downstairs. "Cindy, Trans International has informed me that you'll be returning to Oakland June 28th. That's if there isn't a weather or mechanical delay," the TIA representative stated in the taped message.

The day after we arrived in Hong Kong for the second time this trip, my roommate and I went to visit another crewmember in the hotel. She had flowers and food set out on the table. I didn't think they were for me, but soon found out that they were. I smiled. The crew had planned a wedding shower complete with red roses and chrysanthemums, a vodka punch, cakes, hors d'oeuvres, presents, and a card that was made by cut out pictures from magazines and signed by everyone. They had taken the trouble to buy me perfumed soaps, bubble bath and a cream colored negligee all wrapped up and tied with bows. Later we all went to dinner, then danced at the Polaris nightclub. It took my mind off my worries.

The following day my roommate and I toured the Ten Thousand Step Monastery in Satin, a twenty-minute train ride away. Satin had no busses or taxis so we walked for what seemed like miles before we arrived at the first of the ten thousand steps. The steps led us through a lush jungle area. At the top of the staircase was a tall red open door. Two pairs of shoes were outside the massive door so we slipped ours off and placed them next to the other shoes. Inside was a statue of a monk sitting cross-legged on a four-foot platform. An altar was in front of him with a red and white tapestry cloth under it. At the foot of the platform was a little red bench. Only one piece of cloth covered his thin body and this was tied at the waist. I peered in and a Chinese woman motioned me to come inside. She handed me an incense stick, lit it, and then motioned me to place it in a brass urn in front of the altar. I did as I thought she wanted me to do while she said a few words in Chinese. I presumed it was a prayer. I prayed that I'd get home for my wedding. Then we headed back down the stairs. Famished, we ate at a chain restaurant called Lindy's, which had awful food. We discovered that a Hong Kong bagel was not the same as New York or English bagel. It was small, hard as rock and you could bounce it off the floor. The manager wasn't pleased when I sent it back.

Breakfast at the Sheraton the following day wasn't any better. At least four waiters walked by our table and counted the number of jellies on our plate. We had only ordered coffee and rolls. When my roommate placed two of the unused jellies in her purse, we both got dirty looks.

Later we cruised on a friend's boat to the Queen Elizabeth that had sunk in Hong Kong Harbor—about a fourth of it stuck out of the water. We cruised around the carrier Midway, through Aberdeen and then dropped anchor at Repulse Bay.

June 27th, 1975, I received my wakeup, dressed, packed, and headed for the lobby. I was relieved that I was headed toward home. We landed in Anchorage at 2100, crew rested, and then commercialed to San Francisco on the 28th. I married June 29th, as planned and wore the wedding gown that was custom made for me in Hong Kong without alteration to the collar. At that point, I was thrilled to have made it to my wedding and pinned the collar up for pictures.

Our wedding, June 1975.

CHAPTER 5

VIETNAM, WAR ZONES & AIRLIFTS

1
DRIFTING OVER YUGOSLAVIA 1974

I rarely saw obstacles until I came to them and trustingly embarked to parts unknown. Scheduling would call, spurt out numerous three-letter codes for cities around the world and I'd scribble them down. Then they'd announce the time I was to show in Oakland to begin this journey. I'd appear at the designated time and head out unaware of the possible dangers or political situations of those countries. I was a naïve chess pawn to be moved about the globe and subjected to the political disagreements and mistrust of people from countries I had little knowledge of. It sounded exciting venturing off to Cyprus, Angola, Iran, and Cuba. Yugoslavia in 1974 was an added surprise adventure. TIA briefed us on health issues, safety issues and passenger issues but not political issues, revolts and uprisings.

Dreaming, content, and all curled up with my eight-inch pillow and turquoise airline blanket all warm and toasty; I along with six cabin crewmembers and the three cockpit members ferried the DC-8 aircraft to position for our next live (passenger) flight. I was awakened by our captain's deep voice over the PA.

"We've been asked to land," our captain said. "Hide your Geneva Convention cards. We will be questioned upon arrival and they may think we are military spies." I glanced out the window and saw a couple of gray fighter jets with colorful stripes on the tail. Good grief, I thought annoyed that my dream had been interrupted. Naively, I wasn't concerned for my safety since I knew I'd done nothing wrong. This was all a big mistake. I pulled my Geneva Convention card from my wallet. In big black letters it said, "United States of America Department of Defense Washington D.C. USAF CO. Grd. Off. 111. I turned the card over and read: 'If taken prisoner he, or in my case she, shall at once show this card to the detaining authority to assist in his identification. He is to be given the same treatment and afforded the same privileges as a member of the Armed Forces in the rank category shown." I placed my Geneva Convention card in the seat pocket in front of me, gathered my belongings, and headed for the lavatory. I splashed my face with water, redid my makeup, and dabbed Emeraude perfume on my temples.

We had entered into Slavic airspace. Why? I thought. I glanced at my watch. It had been fifteen hours since wakeup. Was the captain as exhausted as I was and drift over? The small gray jets were still beside our cigar shaped stretch DC-8. I suppose they were concerned we might scoot away. How bizarre. That would be like a chicken out running a roadrunner.

Upon landing, a group of uniformed military men armed with rifles circled our aircraft. Some boarded and escorted us into the terminal. The cockpit members were separated and questioned one by one. I slid my back down the barren hall wall and sat on the concrete floor, as did the other six cabin crewmembers and waited. I was escorted into a room and told to sit. My purse was searched and my passport removed. Then I was questioned.

"Are you employed by the military?"

"No," I replied.

"Where do you work?" he asked.

"On the aircraft."

"What were you doing on the aircraft?"

"Sleeping," I said.

"Where are you going?"

"Italy," I answered. My purse and passport were returned. Two hours later, we were allowed to depart and continued on to Italy.

Once home in the United States I researched the situation.

Josip Broz Tito's Territorial National Defense doctrine was Yugoslavia's official military doctrine when the National Defense Law of 1969 was published. Tito, born a peasant in Croatia led Yugoslavia as dictator since 1953. Tito was unsure whether it's allegiance was with Russia (Warsaw Pact) or the United States (NATO). The Warsaw Pact would eliminate nuclear weapons from United States forces in Greece and the

United States Navy's sixth fleet in the Mediterranean. Tito didn't want this to happen. Yugoslavia wouldn't accept foreign troops of either alliance on its territory. If either country attempted to enter Yugoslavia, that country would be considered the aggressor and Yugoslavia would immediately join the opposing side for the specific purpose of liberating its territory. Yugoslavia's Territorial National Defense (TND) was codified in article 240 of the Constitution of 1974.

This situation was volatile, and our flying into their airspace could have caused an international incident. Scary.

2
CYPRUS INVASION 1974

I worked into Shannon, Ireland July 19th, 1974 not all that tired so planned to hike to Bunratty Castle from the Limerick Inn for the medieval banquet. We were scheduled to fly passengers into Cyprus the following day.

July 20th, our TIA representative informed us that the flight into Cyprus might not happen since the Turkish military had invaded the country this day. We were on stand-by since the passengers arriving in Shannon that evening still wanted to vacation in Cyprus. We turned on the TV and listened to the news.

On July 20th, 1974, Turkey launched an invasion with 40,000 military troops against the island of Cyprus. The island fell to Turkish military occupation and the Greek Cypriots were forced to the Southern part of Cyprus. The reason for Turkey's invasion was to protect its 18% Turkish minority of the island and claim the Northern part of Cyprus for Turkey.

If this flight had been scheduled one day earlier, our crew would have been eyewitnesses to this invasion. The flight to Cyprus was cancelled and we were scheduled to commercial to New York. I was relieved. The crew migrated to the Limerick lounge for Bailey's Irish Cream and Irish coffee's. I'd been a F/A for two years and knew how lucky I was to be born in America.

3
VIETNAM

In 1954, the country of Vietnam was divided in half at the 17th parallel. To the north was the Communist regime of Ho Chi Mien; to the south was the American backed regime of Ngo Dihn Diem. Between November 1963 and July 1965, President Johnson transformed America's limited engagement in Vietnam into an open-ended commitment.

President Nixon signed a peace agreement calling for a cease-fire on January 23, 1973 in Paris. The terms of agreement called for elections for the South Vietnamese; all prisoners of war were to be released, and American forces were to be withdrawn.

"The people of South Vietnam have been guaranteed the right to determine their own future," President Nixon stated.

In late February 1975, the Ford administration attempted to get Congress to vote for aid to South Vietnam. Congress refused. The Communist forces captured Da Nang. By March 1975 the South Vietnamese soldiers retreated. In April of 1975, Northern troops were outside Saigon and on April 29th Tan Son Nhut Airport was under fire. 'The temperature is 105 and rising, followed by Irving Berlins White Christmas,' was the signal that sent the last remaining Americans running for the United States Embassy rooftop.

One ship located off the shore of Saigon, was the command ship BlueRidge. Aboard were a Brigadier General and a two-star Admiral. The BlueRidge was prepared for a barrage of helicopters that collected the last remaining officials on top of the United States Embassy building. The soldiers aboard the BlueRidge were ordered by President Ford not to go ashore and not to interfere. All helicopters that landed on the BlueRidge were pushed over the side after they were searched. This was done to make room for the next helicopters. Also all weapons were dumped overboard per President Ford's orders. One American woman boarded with a few hundred thousand in U.S. dollars. Another couple had two Samsonite attaché cases that were filled with small gold bars and a pair of pearl handled hand made thirty-eight caliber pistols. The pistols were dumped overboard. All valuables were kept in the ship's safe keeping cells (brig). General Nugyen Cao Ky also landed on the BlueRidge. General Ky, an Air Force general, was the vice president of South Vietnam 1967-71. The commanding officer aboard the BlueRidge, assigned him a USMC aid. He refused stating that he was no longer a General, therefore didn't rate any special treatment.

I'd been to Saigon's Tan Son Nhut Airport numerous times. The first time was in 1974 when more senior F/A's chose me and another junior who had not yet earned the title of Pacific Queen to observe the cleaners while the aircraft was on the ground, which we did. The other F/A and I were told to make sure no bombs were placed onboard and the Pacific Queens walked to the terminal. I'd hoped the cleaners were searched before they entered the aircraft since all I did was look for suspicious items, of which I found none.

TIA also flew into Nha Trang Air force base approximately four hundred miles south of Da Nang on the Gulf of Tonkin, the army base at Cam Ranh Bay less than fifty miles south of Nha Trang and Phnom Penh in Cambodia.

I recalled that on descent into Saigon's Tan Son Nhut Airport late March 1975 one crewmember pointed out the rear exit window across from the galley. Smoke billowed up from the jungle below. We were on descent and the smoke wasn't far from the airport. "Something probably just blew up," she had said.

I thought back to a picture I'd seen in the most recent Trans International "What's Happening" magazine. A TIA aircraft emitted black smoke from the rear of the aircraft. Written under the picture was: "This is 65T on its last trip to Phnom Penh." The article stated, "The aircraft was sent to Phnom Penh, Cambodia to deliver rice and supplies in March of 1975. While on the ground it was hit by rocket attack and was temporarily knocked out of commission." Strangely, this only concerned me slightly. Most of the F/A's on this particular flight had made this run numerous times before. This flight route had become routine and so far, we didn't feel as if we were in danger. The young men we transported were in danger. To many of them, we were the last American females they'd ever see.

Late in March of 1975, I was scheduled to work to Saigon again. On this trip, a military officer offered to take our crew on a tour of the military base in his jeep. The furthest he took us was to the large white sign with blue lettering that said, "Saigon Long Binh." We saw numerous small gray prop planes the size of 727's on the ground. Otherwise, the area looked deserted. I snapped pictures of a two story gray and white building where the Viet Cong had stayed during peace talks. It was embellished with numerous red and yellow flags. On a red banner over the entrance were the words Mona Quax Ming (someone's name), Tet Quy Suu (Happy New Year of the buffalo) 1073. No one came or went from the building, at least not above ground.

We were allowed to enter a bunker made of large gray stones and looked through the rectangle slot where guns point out, then visited a cemetery and last of all went to the Vietnamese Officers Club. At 1100, a military officer drove the crew back to the aircraft to prepare for the twelve thirty departure.

Military flights were easier to work than other charters since the aircraft was configured with fewer seats, no alcohol was served, and the majority of the soldiers slept. At noon, two hundred twenty soldiers boarded the TIA DC-8 headed for Travis Air Force Base in California. An army captain introduced himself to me.

"Good afternoon, I'm Captain Coleman. If any of these men give you any trouble I'm in row 6 seat C."

"Thank you," I replied. "I'm a little concerned about the two men in handcuffs."

"They're not dangerous," Captain Coleman said. "They have armed guards escorting them."

The two men in handcuffs and their escorts walked to the rear of the aircraft and sat in the last row of seats on the right. The escorts brought the prisoners their meals and drinks. The F/A's didn't serve them.

Call buttons lit up in the mid cabin area.

"Something's happening mid cabin," I said. I walked quickly toward the activity. Three soldiers were in the aisle, two standing, and one flaying around on the ground. The soldier appeared to be having an epileptic seizure, but his legs weren't moving. It was about four hours into the flight, the point of no return.

"He'll be all right. He's suffering from substance withdrawal due to an injury. Notice his legs aren't moving. If this were an epileptic seizure his legs would be flaying around like his arms," Captain Coleman said confidently.

The soldier on the ground stopped moving. The two soldiers that were holding his arms down lifted him up and helped him back into his seat.

"Can I bring him a cold towel or something?" I asked sympathetically.

"No, he'll sleep now," Captain Coleman, replied.

It had all stopped so suddenly I thought the soldier was probably given something to sleep. I retrieved an incident accident form and filled it out. The ill soldier slept throughout the remainder of the flight and was helped off the aircraft upon arrival.

Early in April 1975, I flew once again into Saigon. This time all Americans were leaving, I was told. The crew remained on the aircraft that afternoon and waited for the soldiers to arrive. A dark gray bus pulled up next to our TIA airplane and delivered our first group of soldiers. All were dressed in their short-sleeved beige uniforms with white undershirts. All the soldiers wore navy blue canoe shaped hats, except one who had on a French beret. I watched out the airplane window as another gray bus pulled up and out came another identically dressed group of soldiers.

The soldiers were instructed not to board the aircraft until they were given the order to board and formed a large semi circle around the airplane's ramp and waited there. I felt this was a historical moment. I walked toward my topside, took out my Pentax zoom camera and headed toward the forward entrance of the aircraft and out onto the ramp to take a photograph. All the soldiers had big Cheshire grins on their faces. I smiled back, clicked a picture, and went back inside the DC-8 stretch aircraft. At that moment, I didn't notice the movie camera in the background recording the momentous occasion.

Upon landing, a military band greeted our soldiers at Travis AFB in Fairfield, California. They were positioned on the tarmac not far from where the airplane landed. The moment the ramp was in place and the main cabin door was cracked open, the air was filled with the famous marches of John Phillip Sousa, "The Stars and Strips Forever," "Washington Post March" and "King Cotton"

It was after I returned home to the United States that I learned I was seen on the evening news taking that photograph of the soldiers waiting to board the flight home. What they had experienced in Vietnam was beyond my comprehension.

Although I'd worked as a F/A for three years, I was also a student at San Jose State's New College and worked toward my undergraduate degree in liberal arts. I had not witnessed Vietnam protesters before or after any of my flights, but protesters did cause grief at San Jose State and interrupted classes. The administration decided on some occasions to cancel classes. This New College program was set up so that classes could continue, sometimes off campus, so that students could finish the semester and in some cases graduate. I had signed up for classes where the professors allowed me to do my airline work and then meet, after my trips, to discuss projects I was instructed to work on.

My next assignment was to fly to Hong Kong, which we did, but not for long.

4
TAN SON NHUT AIRPORT APRIL 1975

On a pleasant evening in late April 1975, I shopped in Hong Kong at a jeweler dressed in my blue jeans, flowered blouse, and blood red beads. I chose a fire opal ring. Wanting a pinky ring, I left it at the jewelers to be sized. I returned to my room at the Holiday Inn and found someone had slipped a note under the door. It read, "There has been a schedule change, meet in room 204 ASAP." I obediently went to the assigned meeting room and knocked on the door.

"It's open," I heard a female crewmember say.

I walked in and glanced around. Everyone-the six female cabin crewmembers and the three male cockpit crewmembers- looked distressed. All were silent and from the tight mouths and worry in their eyes, I knew something had happened or was about to happen.

"What's going on?" I asked.

"Our representative received a telex. They want us to leave Hong Kong ASAP to pick up Americans in Saigon," our senior F/A replied.

"So what's the problem? We've done that for years."

"Haven't you seen the news?"

"No, I've been shopping."

"North Vietnamese troops are heading for Saigon and the people in Saigon are panicking," she said. "They want us to fly in and help take them out."

"Trans International wants us to fly into Saigon when the airport could be under siege?"

"Yes," she replied. "They want us to depart in two hours. TIA says first we're to position at Yokota AFB, Japan.

The Headquarters for US Forces in the Pacific was located at Yokota Air Base about twenty-five miles west of Tokyo. The Yokota Air Base was established July 1, 1957 and was comprised of Army, Navy, Air Force, and Marines who were stationed in Japan pursuant to the US Japan Treaty of Mutual Cooperation and Security of 1960. The United

States was given use of the facilities in Japan for maintaining regional security.

"I called the teamsters union," our senior F/A said. "They said it was up to us to decide but only the pilots would get hazard pay."

I shivered, "If I decide not to go what will happen?"

"They said if you refuse a trip you'll be fired and must find your own way home," the senior replied.

"We're going to Yokota first," our captain said. "You can decide there."

"How can we be sure Trans International won't reroute us directly to Saigon?"

"I've been instructed to go to Yokota, Japan," he replied. "That's the flight plan I'm filing. If for some reason it changes I promise to let you know."

"Does everyone agree to go to Yokota?" the senior asked. "Let's see a show of hands."

Everyone raised their hands.

"Ok, show in the lobby in one hour."

I went to my room to change into my uniform and pack. The jewelry shop closed at six o'clock and it was already after six. I decided to write a note asking them to mail the ring to me in the U.S. Enclosing twenty Hong Kong dollars for shipping, I sealed the envelope and slipped it into my purse. After scanning the room for forgotten items, I flung my purse over my shoulder and wheeled my luggage down the hallway to the lobby.

Not one crewmember was in the lobby yet. I left my suitcase unattended and ran to the jewelers. The hot and muggy air outside made me perspire. I peered into the window. Nobody could be seen. I knocked on the glass. No answer. I knocked again, still no answer. Slipping the envelope under the door and hoping I hadn't wasted my twenty Hong Kong dollars, I raced back to the Holiday Inn. My luggage was still where I left it but the crew bus was now loaded and waiting for me.

The crew arrived at the airport and boarded the Trans International jet for the empty (ferry) flight to Yokota. I completed my pre-flight check and picked a row of seats to relax in. Opening my topside, I removed my book and placed it in a seat pocket. I lifted the armrests and the seats cushions to make a bed. Placing the seat belts flatly under the seat cushions, and propping up pillows behind me, I leaned back against the fuselage and stretched out over the three seats pulling the blanket up over my legs. I figured I had about twenty minutes before takeoff to relax and read, and then a few hours in-flight before arrival in Yokota. It seemed unreal that I'd be asked to go to an airport when there was fighting going on.

We landed in Yokota and were greeted by the Trans International representative. Everyone gathered to hear what he had to say.

"I've been instructed to tell you that you're on standby to fly into Saigon. Stay by your phone." He continued, "You could have only one hour after Trans International gets the ok."

The crew boarded the bus for the Morikawa Hotel. None of us wanted to fly into a war zone and none of us wanted to lose our jobs by refusing a flight. We were in a state of limbo while we waited for the United States Military to give Trans International the contract to evacuate.

On other occasions, I had enjoyed staying at the Morikawa where TIA crewmembers usually made up 95% of the clientele. I could always find a friend to ride down the strip into town on the hotel's mini bikes. Cute little signs were posted around the hotel, more for the crewmembers than for the others. In broken English, the manager of the Morikawa would write something like: "No boys in girls room, no girls in boy's rooms." Inside the hotel rooms, everything was much smaller than in an American hotel. The tub was deeper, but only about four feet long. The beds were short and narrow and the TV was the ten-inch variety. It was like staying in a dollhouse.

Minutes after arrival the crew met in the restaurant and drank peach juice, a favorite of crewmembers. It smelled and tasted refreshing after being locked up on that stuffy aircraft. Today I thought I'd ask how they made it, thinking that it was made from fresh peaches and maybe a secret ingredient. The chef arrived at our booth and told me all he did was open a can of peaches in heavy syrup, pour it into a blender and whip it up. I thanked the chef, and wondered, how many calories were in a can of peaches in heavy syrup?

Today the crew sat in the restaurant until evening. Every time the phone rang at the front desk, we stopped talking and listened. No one had been asked yet to make a decision on whether they were going to refuse the trip.

Time passed and we were deep into discussing the joys of Japan. I'd mentioned I enjoyed being the first customer at the department store in Yokota during one summer day in 1973 since a large number of the employees lined up at the entrance door and bowed to the customers when they entered. The rest of the employees stood in front of their departments and bowed to the shoppers when they passed. It was a great honor to be the first customer of the day. I hadn't known this so glanced around to see if something else was going on; after all, I'd only bought breath mints.

At 2100, we still hadn't heard from TIA, and I went to my room to sleep.

The next morning, in the newspaper, there was a picture of a World airlines aircraft. People were pushing up the ramp to the aircraft that looked overcrowded. The people had panicked looks on their faces. A F/A peered out a crack in the door. She looked terrified. One man had his hand on the forward cabin door. He looked like he was attempting to pull it open. Apparently, Mr. Daly, the owner of World Airlines, had made the decision to fly into Saigon to rescue the Americans. This reminded me of an article I had read at home about World Airlines. "During the Da Nang flight, I was kicked, slugged, shot at, and bitten. That trip and the orphan flights out of Saigon cost me over a million bucks out of my own pocket, and I don't know how many millions in military contracts and fines, and both trips failed. You ask me why I did it? I'll tell you—cocktail circuit bureaucrats, a golf course president and a country club first lady who cries crocodile tears for the poor little orphans."

Later that day the panicked citizens of Saigon were shown on TV. They were running to a World Airlines jet and hung on to it even as it took off. That afternoon TIA sent a telex stating we were to return to Hong Kong ASAP and then resume our initial itinerary. I was relieved.

Two days later, I arrived at my domicile. I'd been away for eight days and had four days off per airline policy.

After my required time at home, I received my next itinerary. I was scheduled for two Atlantic crossings and one Africa (Angola) to Europe (Portugal) leg of the trip before I headed back to my Oakland, California base.

Soldiers waiting to board TIA in Saigon, 1975.

5
ANGOLA AIRLIFT

The military airlift command (MAC) under the direction of General Nash ordered the airlifting of thirty one thousand five hundred fifty-nine Portuguese from Angola to Lisbon during 1975 and 1976. TIA was one of the airlines commissioned to carry out this airlift.

Until the late 1900's, Portugal used Angola as a "slave pool" for its colony in Brazil and extracted gemstones and metals from Angola's land. In 1974, the Angolan armed forces overthrew the Portuguese regime and talks began for Angolan Independence. In 1975, Angola was granted independence and an airlift took place to evacuate the Portuguese. Many of these Portuguese people had lived in Angola all their lives. Almost everything was left behind. Although our TIA aircraft landed without lights including runway lights, the F/A's saw the fire and homes of our passengers burn as we flew over Angola. Some F/A's heard gunfire upon landing. The Portuguese burned their homes so that the people who had evicted them wouldn't claim what they left. TIA did not inform the F/A's that this would be dangerous. No coverage of this evacuation was telecast in the United States until months after the evacuation.

At the time of liberation from Portugal in 1975, Angola had two thousand coffee plantations. Refugees fled and crossed into neighboring countries and abandoned these plantations. Humanitarian agencies stepped in to feed the hungry. TIA was under contract with the Angolan government to fly supplies to an isolated diamond-mining center in Eastern Angola. Angolan rebels captured three TIA pilots on December 29th after they landed in Angola. The rebels shot and killed the co-pilot (Bill Read) and detained the other two pilots then released them. I shuttered to think it might have happened on one of my flights.

6
IRANIAN REVOLUTION 1978

I was scheduled to fly into Teheran, Iran in December 1978 to position for a special hajj flight. I decided to visit my local library and read the United States Government Report on that country. The economic conditions in Iran in the seventies were deteriorating under the Shan of Iran. Revolutionaries, led by the Ayatollah Khoemeini were upset that Iran adopted some Western practices. The revolutionaries fought against the deterioration in moral standards and the partaking of drugs and alcohol. The revolutionaries blamed those problems on the United States supported Shan of Iran.

I visited my parents in Coronado, California in December 1978 and weighed the issue; go to Iran embroiled in political turmoil or sit on the beach. I chose the beach and called in sick. I later heard that the hotel where the crew stayed was bombed while the crew was out on a flight. Friends told me that damage was minimal and they weren't required to pay their restaurant and telephone charges. Friends mentioned that the special hajj didn't take the Muslims to Mecca as TIA had said. Instead, the crew transported wealthy Iranians around the Middle East to spread the Islamic faith.

Iran was a frightening place in 1978. I know of one female crewmember that was raped in her hotel room. United States females were treated like prostitutes in Iran. Many crewmembers were asked why they were there, and told that they should go home. Four months later, April 1st 1979 the Shah of Iran was overthrown and Ayatollah Khoemeini took power. Iran became an Islamic power and we no longer flew there.

Although I didn't make a practice of going on sick leave, I was glad I had chosen to, and felt I had dodged a bullet.

7
VIETNAMESE REFUGEE FLIGHTS

In the summer of 1979, I was scheduled to fly into Hong Kong to transport Vietnamese, Cambodian, and Laotian refugees into the United States. These flights continued into the early eighties. TIA, among other airlines were commissioned by the U.S. military to transport the refugees from Malaysia, Thailand, Hong Kong, and other countries where they had been relocated for months.

I spoke to many Vietnamese refugees during and after the refugee flights. One in particular described the boat trip from East Vietnam to Hong Kong and her stay in Hong Kong. Sue was only eighteen at the time she escaped East Vietnam in 1980 with her fifteen-year-old brother. Her parents hadn't joined them since the North Vietnamese officials would search for them if their home were unoccupied. The refugees came from North Vietnam, East Vietnam, South Vietnam, Laos, and Cambodia. The North Vietnamese were sent to England since they weren't accepted into the United States. The officials in Hong Kong could tell which part of Vietnam they came from because of their dialect. The refugees from Laos and Cambodia sailed to Singapore and Thailand. This was the most dangerous journey since robbers pulled along side the refugee boats and robbed, raped and killed many of them.

It had been nighttime when the eighteen year old boarded the boat with her fifteen-year-old brother. They were on their way from East Vietnam to Hong Kong. The journey was supposed to take two days, only they had no compass to direct them. The journey took two weeks. Boats came along side theirs and sold them food and water for jewelry and anything they had of value. The waters were black and the sea sometimes rough but the boat arrived with the help of a Russian vessel that happened to be in the area. Upon arrival, they were greeted and taken to a high-rise building with large open areas on each floor located near the airport in Kowloon, and given a medical checkup and inoculated. Then they were handed a red card for identification purposes.

Men and women slept in bunk beds three high. Sue took the one blanket given to her and tucked it under the upper bunk for privacy. None of the refugees were allowed to leave the building at any time. Three times a day the Hong Kong officials would count the people in the refugee camp. If someone were missing, they wouldn't feed the entire group the next meal and made them work especially hard around the camp. The refugees weren't aware of the specific time the Hong Kong officials would do these checks. Once, while a friend of Sue's took a shower, the officials came in and ordered him out. He didn't understand what they said since he didn't speak Chinese and they hit him.

A large blackboard was located in a common area. Each day the refugees needed to check the board for their names and then report to the Hong Kong officials. If they didn't notice their name, they'd be hit. On another occasion, one refugee was caught smoking and smoking wasn't allowed. The Hong Kong officials made that person smoke all the cigarettes he had. He became sick and his lips became swollen.

Sue was especially anxious not to be near them since they touched her. She'd dart past them and hide. She stayed in this camp for two weeks before she was moved to a new camp in the area.

Camp two, also near the airport in Kowloon was where she was required to take English classes for two hours in the morning and classes on American culture, which lasted two hours in the evening. Sue saw numerous movies about how to assimilate into the American culture and stayed at this camp for two months before being moved to a third camp.

This third camp was where she was allowed to leave the camp and go to work at a toy factory. Thankful to get out of the camp, she worked hard. Other Chinese employees worked along side her and mentioned that she didn't need to work hard since she was paid by the hour and not by the piece. Sue chose to work hard anyway. Her pay was approximately thirty Hong Kong dollars a week. That translated into approximately six U.S. dollars.

Each morning she would walk down a long road from the camp to catch a bus to work. Occasionally robbers approached her and took anything of value. It was for this reason that all the refugees' salaries were deposited automatically into a bank and checkbooks were handed out. Her fifteen-year-old brother wasn't allowed to work; instead, he was required to go to school with all the other refugees under the age of eighteen. Sue worked six days a week, eight hours a day, plus overtime. Overtime wasn't mandatory. She punched in her time card upon arrival at work and then punch out at lunchtime, then punched in again after lunch. The workers sat at a long table across from each other and assembled toys. If she worked two six-day weeks in a row, she'd be paid for one extra days work. Sue spent Chinese New Year at this camp and was given two weeks paid vacation during this holiday and received a red envelope with two Hong Kong Dollars in it for good luck. Her employer treated her well and lunch was included. Sue was supposed to receive money from the Hong Kong officials to take care of her brother. When she asked for this money they wouldn't give it to her. She never did receive any money and found it difficult to support both of them on her salary.

Another time the locals were helpful. Once she traveled into town to shop and became lost. She asked for help from a Hong Kong police officer who put her into a cab and sent her off to the refugee camp. The taxi driver didn't ask for payment. Sue stayed in this third camp for eight months and then was transferred to a fourth camp.

It was at this camp that she was asked which country she wanted to go to. Her mother's niece lived in Michigan so she chose Michigan. They'd be her sponsors.

I spoke to another Vietnam refugee named Pearl about her journey to Thailand from Vietnam. She told me that after the Americans left Vietnam in 1975, the Vietnamese hoarded gold in case they needed to leave the country. Pearl paid the operator of a small boat in gold so that she might board and be taken to Thailand. The boat, only thirty meters long (ninety-eight feet), and four meters wide (thirteen feet), had one hundred seventy-five passengers on board. The food they ate consisted of sweet potatoes, cakes, and a sour drink. Pearl spent five months in a Thailand camp while she waited her turn to fly to the U.S.A. She traveled alone, leaving four sisters and one brother in Vietnam. Her family didn't choose to join her. Pearl had finished three years of college in Vietnam and planned to go to computer school once in the United States. Her sponsor was a relative in Sunnyvale, California. She mentioned that the refugee centers in the United States wouldn't help refugees who had relatives in the United States find jobs. Therefore, she'd enter the work force the same way as the American public, with no special help.

When I spoke with other refugees about the relocation camps, they stated that boredom was a major problem while they waited for a flight. Some of the camps provided sewing machines and English lessons were given. The Thailand refugees said that the camps were organized and that they usually spent six days to six weeks waiting for a flight to the United States. Before being assigned a flight to the United States, Canada, or Australia (the three main countries the refugees were to be relocated to), they were placed in transit camps to learn about their new country's customs and what to expect regarding jobs, housing, weather and personal acceptance.

In December 1980, I spoke with a woman aboard TIA who had interviewed the refugees. She said the refugees were classified into four categories: 1) children under fifteen years of age; 2) people who had helped the United States during the war; 3) people who were or would be politically persecuted; 4) people with relatives in the United States. These persons were acceptable for entering the United States. She went on to say that if a refugee wasn't accepted in Canada or Australia, they came to the United States since the United States accepted everyone—Canada and Australia were stricter. For example, Canada didn't accept any ill passengers and that included passengers with inactive cases of tuberculosis. Australia only accepted refugees who spoke English and had a good job record.

During this conversation in December 1980, I was informed there were few refugees now, but the people processing the refugees refused to admit there was a slowdown since their jobs would be completed. Therefore, people who worked in the camps searched for more refugees to process so that they would have jobs. Some of the refugees I spoke with stated that they weren't even sure they wanted to go the United States.

Our refugee passengers were boarded in an orderly manner and sat where the flight attendants motioned them to sit. No seat numbers were assigned. They had few bags and large families. A family of eight was the average size. All carried large brown envelopes, which contained their immigration papers. They appeared to be neat and clean. Most of the male passengers were dressed in blue jeans and flip-flop sandals. The women wore Indian print skirts tied at the waist. Pewter colored earrings and ankle bracelets were popular. The refugee camp had provided the clothing.

These passengers looked solemn and slept most of the way across the Pacific Ocean. This was probably due to the Dramamine given by a nurse to each passenger after they boarded, to eliminate the chance of airsickness. Many still became sick.

These passengers looked healthy which wasn't what the crew expected after our pre departure briefing, but there were signs that at one time they hadn't been healthy. For example, one child looked like she was going bald, another's head was shaved; another child had two different colors of hair (red and black) and bald spots. The latter was only seven years old.

I asked the nurse on board about the problems with diseases such as tuberculosis. The nurse said that some of these people had inactive cases of tuberculosis. and that inactive cases weren't contagious. The nurse went on to say that inactive cases might become active at any time if the person was tired, hungry or under stress.

The State Department required a doctor to be present on these flights plus two nurses. I remembered seeing a doctor speak about the refugee flights on KRON TV expressing his opinion of the refugees overall health. This doctor was a special speaker at the University of California Medical Center and said the communicable diseases the refugees carried included measles, tuberculosis, respiratory problems, and skin infections. I was aware of only two nurses on the flights I worked.

The following was a quote from an information sheet given to the flight attendants by Trans International: "Although the crews report the passengers appear clean, many are ill, due to the conditions in which they've been living. The illnesses range from various skin diseases to various respiratory problems. All F/A's should insure their inoculations are up to date. Optional TB tests and Gamma Globulin shots are available through East Bay Clinic in Oakland or the Lynbrook Company Physician Group in New York."

A pamphlet was given to each F/A that stated: There is a base dispensary in Kadena, Okinawa for use in case of crew illness; be sure and take the appropriate insurance forms with you. The dispensary will not, however, administer inoculations so be certain your shot record is up to date before leaving. Plastic gloves will be available in the galleys and it is recommended that F/A's wear them when serving food. It is recommended that you wash your hands frequently with the disinfectant soap provided on the aircraft. Small plastic bottles of this disinfectant soap will be placed on board in Kadena for crew use only. Please do not remove them from the aircraft. Also, you should shower immediately after working a live flight and should keep your uniform in plastic bags. Long sleeved shirts and blouses should be worn in-flight, and your uniform should be dry cleaned upon return to the United States.

On Monday December 1, 1980, there was an article in the *South China Morning Post* newspaper, which stated that the "boat people" suffer dirty water illnesses. "Typhoid and diarrhea are brought on by cooking with the heavily polluted sea water and the presence of worms in the bodies of the young children caused by the polluted environment is also common."

I spoke to refugees that stated that many refugees on our planes had been in Viet Cong concentration camps. The families paid the guards to look the other way when they escaped. The refugee then began his or her two-week journey through Vietnam, and Cambodia, to

Bangkok. All the refugees had stories of grief, disease, and starvation. They spoke of being thrown off their land, tortured and raped. The Viet Cong took their possessions, but sometimes I saw one earring or piece of jewelry worn. Those people had retained pieces of their jewelry by placing them in their bodies.

I spoke to a man in the Cambodian military. He was shot by a sniper while traveling down one of the rivers in Cambodia. He walked for fifteen days to the Thai border and all he found to eat was what the remaining farmers would give him. I asked him what he missed most about Cambodia and he replied his relatives. He went on to say that the majority of the people on this flight were from Laos and only about ten families were from Cambodia.

"The people from Laos had more money than the Cambodians," he said.

Plastic gloves provided by Trans International were worn during the meal service. Approximately a month after my first refuge flight some bumps appeared on my face. I had contracted a contagious virus that appears approximately one month after initial contact.

One hot meal and one snack were served during the ten and one half hour flight from Kadena to Travis AFB in California, along with weak tea and juice. Milk seemed to make them sick and so did the juice. One little girl about ten years old said, "thank you" to me when I handed her the tea and giggled about it when I answered, "your welcome."

The crew blocked off a bathroom for crew only. The passengers watched how we opened the door and locked it again, then did the same. On one occasion, a F/A walked into the crew lavatory and saw a five-year-old child standing on the toilet seat. The F/A grabbed the child from behind and I opened another lavatory and the F/A placed the child on the toilet seat. The child looked at us as if we were crazy.

I was amazed at the number of children on board this day—approximately four in a row so one hundred sixty in all. Many didn't have pants on since their diapers were soiled and their parents removed them. The F/A's handed out diapers and showed the people how to use them, but in many cases, bare bottoms sat directly on the aircraft seats. In their homeland, children don't always wear pants. When they do and the pants become soiled, the parents remove and wash them. These passengers were amazed that the F/A's used a diaper only once before throwing it away. They had never seen paper diapers before. Once in the aft of the aircraft, a little boy came back to the galley without diapers on. I was busy at the time so handed him a diaper and said, "Take this to your leader." He looked at me in bewilderment, then without a word started back to his seat looking at me, and walking sideways all the way. He looked both confused and adorable. I smiled.

The children warmed up to the F/A's since we gave them candy, balloons and toys. The F/A's also gathered the children in the galley after dinner for English lessons. Parents and children alike were fascinated by the movies. They watched with wide eyes, laughed, and pointed at the screen. We had no headsets on these flights so there wasn't sound. The children knelt on their seats and some stood with arms crossed on the seat in front of them, chin on arms, and intently watched.

When the aircraft stopped and refueled, military women came on board with spare clothing, magazines, and coloring books. The children were delighted with the latter.

I spoke with a military official and learned these people weren't allowed take gold out of the country. They were forced to exchange it for cash. The international rate for gold was four hundred-thirty dollars in November of 1979 and the refugees got approximately half that amount. They knew they were being cheated.

In 1979, TIA signed a contract with the U.S. military to fly a 747 aircraft with 520 passengers three times a week for two years. The State Department gave these people money when they landed in the United States depending on what the U.S. government budget could afford at the time. Sometimes they received forty dollars, other times up to four thousand dollars. In some cases, promissory notes were written up to pay back the money needed for the trip to the United States and their care. The notes were usually payable in monthly installments to the refugee centers. The Intergovernmental Committee for European Migration (ICEM) was sponsoring eighty percent of this refugee program. The ICEM program was based in Geneva, Switzerland.

Approximately one year later in October 1980, I experienced yet another refugee flight. The passengers appeared healthier than on my last flight. Only minor coughs and rashes could be detected. Their clothing was more stylish and their jewelry was strings tied around the wrists (looked like kite string). Some had silver bracelets and watches. Others had their toenails and fingernails painted, and many smoked. Most of these refugees spoke English and had cards with them that looked like playing cards but instead of numbers, they had English letters on the top and the Thai translation on the bottom. The American Relief Program gave out these cards. They communicated their needs with the F/A's, such as; "May I have a pillow and blanket? I need to go to the bathroom. I'm feeling sick." They also had Vietnamese songbooks with them so that they could keep a part of their culture alive.

Forty-five minutes into the flight, we served turkey sandwiches on white bread and a banana. The banana was popular but the sandwich wasn't. Many of them took one bite of the sandwich and left the rest. Others removed the turkey and ate it. The F/A's served tea with sugar to the adults and pineapple juice to the children. The tea was popular, but the pineapple juice wasn't. These refugees opened the plastic knife and fork packets, which included a sugar packet, cream, salt and pepper and many dumped the salt and pepper into the tea. When the F/A's saw the pepper floating on top, we returned with a fresh cup.

The children looked at ice in amazement and watched it melt. Some children picked it up and placed it on another's cheek. That person jumped not knowing what it was. The little ones came back to the galley for cokes, but the F/A's soon discovered that they really wanted the ice. They didn't know how to ask for ice, but figured out that when they asked for cokes they got ice as well.

After the meal service, half the passengers got sick. The nurses on board passed out Dramamine but it was too late. Many of our passengers carried Tiger Balm and Tiger Oil, which they placed, on their temples and under their nose's. The aircraft smelt like Vicks Vapor Rub.

Plastic runners on the floor and white plastic seat covers over the seat cushions were now on all refugee flights. On these later flights, the babies, wrapped in blankets still didn't always have diapers on. The F/A's walked through the cabin and handed out diapers to all the moms. Many looked like children themselves, about fourteen years old.

Starvation still was a problem in Vietnam, Laos, and Cambodia.

"In Cambodia rain pounds the paddies, covering the dirt paths that separate the fields of young rice plants and sending rats scurrying for their lives. However, there was no safety outside the rice paddy either. Peasants crowd the roadway, desperate for even a bite of the rodents flesh; dozens of peasants stand in the rain with handmade nets, waiting like patient fisherman for their catch." *San Jose Mercury News*, October 22, 1980.

Speaking with the people of Vietnam reinforced my feeling of gratefulness in being born in America.

9
CUBAN AIRLIFT 1980

In 1980, Trans International, AKA Transamerica was commissioned by the United States military to participate in the Cuban refugee airlift. The United States, under President Jimmy Carter offered to resettle three thousand five hundred Cuban refugees in South Florida. The Intergovernmental Committee for European Migration (ICEM) initiated an airlift from Cuba to Costa Rica and onward to other countries on April 16th, 1980. ICEM underwent two name changes in the eighties; first dropping the 'European' now ICM then renaming itself again as the Organization for Migration IOM.

In April 1980, with only a third of the Cubans transported, Castro cut off the flights to Costa Rica and opened the port of Mariel to all those wishing to leave. Cuban refugees flooded into South Florida and President Carter declared a state of emergency. These refugees included criminals, mental patients, and dissidents.

The Refugee Act of 1980 was designed to be flexible in emergencies. Holding centers in military, facilities outside the South Florida area were opened in May and June of 1980. I worked one of these refugee flights with armed United States military personnel. The refugees were told they were going to South Florida. They were really going to Elgin AFB, Fla., Fort Chaffee, Ark., Fort Indiantown Gap, Pa., and Fort McCoy, Wis. I knew because I asked the military personnel aboard. There was concern that there might be a riot on the aircraft after we flew over Florida, which there was not. That was the reason for the armed escorts in each cabin. Surprise.

I occasionally wondered how I got into these potentially dangerous predicaments and concluded that I must be enjoying myself. Otherwise, why would I continue to fly?

My only other full time job was to check little squares of optic glass for defects eight hours a day, five days a week. I kept that job for eight months, then moved back home in 1970, and signed up for classes at

Foothill College, in Los Altos, California. After receiving my AA in liberal arts, I started flying. Both Bill and I were unaware I might be in danger when I departed Oakland for a trip. Trans International briefed us F/A's about the in-flight circumstances after we departed Oakland on most occasions. Flying with TIA was one big, "What could possibly happen now?"

Trans International was also commissioned by the United States government to return Haitians to Haiti who arrived in Florida illegally.

CHAPTER 6

THE PHILIPPINES

1
MILITARY FLIGHTS

The Philippine archipelago included over seven thousand islands in the South Pacific, six hundred miles from the coast of China and fifteen hours by jet from the west coast of the United States. Most came to the Philippines from Indonesia and Malaysia, except the native Igorots, who settled in the Philippines about 300,000 years ago.

The United States acquired the Philippines after the Spanish American War in 1898. U.S. newspapers reported that the Spanish were abusing the Cuban people so they sent the ship the Maine to protect the Cubans. The Maine sank off the shore of Cuba. U.S. newspapers reported the Spanish sank the Maine although this was not the belief of historians. Historians believed it was an accidental explosion not caused by the Spanish. The United States declared war on Spain and sent war ships to Spain's colonies in the Philippines, Guam, Puerto Rico, and Cuba. Spain lost the battles for all four colonies. In 1898, only months after the start of the Spanish American War, the U.S. acquired the Philippines, Guam, and Puerto Rico as part of the treaty that ended the war. Cuba became free of the Spanish and the United States acquired Guantanamo Bay as a military base.

The Japanese controlled the Philippines from 1942-44 during WWII. In 1941, the Philippines signed a fifty-year military base agreement with the United States, then on July 4, 1946 the U.S. granted the Philippines independence.

Trans International flew military flights from Travis AFB, California to Clark AFB, north of Manila after a crew change in Honolulu. This was a regularly scheduled flight. In 1972, military flights were orderly. Our passengers were military men in uniform; who filled up the last row of seats, and then the second to the last row and proceeded in that manner until the plane was full. What hand carried items these men had were placed under the seat in front of them without instruction from the F/A's. They would fasten their seat belts as soon as seated and no alcohol was served. My 1972 military passengers didn't argue and accepted the rules of the airlines.

The F/A's lucky enough to work these trips were the most senior F/A's. The other F/A's called them Pacific Queens. If a F/A with seniority went on sick leave, a F/A with no seniority might fly to the Philippines in her place. Occasionally I was that F/A.

I noticed a change in these flights after 1975 when TIA started boarding families. Families were boarded first and the massive amount of hand carried luggage no longer fit under the seats. When the F/A told the families that it must go into the cargo hold with their other luggage to be collected upon their arrival, they insisted on keeping it. Some of our 1975 MAC (military) passengers hid things in the overhead rack so the F/A's wouldn't take the items and place them in the cargo hold. The overhead racks on the DC-8's were open in the seventies, and only blankets and pillows were allowed up there.

TIA began serving liquor on military flights in the late seventies and the soldiers would gather in the aisles and party. They didn't seem to care if the F/A's had to push by them to do the meal service. Things had changed.

I took notes on one of my typical military charter flights in the early seventies.

We commercialed from California to Fairbanks, Alaska, and joined our passengers who had recently arrived from the Philippines, flew to Hopkinsville, Kentucky, then on to our final destination Atlanta, Georgia. It was a sixteen-hour duty day if all went well. Eleven hours of flight time. I was assigned to the galley this day and when I arrived at the galley the caterers had already catered and left. I checked to make certain that we would have enough food and beverage for this flight and noticed that the number of presets didn't match the number of entrees. Presets were the trays we placed the hot meals (entrees) on. I counted one hundred sixty presets and one hundred twenty entrees. We were supposed to have one hundred twenty-five of each. One of our liquor kits was missing also. Some of the trays had no cups, no plastic forks, and spoons and had no desserts. No wonder the caterers ducked out. This night we transported military personnel and it was a long, long night. Snacks with liquor were to be served at 0230 in the morning out of Fairbanks. Then at 0430 we served them another meal. If the bright cabin lights didn't awaken everyone, the F/A's were required to ask them individually if they wanted a meal. That was military regulation. If we got no reply, we placed our hand on their shoulder and shook them awake. I called this the TIA torture system. The poor guys don't know what they were in for and would hate us before we landed. The F/A's felt bad about this but we had been 'written up' for not awakening everyone.

Three hundred seventy-six military men in green outfits with rifles boarded in Fairbanks. The pins were taken out of the rifles and given to the officers who kept them in a box on their belts until after the flight. The rifles were placed along the fuselage of the aircraft. Most of these passengers had arrived in Fairbanks an hour before from the Philippines, and were now continuing to Hopkinsville, Kentucky. Most had fallen asleep before we leveled off. Then per military regulation the bright cabin lights were turned on, and the waking of the soldiers for the meal service began.

Bill and I at Travis AFB, California.

2
THE MAHARAJA AND OASIS

In 1975, I had started working to Clark AFB in the Philippines on a regular basis.

The flight to Clark was routine, so departure and arrival times were the same week to week. The crew was scheduled to leave Honolulu at 0200 Hawaii time and arrived at 0900 Clark time. The F/A's served a hot meal out of Hawaii, a snack before landing in Guam, then another hot meal from Guam to Clark. For a number of years, I worked the Travis, Honolulu, Clark AFB flights, with four-day layovers in Clark. I wouldn't be surprised if I had spent six months of my life in the Philippines.

Everything was used to its max in the Philippines including the vehicles. A rusty dirty bus with brown seats that had stuffing protruding out, as usual, greeted the crew at Clark and delivered us to our hotel. It bounced and sputtered on its way. The bus would probably have to burn up or fall off a cliff before it would be scrapped.

In the Philippines, in the late 1970's, the F/A's stayed at the Maharaja Inn outside Clark AFB at the foot of the active volcano Mt. Pinatubo. Clark was one of the places we were allowed single rooms. The small bedroom had a large sitting room, a refrigerator, TV, and air conditioning. The latter posed a problem. It was a little square above the bed with a metal sliding plate in front of it. A string hung down from this metal plate. To turn down the air conditioner I needed to move the string back to pull the plate across the square. To turn up the air conditioner I needed to pull the string forward so that the square wasn't covered. Sometimes when I pulled the plate over the square, condensation built up around the perimeter of the plate. Cold air escaped and the plate blocked it. This caused little droplets of water to form around the plate that dripped on the bed. As the drops of water soaked through the blanket, I'd wake up. It wasn't possible to move the bed since it was in a little room partitioned off from the large sitting room, so I'd cover the damp area with a towel, and scoot to one side.

Not only was the air conditioner a problem but the critters of the Philippines were also a problem. One critter was the cockroach. The F/A's knew they were in the walls. We'd hear them scurry about. The rooms were sprayed after each person checked out, but they were still in the walls. These cockroaches were sometimes five inches long. They didn't seem to bother the Filipino people. Mice didn't seem to bother them either. I screamed and ran a lot. Once I slipped out of bed in the middle of the night and walked to the bathroom in my bare feet and was rudely awoken by the sound of a crunch under the ball of my right foot. I had crossed the path of a huge cockroach and smashed it. As I eyed the cracked critter, a shiver extended throughout my body. Afraid it wasn't dead, just stunned. I moved toward the bathroom to get my extra hold hair spray and froze that massive critter stiff before reaching for my closed toe uniform shoe to finish it off. Once I'd reached into a burp bag innocently thinking it was clean and touched something disgusting. That experience ranked up there with the experience of stepping on a cockroach in my bare feet.

In the early and mid seventies, on Pacific routes, a F/A, just before landing, would walk down the aisles of the DC-8 and spray a DDT insecticide in the overhead racks. Instead of tossing the small blue and white canister in the trash, I'd place it in my topside. I'd position the canister by my bed in the Philippines in case one of those monster cockroaches decided to venture by. With one leg forward and one leg back, I'd aim and shoot these prehistoric critters. This spray stopped them dead. The DDT in this insecticide was originally created to control the spread of malaria during WWII. In the mid seventies DDT use was banned in the United States and we were no longer required to spray the chemical in the aircraft due to its toxicity. The F/A's then started using extra hold hair spray for pest control. This froze them in place. Since the cockroach had difficulty scurrying away I had time to inch closer and smash it with my white uniform shoe. The only closed toe shoe I packed.

Before 1975, the crews stayed in the Oasis hotel outside Clark AFB. Although we ate at the Oasis' restaurant, it wasn't tidy and I was thankful I had an iron stomach. I'd heard that a mouse lived near the grill, and drank the cream in the restaurant. This was a little hard to believe, but one day Bill and I saw a mouse run across the grill and take a drink out of the pitcher or at least stick his head in the pitcher, then run back. I brought this to the manager's attention but he ignored me. As I mentioned before, my husband Bill occasionally traveled with me, and at times like this I was grateful he did. He worked for his father in their electronics business.

Another time I noticed something black in my ice cube. It looked like a black spider so I called the waiter over to show him. He said it wasn't a spider and left. I took the ice cube out of my drink and placed it on the table to melt. Later I examined the little black unidentified object. The waiter was right, it wasn't a spider, it looked more like a hairy cockroach leg. Soon after that, the crews moved to the Maharaja Inn.

The restaurant at the Maharaja wasn't much cleaner than the Oasis restaurant. Here I saw an occasional cockroach stroll by, but no rodents. Actually, the crews enjoyed the flavorful foods at the Maharaja. The aroma of fresh garlic enticed the crews and sometimes the quantities were so great that it would exude out our pores. We sat, talked, and listened to the 45 records play in the jute box for hours: I heard Once, Twice, Three Times A Lady, play over and over again in the Philippines. The records never seemed to be updated.

Numerous scrawny felines lived around the Maharaja hotel. I'd place milk in a saucer a few feet away from my room. The cats refused to drink. They also refused to eat chicken or beef. I had no fish. The only nourishment that the cats would bother with was bread. For a short period, the incoming crews to Clark AFB removed the left over milk and entrees from the flight for the maids at the Maharaja. Base milk was powdered and tasteless. The F/A's were informed that this wasn't allowed and were ordered to toss the extra entrees and milk in the trash before arrival.

As our soldiers deplaned at Clark AFB on one occasion, the ramp stairs started jerking backward away from the aircraft. I attempted to hold the ramp but wasn't successful. The soldiers clung to the ramp as it jerked back. Apparently, the car that pulled the ramp stairs up to the aircraft was left running and it popped out of gear and started moving back. The soldiers were concerned but no one was hurt.

On another occasion when the crew arrived at the Oasis hotel, actors were attempting to film a movie by the pool. It looked like a comedy, but I thought it was probably supposed to be a serious movie. Everyone was dressed like "super-fly" in tight leather pants, loud shirts, hats, and sunglasses. This was quite a sight for us F/A's after being up all night. We stopped and watched the action. The actor waiter who brought the drinks to the actors at the pool was so nervous he tripped twice. The third try he did it right but as he was finishing the scene "Bus number three is now leaving for Clark" came over the loud speaker and the whole scene had to be redone. We laughed uncontrollably.

All crewmembers male and female enjoyed the beauty parlors outside of Clark AFB. It cost one U.S. dollar for a manicure and a pedicure, one dollar fifty cents for a haircut, and two dollars for a perm and conditioning. They also gave massages, waxed legs, gave facials, plucked eyebrows, put on individual eyelashes, dyed, and styled hair. A full day in the beauty parlor cost about seven dollars in 1980.

We shopped no matter how hot and humid, diet soda in hand, short shorts, tank tops, and accessorized with a hat, sunglasses and puka shell necklaces. We shopped for handicrafts made out of monkey pod, wicker, and shells. The Filipinos take pride in their work but on their own timetable. I had on many occasions contracted with shops along the strip outside Clark AFB and had items repaired and made. When I went to pick up my items at the agreed upon time, the shopkeepers would say, "Come back tomorrow." When I returned the next day, I'd be told to "Come back later." I would return later and they'd say, "Could you pick it up tomorrow?" Sometimes I was required to return three or four times to even get them started on a project.

I continued to get things made and repaired because the quality of work was good and I had patience. My patience was rewarded with lovely clothing, oil paintings and custom made frames.

Looking for Wentletrap shells on one occasion, I was unable to find them. The Precious Wentletrap shell was a rare and valuable shell less than two inches long. These delicate translucent white shells commanded such a high price that the Chinese would make copies out of rice paste. I spoke to the owner of a Philippine shell shop outside Clark AFB and he sent a diver to collect me some. The shell shop boxed them for me and I picked them up the next day before the flight. When I reached Hawaii and checked into the hotel I opened the box. As the box was opened, an obnoxious odor emerged. The animals were still inside the shells. I hadn't thought they'd be alive. I called a shell shop in Honolulu and asked them for advice. I was told to buy a bottle of Clorox, pour it in the bathtub, and stir the shells until the little bodies came out. I purchased four of the gallon bottles of Clorox and poured it all into the tub at the Kuhio Hotel. I stirred and stirred with the handle of my hairbrush, but nothing came out of the shells. The fumes of the Clorox were noxious and I hoped that the bodies would fall out before I passed out. I let them soak all night but the critters refused to fall out. A friend helped by suggesting they pluck the little bastards out with tweezers. We sat on the bathroom floor for hours plucking away. Now whenever I purchase shells overseas I peek into the box and examine the shells just in case they're alive.

The mode of transportation in the Philippines was busses or jeepney's—colorful jeeps that were modeled after or left in the Philippines during World War 11. These jeeps were restored by the Filipinos, painted bright colors, and decorated with hood ornamentations. The Filipinos used these jeeps as their major source of transportation. The cost to ride was seventy-five centavos in October 1980. This equaled approximately twenty U.S. cents. These jeeps ran a regular route everyday for this fee, but if anyone wanted to venture off this route, they paid extra. Sometimes crewmembers hired a jeepney and driver. The fare was about five US dollars for a full day of shopping or whatever, in your private jeepney. I purchased monkey pod in every size and shape imaginable, baskets, shells, clothing, tablecloths, place mats, napkins, and furniture made of wicker, always ready with presents for special occasions even though I might not make the occasion myself.

In the late seventies, the owners the Maharaja Inn, invited the crew to go to a New Year's party in the country. We arrived to the wonderful aroma of a pig being roasting over a pit filled with hot coals. Two Filipino boys were positioned on either side of the pit and turned the pig on the spit. A Filipino vocalist sang American songs in perfect English. When I asked the vocalist a question in English, she looked at the other band members and shrugged her shoulders. They had no comprehension of the English language. They'd simply memorized the songs.

Rarely, I participated in the nightlife of the Philippines. Other crewmembers would go to the seedier part of town in Angeles City, Balibago. This area close to Clark AFB was famous for its bars and nightclubs. I was encouraged to go since the acts at the clubs were so unusual. I just had no interest in seeing woman shoot ping-pong balls out of their vaginas and other obscene acts. Prostitution was rampant in the Philippines. The haves lived in luxury, the have nots sold their daughters into prostitution.

Susan, a friend, relayed a situation that happened on one of these nightclub outings. She sat at a rectangular wooden table in a club with aged wood walls and rafters when a gecko fell from the rafter above her head and landed in a women's French onion soup. As the gecko hit the soup, the woman screamed and pushed back from the table with great speed. The women's bent wood chair tipped, fell and she landed on the grungy floor. The gecko scampered out of the soup and raced down the wooded table causing more screams and commotion. Employees appeared and demanded to know what had happened. Ordinarily we welcomed geckos since they eat the insects, only not in our soup. I was disappointed I'd missed that evening out.

The tennis lessons in the Philippines were enjoyable and inexpensive. A friend and I would leave for Clark AFB at 0600 for tennis lessons. At that hour, the Filipino coaches keep the entire two dollars an hour for the lesson. After eight, they worked for Clark AFB on salary. He would hit the ball directly to my racquet so I got a false feeling that I played well. Once home, if I played with someone proficient, I discovered I needed to run after the ball and learn to aim, which was exhausting.

In the early seventies, F/A's weren't allowed to mail packages from the Clark AFB post office. Instead we were required to get a letter from the main office in Oakland, CA stating what we wanted to bring home, how large a box would be needed and to which airport we would be flying. Once my roommate didn't know what she wanted to buy in the Philippines but she knew she wanted to find something, and she got a letter from Oakland stating she'd like to carry a box of china home with her. China wasn't a big seller, but wicker was. She shopped along the strip in Clark and found a princess chair that she wanted to purchase. She then went on base and typed princess chair onto her letter and copied it so that it would look like the original. I was with her at the time.

When she boarded the aircraft with the chair, our representative asked for her letter, which she handed to him. When we arrived in Oakland, we were called into the office and the head supervisor of F/A's asked us what we had done. Apparently, Trans International compared the original letter with the copy and they differed. We confessed and weren't penalized since we'd told the truth.

On Thursday, April 6th, 1975, I had the opportunity to visit a faith healer in the Philippines, Doming, a thirty-year-old Catholic. Doming said he found he had the power to heal without knives in 1973. With no medical experience, he discovered this power while working on muscles with oils. He said he acquired his power from the Holy Spirit. Doming worked out of his residence in Pampanga, a short drive from Clark AFB. This day we visited him.

The jeepney stopped at a gray cement house with a v-shaped roof made of bamboo and wood shutters. There was an old gray crooked fence and banana trees in the front. This house looked no different than the rest of the houses in the village.

We went inside and up the stairs. There were four rooms divided by pink print curtains. The windows were open spaces—no glass or screens to keep the bugs out. The pictures on the wall were of Christ and the statues and pictures presented him as a Filipino.

The waiting room where we sat with twenty others was twelve feet by twelve feet. An electric fan circulated the hot moist air. Finally, we were ushered downstairs for a guided tour. A statue of the Pope dressed in gold robes with silver angel wings was on one of the many altars along with a statue of Mary which was adorned with a silver crown, white dress with gold embroidery, and a red robe.

A life size statue of Christ lay on a bed with a white robe over his body and his hair. Mary kneeled next to him and had tears on her face. The dimly lit room had one uncovered twenty-watt light bulb that hung from the ceiling. It gave the impression that we had stepped back in time and were viewing the cave where Christ had risen.

Next to the room with Christ was a dusty room, which contained numerous crutches, canes, and braces. "These were left by people who had been crippled, but walked out of Doming's home healed," our jeepney driver said.

Doming couldn't communicate directly since he spoke little English. A friend from the hotel and our jeepney driver acted as the interpreters.

"What do you use to anesthetize the patient during surgery?" we asked.

"All medicines and herbs are collected from the mountains in the Philippines," he responded.

"Does he operate on anyone?" we asked.

"He will only operate on people who are no longer acceptable at their doctors, or when someone cannot afford to go to a doctor."

"How much does an operation cost?"

"Doming takes donations only. The patient does pay for the after operation medicine which costs 1,000P on the average which is one dollar fifty cents U.S."

"Is there anything the patient has to do before they are operated on?"

"The patient must believe in God. If the patient doesn't believe, the operation will not work."

"What do you do with the organ after it is removed from the patient's body?"

"The organ is put in alcohol, and then it is placed for three minutes next to any image of Christ."

"What religious denominations are accepted for psychic surgery?"

"All denominations are accepted."

"How long does an operation take on the average?"

"It takes ten to fifteen minutes."

"How long does it take to make someone walk who cannot?"

"About three visits of about five or ten minutes each."

I stood about six feet away while Doming operated. He had two assistants who helped him. He waved his hands around and a small two-inch red line appeared on the area that caused the pain. He then appeared to push his hands through the body of the patient and pulled out something. There was much blood, but no apparent pain to the patient. He then cleaned the area with Queen Elizabeth and St Johns Wort herbs. Although I'd witnessed this operation and had no reason to not believe, I felt it was slight of hand.

A couple of year's later Efrin—the jeepney driver—drove me to another faith healer whose specialty was bone and muscle problems since I had back pain. On the way, I purchased two packs of cigarettes named 'Hope.' This was what the psychic wanted as payment.

We arrived; Efrin introduced me and told the healer about my back problem. The healer didn't speak English. He touched my back, around my shoulder blades and the center of my back. This was all he did. I felt a tingling sensation afterwards and my back didn't bother me for about two months.

A few years later, I thought it might be interesting to return to the faith healer whom I had visited previously. I went back to the jeepney driver who'd taken me the first time and asked to see Doming. The jeepney driver denied that he knew him or had ever taken me before. I referred to my notes that I'd taken. He was certainly the person who had taken me. I never saw Doming again.

The crew was scheduled to depart for the United States the following day. The weather was stormy. The lights at the hotel flickered on and off. The sound of thunder then the quick flashes of light made it clear that the storm was close to the hotel.

The aircraft can't take off in this weather. I thought.

The lights went out completely. Thunder blasted down. Someone knocked on the door.

"Pickup is in one hour," the voice said.

What were they thinking? MAC rules stated that the aircraft can't depart in a rainstorm, but I got out my flashlight and dressed. And though it continued to storm, we were driven to the aircraft where we sat, as the rain pounded down, just moments away from the hotel. I reached into my topside for my book, "I'm OK, Your OK" and started reading. An hour later, we returned to the hotel and crew rested until the weather cleared. This storm wasn't as intensive as when Typhoon Irma hit the Philippines with ninety- five miles per hour winds 11-28-74, but it was scary. We departed the Philippines for home twenty-four hours later.

3
THE HARVEST IN CAVITE

In the Philippines, in the spring of 1978, our crew was invited to visit the family of a crewmember on this trip, (Remy's family). We arrived in the Cavite Province, south of Manila, at eleven o'clock after a six-hour jeepney drive through the Philippine countryside. The ride was long and bumpy and each time I inquired how much longer, the driver would reply, "one hour."

After arrival and the initial greetings, a delicious fruit salad made with coconut, mangos, and pineapples was brought out of the kitchen. The milk of the coconut was used as the sauce and the coconut itself was chopped into one-inch squares. The coconut squares were placed in the coconut milk for a few hours until they took on the texture of a grape.

While we ate, our host family told us we were just in time for the Harvest Festival. Each town in the Philippines had a festival twice yearly to celebrate the harvest. Every landowning family made food for hundreds. People started to party at dawn. I ate raw oysters in the shell, fresh crab, prawns, sweet and sour pork, rice and numerous other dishes. We walked along side a parade of brightly dressed dancers and townspeople along with floats that led us to the harbor. A boat decorated with flags made from different colored cloth awaited the crew and the rest of the afternoon we swam, drank, and ate on the boat just off the shore of Corregidor Island.

Thirty-six years before in May 1942, the Japanese had bombed Corregidor Island, a rocky island in the Northern Cavite Province, to the extent that General Macarthur had ordered an evacuation from his underground headquarters. Now, in 1978 we Americans and Filipinos danced in the streets.

Numerous family, harvest, and religious celebrations took place in the Philippines during my stays. During the Christmas season colorful lanterns called parols decorated the city. These star shaped lanterns symbolized the star of Bethlehem.

It was traditional in the Philippines that generations of families lived together in little stucco, clay, and wood houses separated from the other families by a wall. All the family's homes were built only a few feet apart and were connected by dirt pathways. Everyone in the family unit knew everyone else's business and most Filipino's considered divorce a taboo. The exceptions were those who were exposed to the American ways. The husband was allowed to see other women, but the wife wasn't allowed to see other men. Women married young, usually in high school, and the ceremony was always held in a church, on a Sunday. All townspeople were invited. The regular Sunday service was held, and then the special service for the marriage took place. The church would be decorated with flowers, bows, and streamers and only traditional vows were exchanged. The bride wore a long white wedding gown and veil and the groom wore his best suit. Once married, Filipino women stayed home and had children.

Almost all of the children in the Philippines graduated high school at age sixteen. Only the children whose parents had money went on to college. Essay exams were given weekly along with other tests. Students were educated in everything but sex education.

Women who worked in the Philippines were maids, dressmakers, or beauticians. If the women had money, she started her own beauty or dress shop. A Filipino took home approximately fifteen dollars (U.S. equivalent) a month in 1978.

The local people I spoke with (bus drivers, maids, bell boys and dress makers) would all like to visit the United States; only President Marcos made it difficult to leave the Philippines.

"Why?" I asked.

"President Marcos is afraid his enemies would leave and then he wouldn't be able to watch them," was the reply. "The only way for a Filipino to leave is to enlist in the military. Filipinos in the military are considered rich and important. Also, before President Marcos put the ban on people leaving, educated people who went to college would leave the Philippines and take up residence in the United States."

Later, I heard a story that five Filipinos leaving the Philippines were seated in the aft of the aircraft on the way to the United States and stayed aboard until the cleaners boarded. Upon arrival of the cleaners, the Filipinos went one by one into the aft lavatories and exchanged clothes with a cleaner. The cleaners went though customs with their U.S. passports and the Filipinos left as cleaners and didn't pass through customs. The passenger who witnessed this didn't report it.

During my discussions at the harvest party, I inquired about the Black Market which was well known to the Filipinos. A person could go downtown and buy almost any United States product at an inflated price. Items were smuggled off the United States military bases and sold at the 'Black Market'. If a military person was caught smuggling, all military base, privileges were revoked, and the husband of the wife would be demoted one rank, if she were the one doing the smuggling. The commissary (food) and the PX (clothing, drug store items, knick knacks) had strict rules about how much a person could spend for food and supplies each month. If a person were constantly going over his or her limit, he or she would be watched.

After my visit, I boarded a bus and went to this 'Black Market' area. I was amazed at the cartons of United States products. I'd only been there for about five minutes, when a woman walked up and ushered me to the bus stop. The woman either thought I shouldn't be in that part of town or didn't want me in that part of town. I obliged and took the next bus back to the Maharaja Hotel.

Some time after my visit in Cavite, I received an invitation to visit Balibago for the fiesta celebrating the harvest. My roommate and I took a bus into Balibago and caught a jeepney to the home. The harvest table was set with about thirty different dishes: ham, pork, turkey, five different types of salads, much seafood, bread, and wine. Their home looked like a mansion compared to the typical homes in the Philippines. During the course of one of our conversations, I asked if the boxes, which were piled high to the ceiling, were presents or donations for the needy.

"Those things were to be sold on the Black Market and all the people who were at the party had brought items from the United States Air Base," she said.

Not all the people, I thought.

4
MAD MARCOS IN BAGUIO

On yet another excursion in the Philippines, I traveled north to Baguio where Camp John Hayes airbase was located. We boarded a white bus with red and blue stripes called the Overland Express and sat down in one of the few vacant seats, next to a woman with a chicken in her lap. The driver zipped around corners, picked up speed, and careened over winding mountain roads. I glanced over the cliffs and saw buses that actually had fallen. Baguio was about three hours from the Clark AFB so this was a long terrifying ride.

We breathed a sigh of relief when the bus pulled into the station in Baguio, jumped out of our seats, and were the first off. We ducked into a restaurant and discussed how we were to return to Clark AFB. Over two freshly squeezed orange juices we consulted the waiter about what other mode of transportation there was down the mountain.

"You must have gotten Mad Marcos as your driver," he laughed.

"Well, Mad Marcos isn't going to get us as passengers on the return trip. We'll stay in Baguio before that happens."

We regained our composure after our near death experience and walked toward the sound of music. A Filipino military band dressed in milk white pants with crossed white suspenders and royal blue shirts played march music in a park close to Session road, the main road in Baguio. We stopped in the shade of a monkey pod tree also known as a rain tree since the leaves close up on cloudy days allowing the rain to rush through, and listened. Igorot natives indigenous to Baguio lived in the mountains behind us but they rarely came to town.

The small town of Baguio was made up of modern seven story white stucco and cement buildings and some older one-story businesses with brown wood roofs and awnings. We made the rounds in a couple of hours then ventured back to the Baguio bus terminal to check on Mad Marcos' work schedule. He wasn't our driver so we boarded. Even without Mad Marcos driving the bus, it was scary winding down the mountain. This driver also drove at a speed that wouldn't be permitted in the United States.

5
MUSLIM GOLD IN OLONGAPO

Northwest of Manila on the South China Sea was where Subic Bay Naval Base was located. The name of the city was Olongapo, White Rock. Although this area was considered safe, three United States Navy Seabee officers were slain on base on April 15th, 1974 when inspecting construction along the eastern boundary road.

I'd heard that Muslims sold gold outside the Subic Bay Base for small amounts of money and wanted to investigate. This time we boarded the Philippine Rabbit Bus Line along with the locals and their livestock and traveled south through the Philippine countryside. Glancing out the window of the Rabbit Bus I noticed a woman dressed in canary yellow with a white apron and scarf. She held a long yellow pole and had her back to the road.

"What's that lady fishing for?" I inquired of a fellow passenger.

"She's fishing for frogs," the person replied. "Their especially good to eat."

We passed by numerous wooden carts full of items and families that were pulled by oxen. As we bounced down the dirt road during the three-hour ride to Olongapo, I saw few signs of civilization.

Upon our arrival, we found an English-speaking Filipino taxi driver who was willing to take us to see the sights. He was about twenty years old and wore navy blue slacks and a short sleeved white tee shirt with an unidentifiable cartoon character on the back. He knew where the Muslims sold the gold.

We arrived at a dirty part of town (much trash in the streets) outside the Subic Bay Base. As soon as we were detected as tourists, twenty Filipinos rushed over to the taxi. I rolled up my window and locked my door. I noticed that the venders appeared harmless so unrolled the window a couple of inches and told them what I was interested in purchasing. They knew what I was talking about and a young man ran off to get someone who dealt in gold. It got hot and muggy in the taxi so I unrolled the window. Immediately, the venders put their hands, arms, and goods, about six inches from my nose pleading for me to buy something. I bought a necklace and they left us alone for a minute. Then it started all over again.

An older Filipino man arrived with some coins that looked like gold and handed them to us.

"Why do you have so much gold?" I asked.

"During World War II American soldiers would trade gold to the Filipino's for food, shelter, and weapons," the man replied.

My friend and I examined the coins and weighed them in our hands. I had a five dollar gold piece on a chain around my neck. My five dollar gold piece seemed heavier than the twenty dollar gold piece I was handed. The Filipino man agreed to meet at a local jeweler in White Rock to get it appraised.

The jeweler's shop was a wooden table on the sidewalk. The jeweler, dressed in a short-sleeved pink shirt and pink and brown print pants had his left bare foot resting in the pull out drawer that was connected to the wood table. First, the jeweler placed the twenty dollar gold piece on one side of a two-sided metallic scale. Then he placed my five dollar gold piece on the other side. My five dollar gold piece was heavier.

"This is a false gold piece that was used as tie clasps during the war, and were really silver dollars dipped in gold," the jeweler informed us. We thanked the jeweler and handed the false gold back to the disappointed Filipino man.

Hungry, we asked our taxi driver to drive us to a restaurant and I invited him to lunch, my treat. We sat and talked and ate for almost two hours. When we returned to the taxi I noticed that the driver had left the meter running. He hadn't told us he was going to charge us and didn't look at all guilty for keeping the meter running. I was furious and made my feelings known. The taxi driver could care less and demanded his money. I felt betrayed; I had treated him like a friend. Bill paid the fare and nudged me away from the situation. The taxi driver accepted the money without a word spoken and drove away.

The Filipinos were excellent copiers of coins and other merchandise both legal and illegal. On one occasion, I brought travelers checks to the Philippines only to fine that they had machines to make false travelers checks. For this reason shops were skeptical about taking travelers checks for payment. I took mine to the Clark AFB bank. The bank teller refused to give me cash. I was amazed since I was an American, this was an American bank, and I had plenty of ID. All I wanted to do was cash a twenty-dollar traveler check. I waited an hour to speak to the bank manager, who said I could cash the travelers check since I had an American Express card. The bank manager said that these travelers' checks were duplicated in such a quantity and done so well that it was difficult, if not impossible to tell a phony one from a real one. I also learned that the Filipino twenty-five centavos coin was the exact size and weight of a twenty-five cent United States coin. Twenty-five centavos equaled four cents U.S., if that. Curious, I put the twenty-five centavos coin in a base vending machine that was supposed to take quarters and the bank teller was correct. A soda dropped out.

I was grateful to be able to have the opportunity to visit obscure places such as Olongapo and looked forward to visiting other equally as obscure places in the future.

Bill checking the gold coin for authenticity in Olongapo, Philippines.

6
MANILA BAY

On yet another long layover in the Philippines, I visited Manila. I'd heard from my father-in-law who was a Sea Bee in the U.S. Navy, stationed in Manila during WWII that Manila Bay was littered with sunken ships some that were visible from the shore. A friend and I boarded the Victory Bus Liner and drove the two and one half hours to Manila from the downtown area near Clark AFB. We drove through the lush Philippine countryside bouncing and rocking all the way down the dirt and rock road. Manila was considered a big city, but it had only one high rise building in 1976. Most of the concrete buildings in the mid seventies were only four or five stories high.

I stepped off the bus at Manila Bay. The Bay was calm when we arrived and the visibility good. I saw no sunken ships that had made such an impression on my father-in-law. All I saw were a collection of fishing boats off shore and the calm dark blue water.

I turned toward the sound of a horse trotting on the pavement. A yellow and white stagecoach pulled by a horse clip clopped by, then stopped to let passengers off. My friend and I paid the fare to ride in the stagecoach and trotted off to the National Cemetery.

All the structures in the well-manicured National Cemetery were squares and rectangles. I saw an American flag flying high above the cemetery and walked toward it. I was looking for the Memorial dedicated to the Americans who had lost their lives in the Philippines during WWII. I approached a memorial and noticed the numerous names of the men who died listed in alphabetical order. Next to the name was the rank or duty area where the service member was assigned on the day of his demise. I clicked a picture of my paternal grandfather's name, (Captain Lyman Knute Swenson) etched on the cement memorial; sat down on a bench, and thought long minutes about him and the others who had given their lives for their country. Grandfather Swenson was the captain of the cruiser Juneau that was torpedoed in the South Pacific during WW11, with the five Sullivan brothers on board.

Next, we visited the Chinese Cemetery. A man was cutting the tall grass in front with a long machete. He wore a cream colored scarf over his face, and a straw hat. The buildings were less geometrical than the National Cemetery. Some of the mausoleums in the Chinese Cemetery were air-conditioned.

The Republic of the Philippines Congress, a large impressive Greek structure was our next stop. Four tall columns topped with agapanthus leaves were located at the main entrance. A green army jeep sat empty, not on the street but in front of the entrance stairs.

We walked past a primary school near the Philippine Congress. In the yard, about thirty kindergarteners dressed in canary yellow shirts with the capital letters PE on them and black shorts were watching their teacher jump up and down. The teacher faced forward and probably wanted the children to jump up and down also, but as I watched, the children were not cooperating. One young fellow in the front looked like he was making fun of the teacher as she jumped. Everyone else looked bored. I giggled.

The day after we visited Manila, we left the Philippines for Travis AFB in California. I'd noticed on numerous flights back to the United States, Filipino women would run to the aircraft and try to climb the stairs. I asked the Trans International representative what this was about.

"Many military men marry Filipino women while in the Philippines," he told me. "Then many of these men get second thoughts about their wives when transferred back to the United States. Sometimes the servicemen don't tell their wives they're leaving and just disappear. Other times the wives find out. When their husband shows up at the airport they scream and cry and hang on to them knowing that they wouldn't see their husbands again."

Once a young women made it out to the aircraft while I was at the bottom of the ramp greeting the passengers. The young woman hung on to this soldier, and cried hysterically until a ramp agent pulled her away. It made me sad.

We made the usual stop in Guam and boarded a couple passengers. One was moving to the United States with his tropical fish on board in a plastic bag. Apparently, he hadn't thought about the number of hours it would take to reach the U.S. and the small amount of oxygen in the plastic bag. The plastic bag that held the fish was the size of two bread bags put together. During the flight, the passenger realized that there wasn't enough oxygen in the bag to last throughout the flight so he asked the F/A's if they could do something to help his oxygen deficient fish. Although we F/A's knew it was against company policy to use oxygen for any reason other then an emergency, we removed the oxygen canister, and took the fish to the cockpit.

We opened the plastic bag, then put the tube from the oxygen bottle in the water, and turned the oxygen on until it blew bubbles for a minute. We then tied the plastic bag closed and brought the fish to the passenger. He was delighted to see that his tropical fish no longer swum sideways.

We stayed in Honolulu, Hawaii for twenty-four hours and then commercialed home to California to end trip. I had five days off before my next assignment.

CHAPTER 7

DC-10's, Japan & Strikes

1
McDONNELL DOUGLAS DC-10'S

The first McDonnell Douglas DC-10's rolled off the runway in 1971. Mid seventies, the DC-10-30 CF standing for convertible freighter was manufactured. This aircraft could be configured for cargo or passengers. Trans International and Overseas National (another charter airline) were McDonnell Douglas's first DC-10-30 CF customers. The McDonnell-Douglass DC-10 was designed and built in Long Beach California by the Douglass Aircraft Company.

Trans International purchased three DC-10-30 CF aircrafts in the mid seventies. This aircraft along with the standard DC-10's had more than their share of mechanical problems and interior problems as well. The ovens, meals, food carts, liquor carts, and all galley supplies were located downstairs. The F/A's went downstairs by an elevator (cart lift) and when these elevators were inoperative, it was difficult.

August 15, 1981 while ferrying to Cherry Point, North Carolina on the DC-10, I overheard our engineer speaking to Operations about our galley elevators. Seated next to the galley I heard that this day's elevator moved up and down no matter what position it was in or if the elevator door was open downstairs. Therefore, if someone opened the elevator door downstairs and started to roll the cart in and someone pressed the up button upstairs the elevator would move up. This happened and the cart wasn't altogether in the lift yet and tore off the cart door.

In July 1981, many items needed repair on this day's DC-10 #103. I checked the F/A's discrepancy log: There was no handle inside the passenger lift, the F/A's needed to kick the door open when inside, or someone needed to open it from the outside. Three-area call light buttons were in-op in service center upstairs and one area call button in-op downstairs. These buttons were needed to work the elevators. Seat #5F reading lights flashes on and off. Cabin C—all "bells" ringing by landing. This and more needed attention.

Once when working the galley, I had to pass the food up through a hatch in the ceiling of the galley to the floor of the passenger compartment. Usually the F/A's utilize carts to serve the passengers—this time we devised a relay system since the carts were trapped downstairs. One F/A handed the meals through the emergency hatch to another F/A who handed it to another F/A about twenty feet away, who handed it to another F/A until the passenger was reached and served. The passengers never gave us the impression that they thought this was unusual.

The DC-10 food and beverage carts were massive and extremely weighty. Sometimes the cart had more control over where it was going than the person guiding it. I was accustomed to the undersized fold down beverage carts on the DC-8. The F/A's on the DC-10 had a difficult time getting these carts off their mushroom-shaped latches in the galley floor. These latches kept the carts from falling over in turbulence. There was a lever on each side of the cart that when pressed was supposed to release the brake, but it didn't always work. Finally, the F/A's discovered a release lever under the cart in the center. I'd get down on my knees in front of the cart, shoulder plastered to the bottom of the cart, reach my arm as far as possible under the cart and grasp the stuck lever and push it down

We were trained that all we needed to do to move the carts up and down the aisle of the aircraft was push down with the palms of your hand on the waist high lever located on either side of the cart.

In the late seventies TIA tried to improve on this system and devised another cart. This new cart had no lever underneath to push down if the cart stuck on the mushroom in the galley. I called the engineer on numerous occasions to release a cart stuck in the elevators. He'd take off his uniform shoes and hat and climb on top the cart as if it were a bucking bronco and try to release the jammed lever on the other side of the cart with a broom. Sometimes this worked sometimes it didn't. This time nothing seemed to work so after jerking the cart back and forth out of desperation the engineer gave up, climbed down from the cart, picked up his shoes and hat and returned to the cockpit.

Once again, we used the relay system. Only this time the F/A's loaded the stuck cart with meals and sent it up since the elevator was operating. The F/A's then relayed the food trays to the 376 passengers. The passengers adjacent to the galley thought this was all very entertaining.

There were eleven F/A's on the DC-10 and each one was assigned a number for each flight. Specific duties were assigned for each number. On October 9th, 1981 a memo was received from the supervisor's office stating that F/A number seven would be responsible to pre-flight the galley elevators and insure the interlock systems on the carts were operating.

Our charter airlines had narrow aisles. We had about two inches on each side of the cart as we tooled down the aisle kicking passenger's items completely under the seat. Every now and then we'd hit an elbow or foot and repeat our "excuse me's" repeatedly to exclamations of AWH! OUCH! In addition to an occasional, four letter word.

When our DC-10's were new, the interior lights would blink on and off. This was joined by a ding, ding, ding sound like a kitchen timer for cooking. Every now and then, this occurred during the middle of the flight, but more usually on landing. This combined with the problem of condensation on landing created quite a show. The condensation was caused by the differences in temperature inside and outside the aircraft. Rain started to fall in the cabin areas around the doors and by the bulkhead (walls). Often water dripped right on a passenger who's confined by his seat belt. Passengers would look at me and ask, "What's happening?"

I would smile and say, "This is a new airplane, all the quirks haven't been worked out yet."

"Aren't you afraid to fly?" they would ask.

"No," I would reply. The passengers would accept this answer as yet another part of travel and go on with whatever they could in those tiny seats.

There was an excerpt in the F/A manual about what to do when condensation dripped on passengers: *Once a F/A notices water dripping, she is to grab some paper towels and masking tape and tape the paper towels to the wall to absorb the water.* This worked until the tape got wet and the soggy towels fell.

In the eighties, TIA ordered thinner, smaller seats to give the illusion of more spaciousness and to place more seats on the aircraft. The passengers' seats became as uncomfortable as the crew's fold down jump seats.

I preferred to work the DC-8 aircraft. Once after landing in Anchorage, Alaska on the DC-10 the captain said as usual, "Disarm your doors." Most of the F/A's did, but a couple of the doors could not be disarmed since the disarming lever was frozen down. The lever was frozen at the main cabin door where the ramp pulls up to let the passengers deplane. The F/A stationed at the main cabin door chose to enter the cockpit and inform them of her problem instead of calling the cockpit, (a phone is by each door). In the meantime, another F/A looked out her window and saw the ramp in place and the door was still closed so she proceeded to the door to see why it wasn't opened. She pulled the handle to open the door not noticing it was still armed. This lever was not frozen. A hissing sound started emanating from the door. The pneumatic bottle in the door was activated and the door flew open and the slide fell out on the ramp with a thud. This also triggered the alarm system to go on throughout the cabin. The passengers became restless.

"Is this an emergency?" they asked.

The F/A's knew the ramp was in place since they could see it through the window. They also knew that the DC-10 disarming lever sometimes froze in Alaska so informed the passengers of these facts. The alarm system stopped after a couple minutes and the slide was placed back in the door, which took hours, and the aircraft was ready to go again. The passengers waited in the terminal while maintenance replaced the side packet.

Occasionally the F/A's boarded the aircraft even though there was a delay, per Trans Internationals instructions. It was one of those icy cold days on the aircraft in Anchorage when a F/A had what she thought was a great idea. She went to the galley, turned on the ovens, and warmed her hands. Then another F/A took off her shoes and placed her feet close to the warm and toasty heat of the oven. Then yet another F/A took it one step further and placed her shoes inside the oven to take the chill off. It was only when a F/A's shoes caught fire that the supervisors office back in Oakland got wind of this. I remember a memo that stated F/A's weren't allowed to place anything inside the ovens except the meals and that the FAA (Federal Aviation Administration) would contact the crews. TIA never found out who that person was and the incident was never repeated.

2
SITUATIONS IN FLIGHT

In February 1981, aboard the DC-10 aircraft headed from Osan, Korea to Yokoto, Japan to Oakland, California, a cigarette ignited the paper towels in the lavatory next to the service center. A F/A grabbed a full pot of coffee and put it out. Scary.

Also, during this flight two meal carts had in-op brakes. No one could budge them. I'd been flying for nine years now. This wasn't the result of inexperience as maintenance stated later.

My back ached. I could bend over, but it was difficult to straighten up.

The F/A I worked with had an ear block so couldn't hear. She kept shouting at the passengers CHICKEN? or BEEF? and since she couldn't hear the reply she'd yell again.

The F/A across the aisle from us couldn't speak. She had laryngitis. We three had quite a time finishing the service. I couldn't pick up trays and the other two couldn't communicate. We were headed into Oakland to end trip. By the time we arrived in Oakland, I was bent over and couldn't straighten up.

Our representative greeted us with news that we must continue this trip due to a lack of F/A's in Oakland. TIA sent me to a chiropractor in Oakland by taxi. He adjusted my back and I was off again after fourteen hours of crew rest. After I arrived home and ended trip, I laughed about the situation.

Three embarrassing incidents happened to me on my next flight. The first happened when I wheeled the cart down the aisle and had my back to the passengers so couldn't see where I was going. A woman was fastening her shoelace in the aisle and I sat on her head. I didn't hurt her but the surrounding passengers laughed. So did I, only later.

The second incident happened when I placed my topside in the bathroom and locked it in., Later I took out my cockpit key, placed it in the rectangular opening on the occupied sign and switched it to open.

A man was seated in the lavatory at the time and looked at me surprised by my appearance. My topside was at his feet. I closed the door immediately inserted my cockpit key in the latch and locked the door again while apologizing profusely.

The third incident was more annoying than embarrassing. A piece of plastic on the aisle side of the seat came loose. When the carts were pulled down the aisle the cart pulled this flexible piece of plastic forward. When the cart passed, the plastic would fly back again and whack me in the leg. I pulled the masking tape out of my apron pocket and attempted to tape the wayward piece of plastic flat but to no avail.

The aircraft landed in Oakland and we proceeded to baggage claim. Our large bags were nowhere to be found. We returned to the aircraft to retrieve them ourselves. The aircraft baggage door that held our luggage was stuck closed. No one would help us open it since it wasn't his or her job. Our company representative said it wasn't his job either. It took us an hour to open the luggage compartment ourselves and retrieve our bags like Ellen Marshall Church (the first airline stewardess) did in 1930. During this time, an Air Cal aircraft pulled up feet from where we were retrieving our suitcases and startled us.

The cockpit members went through the customs line first as they sometimes do. This day, as soon as the three cockpit members finished with customs they climbed in the limo that waited for the entire crew and told the driver to leave—so he did. The F/A's didn't arrive at Oakland crew scheduling until almost noon. We woke up at 0930 Korean time. We had been up and on duty for nineteen hours and thirty minutes and were completely exhausted.

Horrific incidences happened on the DC-10 during the seventies:
November 1973 a piece of the engine struck the fuselage and broke a passenger window.
March 1974 a cargo door, which was improperly closed, blew out.
March 1978 a tire ruptured and the aircraft ran off the runway.
May 1979 the left engine and pylon separated from the wing.

October 1979 the pilot landed on a closed runway perpendicular to the active runway.

November 1979 navigational error, the pilot flew into a mountain during whiteout weather conditions.

By the end of 1979, the Federal Aviation Administration temporarily grounded all DC-10 aircraft due to mechanical problems and numerous accidents.

A DC-10 aircraft I taxied out on lost an engine in Naha, Japan in 1978. The engine quit working so the airplane returned to the gate. Everybody on board the TIA DC-10 was thankful it hadn't happened after takeoff. I also experienced two other engine problems in 1979, nothing serious though, just long, long delays. On one of those delays, a military man in Japan offered his home to the crew so that we wouldn't need to sleep on the aircraft while it was being repaired. We accepted the offer.

There were other problems too. In February 1979, the crew noticed that the water smelled and tasted different on a DC-10 aircraft we were flying on. A different water company in Utah had filled the tanks. Since the water tasted strange, the crew didn't serve coffee and tea. We also placed a masking tape X over the cabin water dispensers. The crew informed the captain that the water tasted strange and asked if Public Health could meet the plane. Our senior filled a flask for Public Health, but they never showed up. Once home our senior F/A had the water tested. As it turned out the water contained 15% methane. She found out that methane could cause dizziness, nausea, and sometimes blindness. TIA said that this was just a fluke thing and it would never happen again. The company also said that the F/A's were extra safety conscious which is an allegation that I'm proud of.

Another unusual situation happened on the DC-10 out of Cairo, Egypt. TIA boarded a full load of passengers and encountered a delay at the end of the runway. It was a stifling hot day, so a F/A cracked open a cabin door for air. A light was supposed to light up on the cockpit panel when a door was opened. Later an announcement was made to close the doors for takeoff, but the F/A in the rear of the aircraft didn't hear the announcement. The DC-10 started down the runway with the aft door cracked open. The cockpit was immediately informed by phone even though at this point in departure the F/A's were trained not to contact the cockpit (sterile cockpit). Rumor was that they ascended to about one thousand feet when the engineer walked back to close the door. The door was closed and the aircraft continued on to the United States.

Yet another incident happened on the ground on the DC-10: The galley girl needed something upstairs so opened up the escape hatch in the ceiling of the galley to the floor of the upper cabin. A caterer was coming up the elevator at that time, opened the elevator door, and stepped out. He took a couple more steps and fell through the escape hatch to the galley below (about seven feet). The hatch should have been closed immediately after the conversation was finished; actually, it wasn't supposed to be used for anything except as a means of escape from the lower galley if the elevators were inoperative. The caterer wasn't hurt badly.

After a flight to Anchorage, Alaska, the crew was scheduled to go to Chicago on May 26th, 1979. This was the day after a DC-10 crashed in Chicago when the left engine and pylon separated from the wing and damaged the hydraulic system. As our TIA aircraft descended into Chicago, the crash sight could be clearly seen. Once at the airport hotel I opened the hotel room curtains and there was a view of the crash sight. I pulled the curtains closed again. A chill ran through me.

On a flight to Anchorage, Alaska on the DC-10 in 1983, our senior gathered the F/A's in the forward galley and informed us the aircraft had a hydraulics problem. The pilot was concerned that the landing gear wouldn't drop into place. We prepared the cabin for an emergency landing. We were assured that emergency vehicles would be nearby upon landing. We went through the cabin and told the passengers to place all sharp objects into the white bag located in the seat pocket in front of them, including dentures and jewelry. We stowed all personal items completely under the seats and removed all items that might have had a tendency to fly upon a hard landing. We also went through the briefing of passengers so they would be certain to know where the closest exit was and how to open that exit. We were told in training that passengers usually go to a forward exit in an emergency, even though there might be an exit two rows behind them. We told the passengers to take nothing with them. We showed them the brace position and told them to listen carefully to what the F/A's said upon landing. The F/A's would yell when the aircraft came to a complete stop, UNFASTEN SEATBELTS, COME THIS WAY, JUMP, JUMP, JUMP THEN RUN AWAY FROM THE AIRCRAFT. Fortunately, our TIA pilots found a way to drop the landing gear and we landed safely. Trans International had never lost a passenger and I commend the ability of our pilots.

3
JAPANESE ADVENTURES

On July 16, 1978, the crew was informed that after this leg of the trip into Anchorage we were going to commercial to Tokyo instead of Boston. What a switch. We commercialled to Tokyo ASAP and landed at the new airport in Nirita. The one the protestors threatened to bomb. The locals had protested the new airport in Nirita because the Japanese government had taken the land from the Japanese farmers to build the airport. Other than this, I thought of Japan as a safe place to stay.

We checked into the Holiday Inn in Tokyo and I walked over to the concierge desk.

"Are there any special activities going on today?" I asked.

There's a Japanese tea ceremony at the pool." the concierge replied.

I signed my roommate, and myself up for the tea ceremony.

A short time later, we joined a group of tourists gathered around a platform covered with a red sheet and shaded with a red paper umbrella. A woman wearing the traditional Japanese fashion was seated on her heals on a platform, her hands gracefully placed in her lap. She looked like a china doll with her white makeup, cherry red lips, kimono, and her jet-black wig in a loose bow shaped bun with a chopstick through it. The kimono draped to the ground and her feet were barely visible. She wore red cloth flip-flop sandals and thin white socks.

Slowly and gracefully, the hostess poured hot water into a small porcelain cup. She placed some green powder in the cup, and then slowly stirred it. The tea was offered individually to each guest after the hostess bowed before them. The mixture was thick, green, foamy, and tasted like spinach.

Another Japanese woman carried a small saucer with diminutive sugar candies that were lime, rose, winter white, and lemon yellow. Some were shaped like stars slightly larger then the stars teachers place on student's papers and sugar balls the size of a small cherry. A toothpick was placed through each center for easy access. Carefully she placed them on rice paper, bowed to each of us individually, and held out the candies. When she came to me, I bowed back and then the hostess moved on to the next guest. No words were spoken. The ceremony turned out to be very interesting.

After the ceremony, I asked the hostess if she could take a picture, only I didn't have a camera. The hostess bowed and walked away taking little baby steps. She returned in ten minutes with a camera and clicked some pictures. I handed her my address and a few yen for the pictures. The hostess wouldn't accept the money. About a month, later I received the pictures.

The Tokyo Holiday Inn had both Japanese and American rooms at the same price. The rooms were the same size, but the atmosphere was different. My roommate and I had chosen the Japanese room. As we walked into the Japanese room we took off our shoes, then stepped up to the living room area. No bed was in sight, only a small table and two pillows to sit on. Under the table was a bamboo mat. A small black dresser about three feet high with a mirror on it was located in the corner. A bamboo screen was on the other side of the dresser and it partitioned off another area of the room. We stepped down to this area and sat on pillows in front of a little table about twelve inches from the ground. Even the window was smaller in the Japanese style rooms. We found kimonos and slippers in the closet. The bathroom in the Japanese room was the same as the American version.

Upon our arrival, a pot of green tea was brought to the room. I was instructed to call the front desk when ready to sleep. I called and a Japanese woman dressed in a kimono came to the room bowed and said, "Sumimasen O-negai shimasu," (excuse me please) and then removed a futon (mattress) from the closet. The Japanese woman then moved the table and pillows to the side and put the futon down in the middle of the room. She made the bed with linen sheets then bowed and left. It was great fun experiencing different cultures and sleeping on a futon felt good on my aching back.

In 1979, my roommate and I decided to go to a health club outside of Yokoto, Japan that the reception desk recommended. I had been flying for seven years at this point. We drove by taxi toward the Japanese hillside and arrived at what looked like an old mansion. We attempted to inquire whether this was a private health club, but no one spoke English well enough to answer our question. We each paid a small fee (three U.S. dollars) and entered. The Morikawa hotel must have had a special agreement with this club for their guests. The first floor of the health club had numerous baths. The water was green and smelled awful. At first I though they hadn't been cleaned, then we realized that the Japanese put herbs in the water to make it smell and look this way. We had brought our bathing suits so changed and jumped in with the Japanese people. My roommate and I were the only blue-eyed, blondes, but that didn't bother us.

After a while, we ventured upstairs and found every type of exercise equipment imaginable in a room about two hundred forty feet long. Mirrors covered the walls and large windows overlooked the extensive garden outside. I climbed on one of these machines and pushed a button. The machine was set in motion. We sat on seats that moved us back and forth, lifted our legs up and down, moved our ankles in circles, and moved our necks and arms in circles. How much good these machines did was debatable. My roommate and I had exercised before we left the hotel. I always brought my "Body Design" exercise tape on trips and exercised an hour each morning. My exercise tape made me perspire; these machines didn't. After we played in the exercise room, we started to smell an odor that was unfamiliar and decided to investigate. We ventured up a stairwell to what appeared to be a doctor's office. People were seated in room that had other rooms opening from it. All doors were open. We peered into one of these rooms and discovered where the smell came from. A person was lying on a table—little pyramid shapes of a dust-like substance covered different parts of his body. This substance was lit and smoke was coming from each little pyramid giving off a strange odor.

A Japanese doctor appeared, opened a leather case with long thin needles in it, and then proceeded to stick a needle in the patient's body. The needle stuck out about six inches, but the patient didn't show any discomfort. He was awake and lay there quietly as the doctor placed another needle about one inch from the first. This was continued until six needles were placed in a circle. The doctor then placed needles in the same manner elsewhere on the patient. We were watching an acupuncture operation. The doors were open and others watched also. A Japanese man asked us if we'd like to speak to a doctor.

"Yes," we said.

I was handed a phone and introduced myself.

"What is the powder made of that is placed on the patient?" I asked.

"It's the anesthesia made from herbs. No other anesthesia is necessary since the patients feel no pain with this. Sometimes a patient will bring in a bottle of liquor and drink it. Nothing such as pills or injections are necessary. The patient is awake during the operation but sometimes closes his or her eyes and naps. After the operation, the patient gets up and goes home with no after effects unless they have drunk too much. There's no recovery room since none is necessary. The patient may need to return for further operations according to the type of illness."

I thanked the man on the phone and then watched the final steps of the operation. The doctor removed the needles from the patient's body. When this was completed, the pyramid piles of herbs were removed. I could see red spots where the needles had been but no blood. The patient lay there for a few minutes, then got up, spoke to the doctor and left the office.

The doctor turned to us and asked, "Do you have any ailments?" He also stated that the operation was included in the price of the health club. We declined his offer and returned to our hotel.

In 1977 during one of my many layovers in Yokota, Japan, all the crew traveled by train to a stage show in the Tokyo Ginza District. With pencil in hand, I wrote down each stop, so as not to get lost. Japanese character rather than letters indicated the stops. We arrived at the Tachikawa District after a two and one half-hour train ride; changed trains and headed for the luxurious Ginza District.

Upon arrival in the Ginza, I noticed a four-foot high pile of white crystals outside a restaurant. Curious, I entered the restaurant and asked what they were. The proprietor said it was salt, put there to purify everyone who entered the restaurant. Interesting.

We taxied to a nightclub, much like an American nightclub with one exception; all spoke Japanese. It was my roommate's birthday, so I asked the waiter for a birthday cake. He returned with the tiniest birthday cake I'd ever seen— about six inches around. The crew sang happy birthday and Marilynn blew out the candle. The waiter then proceeded to cut it into twelve pieces. Unlike in the United States where the dessert is sometimes free for the birthday person, this cake cost seventy-five dollars.

By the time we were ready to leave, the last train had departed from Tokyo to Yokota. We had missed it. Yoshida, a friend lived in Tokyo. It was midnight when I showed his address to a taxi driver and he nodded. Marilyn and I got into the taxi and headed down the pitch-black streets of Tokyo in search of Yoshida. The other crewmembers stayed in a hotel.

Unfortunately, numbers were rare on the streets of Japan and individual apartments were difficult to locate. We searched for two hours before the taxi found the correct address. My friend Yoshida didn't seem in the least perturbed about having visitors at this unusual hour and pulled out a couple of futons for us to sleep on. The next day Yoshida and his roommate showed us Tokyo by taxi. At one temple, he handed a little piece of red paper with Japanese characters on it to me and translated it. "You will have a happy, healthy life," It said. It was a good fortune so I was instructed to tie it to a tree that was already full of red paper fortunes. This was done so the fortune would come true. That evening we returned to Yokota, Japan by bullet train. I was always amazed at the variety of places, people, and things to do in each country and since they all were unique, it was difficult to pick one as a favorite.

4
TRANS INTERNATIONAL STRIKES

The day after our excursion to Tokyo the crew was greeted with the feared telex. I hadn't yet received a telex that was good news. No matter what our plans may be, it can always be changed by the feared telex. This one stated that the Trans International flight crews were on strike. The telex also stated that the flight attendants would be responsible for their hotel bills and any other charges. The crew had already spent four days in Yokota and it was quite probable that we would spend another four here while we planned our route home to California. The F/A's had been without a contract since April 1976. Issues included wages, working hours, and grievance procedures. Trans International did mention in the telex that the crew could bump military personal off the first military flight through Yokota. The military wouldn't allow this though, so three days later our captain got the crew passage on a U.S. Air Force C5 Galaxy cargo plane going to Travis Air Force Base in California.

Before the crew boarded the C5 Galaxy, we were asked if we would like to buy a box lunch—it didn't look appetizing but I purchased one anyway. It contained a roast beef sandwich, hard-boiled egg, juice, milk, cookies, and an apple. Before the crew boarded we were told that our Trans International life insurance was void when we flew on military aircraft. Maybe the pilots had Trans International life insurance policies, but the FA's weren't given that option.

When the time came to board this huge C5 known as the Guppy, we marched through the inside, then up some stairs (that went almost straight up) to the passenger compartment. The only window was by the door and all the seats, thirty total, faced backwards. I had just buckled in by the door when one of the two male stewards dressed in military uniform came over.

"I'm sorry but children aren't allowed to sit by the exits," he said.

I thought he might be joking but replied I was a flight attendant. He was probably accustom to have military men sit by the exits, not one hundred ten pound, five feet two inch females.

He smiled and returned to his duties.

When the engines started, the C5 cargo plane almost immediately started filling up with condensation,. The thirty passengers were encompassed in a cloud inside the aircraft. No food was served on this thirteen-hour flight.

One day after we arrived home, this wildcat strike ended. Then again, in 1977 the F/A's went on strike and once again, I was stranded in Yokota, Japan. Good grief.

On October 26th, 1977, during the strike, I arrived in Yokoto on a TIA DC-8 aircraft. On October 31st, our Trans International representative in Yokota gave each crewmember a copy of a telex he wanted us to read. I read the telex as requested, which said that we must fly military flights. I flew a military flight into Yokota so thought this wasn't important. Our representative in Yokota asked the F/A's on the crew to sign the telex. All the other F/A's signed. I didn't, instead I continued with my plans to go shopping. Of course, I'd fly military flights, after all that's what brought me to Yokota. Within only a few hours, our airline representative was back at the Morikawa Hotel with another telex. It stated that I was terminated for refusing a military flight, and responsible for my own affairs. I told the representative that I wasn't refusing a military flight. Wouldn't I have refused the flight to Yokota if I weren't going to fly military flights during the strike? The telex stated that I had refused to operate (refused a flight). I wasn't allowed on the flight home. The crew didn't want to work one F/A short and I didn't want to stay in Yokota. It didn't make sense to me.

I called the Union (Teamsters) and they told me a company who sends a person out of the country on business has to return that person to the country she or he started from (The Shanghai Act). This law did me no good whatsoever. The Teamsters did telex a ticket for me to take Pan Am home to California. What upset me was the fact that my friend Sorenson would need to replace me on this flight. She was on her way to Yokota from Travis AFB in California. That meant that she had already been on duty for at least sixteen hours and as soon as she landed she would be ordered to work back to Travis again (continuous duty). If she refused the trip, she would be fired.

Although the lack of control over the situation was disturbing, I was determined to make the best it. I 'd always wanted one of the large four-foot clay cookers but would have never been able to carry it to the aircraft since it weighed one hundred and fifty pounds. I thought that this would be an opportune time to purchase it since I was traveling alone on a commercial airline.

Before I got into the taxi that was to take me to the airport, I asked the driver if he knew where I could purchase a clay cooker large enough to cook a thirty-pound turkey. He did, so we headed off to shop. We arrived at a business where clay cookers were located outside. I purchased a green one and counted out the yen I had in my wallet.

The next challenge was to get it into the back of the taxi. It would have been impossible for me to lift it, so I stood to the side and watched as two one hundred pound Japanesse men lifted it into the trunk. We headed off toward the airport with my clay cooker sticking out of the trunk. Once at the airport I checked the clay cooker in with my big red suitcase. They put a fragile sign on it.

Once home I received a letter stating, I was fired. I took this letter along with the original telex I received in Yokota to the unemployment department. The unemployment office called Trans International.

"I had a job, only I was on strike," Trans International replied.

The unemployment office then docked me three weeks unemployment pay for saying I didn't have a job when I did. My letter stating I was fired meant nothing to the unemployment office.

After Trans International told the unemployment office that I had a job, they sent another telex to me stating that I was fired. These telex's were dated and signed but still the unemployment office wouldn't give me unemployment pay.

I never did get unemployment, back pay or any compensation for being fired by mistake in Yokota. Trans International Airlines owned by the mighty Transamerica Corporation did admit my firing was a mistake.

Here were some of the details regarding the strike; More than five hundred fifty F/A's for TIA walked off their jobs on September 9, 1977, five hours after a federal judge ordered them not to strike. TIA was the world's largest charter carrier and provided service to Europe, Asia, South America, Africa, Mexico, and the rest of the world. The F/A's were members of the International Brotherhood of Teamsters, Local 2707, but the Union, which also represents Trans International engineers and F/A's for other airlines, had not sanctioned the strike because of the court order that said everyone must fly military flights. It was a national safety issue.

The United States District Court Judge, Robert Peckham, located in San Francisco, wished to restrain the F/A's from striking until a September 15th hearing.

About three hundred fifty F/A's were based in Oakland and two hundred in New York. Our main grievances were scheduling, wages, and working conditions. I netted two hundred twenty dollars on my 9-16-77 to 9-30-77 paycheck. Foremost in our demands were health and safety issues, including workdays shortened from the current sixteen hours and a guarantee of five known days off each month. I'd never spoken to a F/A who wasn't upset about the twenty-four hour continuous duty days, and that was an issue as well.

On the same day the strike began, the United States District Court ordered TIA to operate all military flights. Before September, military operation comprised eighteen percent of TIA's total business, since the strike, it had increased four hundred percent. This information was given to the flight crews through pamphlets distributed by the teamsters. Trans International was sub-servicing many other airlines' military flights in exchange for their charter flights. Judge Peckham threatened to impose severe penalties on the union if the F/A's didn't fly military flights. The Department of Defense elected to increase the number of military flights so TIA made more money during the strike than before the strike. Trans International hired scabs to fly the regular flights it couldn't sub service. I watched them go through training in Oakland, California while I stood outside with my strike sign in hand and picketed. The F/A's, members of Teamster Locals 2707 and 732 brought their case to the nation's capitol urging their senators and congressional representatives to insist that the Defense Department remain neutral in the labor dispute.

This action accomplished nothing whatsoever. TIA was still allowed to take on extra Military (MAC) flights. It was upsetting to all of us, but we didn't disrupt any flights.

During this strike, many articles were written about TIA in magazines and newspapers. One I found interesting was written by Herb Caen and read:

"Corporate Life" states that first you have to know that Trans International Airlines is owned by mighty Transamerica, and that the airlines' flight attendants have been on strike for some three weeks. Negotiations are moving so slowly that on Monday sixteen stewardesses in uniform decided to confront Trans International's President, in his 25th floor suite in the Pyramid. As they entered two elevators with other passengers also aboard, a voice demanded over a hidden speaker: "Who are you?" When they did not answer, both elevators rose to the 17th floor, at which point the lights went out. The elevator then returned to the lobby, where uniformed guards 'invited' the stewardesses to leave the building: thank you, muttered one of the other passengers. 'Well that's the first time I've ever been hijacked in an elevator and by stewardesses, at that,' she said."

This Trans International airline strike lasted four months. We were awarded a small wage increase, but other than that, I noticed no changes.

After 1977, the F/A's changed from the Teamsters Union to the Association of Flight Attendants. We, the Trans International F/A's, threatened to go on strike again in 1982. The Association of Flight Attendants distributed Trans International's company proposal to each F/A along with a ballot that was to be postmarked no later than July 23,

1982. These ballots were counted on July 30th. The F/A's agreed not to strike. We'd receive no less than thirteen dollars an hour for sixty-five to eighty-five hours of flight time per month; fifteen dollars an hour for eighty-six to one hundred hours of flight time a month and seventeen dollars an hour for working over one hundred hours of flight time a month. Also, if the F/A's worked fifteen to seventeen hours in one day they would receive twelve dollars an hour for those two extra hours over fourteen. If the flight attendant's day was extended from seventeen hours to twenty hours in a day, we would get fourteen dollars an hour for three of those hours. On the occasions that we were required to work over twenty hours in one day we would receive twenty dollars an hour over duty for each hour over twenty. Our per diem was raised from one dollar fifteen cents an hour to one dollar twenty-five cents an hour.

With the signing of this new contract, we would not be required to work over one hundred-twenty flight hours per month. We would get no less than twelve hours block-to-block rest and we would no longer be turned around at our domicile. The F/A's weren't pleased with this proposal but the general opinion was that scabs had replaced us already so we had better accept whatever we could get if we wanted to continue working for Trans International. We accepted TIA's terms because we didn't want to lose our jobs as F/A's

Picketing at Oakland International Airport, 1977.

5
THE BLACKBIRD

We landed in Okinawa, the largest island in the Ryukyu Islands archipelago, after a fuel stop at the naval base on Midway Island in Oceania. Midway was four hours fifty minutes flight time from Hickam Field in Hawaii. The albatrosses otherwise known as the Gooney birds resided exclusively on Midway Island. This day our final destination was Kadena AFB, Okinawa, a military facility established after World War II.

It was 1981, and I had been a F/A for nine years when an officer offered to take our crew on tour of the SR-71 aircraft. Few of these tours were given since this was a new top security aircraft. SR stood for strategic reconnaissance and the aircraft was referred to as the "Black Bird." It flew at an altitude of 80,000 feet and special flight suits were worn. The F/A's needed a United States passport to be allowed to view the blackbird. One of our crewmembers didn't have a United States passport so wasn't invited.

One of the pilots asked if I'd like to try on a flight suit—the ones they wear while flying this SR-71. The same suits were used for space travel. It was a bulky yellow suit.

I thought this would be interesting so said yes.

First, I slipped on long white cotton leggings and a matching white top. Then I sat down and pulled the flight suit on feet first with help from two pilots. A person can't get into it alone since it zips up the back, and the arms were too stiff to reach behind to do this. After this bulky yellow plastic suit was zipped, I felt a bit hot and sticky. That's when the pilots placed on the large white helmet over my head and snapped it down around my neck. I felt claustrophobic. Someone flipped open the front visor.

"Don't worry we'll have you hooked up to the air ventilation system shortly," he said.

I was turned toward a brown leather chair where the air hose was located.

"Get me out of this!" I yelled. I hadn't expected my claustrophobia to get the better of me.

The pilots immediately unsnapped the helmet, removed it, and had me out of the suit in seconds. I was relieved, but extremely embarrassed and apologized.

"Lots of people become claustrophobic when the helmet is snapped down, "a pilot calmly remarked."

A week later, we arrived back in Oakland and after the allotted time off; I was called to go through recurrent training. Recurrent training was a yearly three-day class, sometimes more if a new aircraft was added to the fleet. This was the time we updated our skills and knowledge along with being briefed on new equipment, and situations. For example, many airplanes were hijacked in the seventies so we were trained to deal with that situation. This year's recurrent was three days long, 9am to 5pm.

Monday the scheduling department called to give me a trip alert for the evening after recurrent training. She asked me to bring my suitcase to class so I'd be ready to depart immediately for a trip.

"What do you have planned for me?" I asked.

She just giggled then remarked, "Put clothes in it."

She wouldn't tell me anymore about it so I asked to talk with someone else in scheduling. The other scheduler explained that due to the storms in the area they were afraid crewmembers might not be able to show for this trip.

"Where is the trip going and when will I return?" I asked.

This scheduler answered my questions and I called friends and family to tell them I was leaving tomorrow.

I put my suitcase in the back of my car and started for my last day of recurrent training.

A F/A in recurrent was handed a note from the scheduling department. Scheduling wanted her to take a trip this morning and not finish recurrent training. She went on sick leave. I was then called to the phone and asked to take this new morning trip. I'd no longer be required to take the afternoon trip. I went back to the recurrent training class to pick up my things. I pulled my suitcases out of my car and the limo driver placed it in the limo that was taking me to the airport. The secretary of the training department came running out of the building and yelled to me that the other F/A had shown up and that they no longer needed me. I took my suitcase back to my car then went back to recurrent training class. Another F/A was pulled from recurrent training to take my evening trip and I drove home. Some days I didn't know if I was coming or going and nobody else did either.

The FAA reviewed TIA's training in January 1981 and remarked that our training surpassed all others by leaps and bounds. This didn't surprise me. Our training was so intensive that I dreamt about it at night.

A few days later on Sunday January 10th, I showed in Oakland at 1630. I arrived to find no other crewmembers were there. Wondering what was going on I asked the schedulers.

"1830 is the show time," the scheduler said.

"I was told 1630 three times. Once the last day of training, second time when I was called for my pre-alert and the third time when I was called for my final alert," I replied.

The scheduler checked the sheet and noticed that the show time on the piece of paper she had in her hand had been erased and 1830 was written over it.

"Sorry," she said.

"Why wasn't I called if the show time changed?" I asked.

"I don't know," she replied.

I settled down to wait.

We were scheduled to commercial on Pan Am to Honolulu tonight and then work to the Philippines after crew resting. Apparently, both Northwest Orient and United had flights to Honolulu at that time too; but those airlines were encountering weather delays in the Midwest. Therefore, all those passengers on Northwest and United went to Pan Am to fly to Honolulu. I had an awful seat next to the lavatories between two large men who shared my foot space since their legs were so long. I sat with my arms crossed in front of me hoping the time would pass quickly. I was too uncomfortable to sleep and couldn't see the movie screen.

We landed at 2330 Honolulu time and when I picked up my big red suitcase off the luggage carousel I noticed that one side was smashed in. It looked as if something heavy had been put on top of it. The crew had been anxious to get to the hotel and I didn't want to delay them so I also boarded the crew bus for the hotel.

I tried to call Pan Am and report the damage; only Pan Am had a telephone message recording on, so there was nothing I could do. The Marimar where we stayed in Honolulu charged fifty cents for local phone calls in 1981. All the numbers I called were recordings. Finally, I trekked out to the airport and I went to Pan Am's baggage assistance room. They wrote up a damaged bag form and said to bring the receipt for the repair into any Pan Am office or the airport and they would give me cash.

We left for the airport that night Tuesday January 12th, 1982. The TIA aircraft that we were to take to Clark AFB in the Philippines, landed forty-five minutes after our arrival at the airport. When it arrived, the compass was broken in the cockpit, so we took a mechanical delay to wait for a replacement compass. The aircraft was repaired by sunrise and we departed. Now our paid duty day began.

One F/A received a love letter from a passenger on this Guam, Clark AFB flight. She brought it back for me to read. I read it on the aft jump seat and she sat next to me. He also included his picture. I looked up, then looked at the picture, and was silent. She looked up and saw him watching us as I read her letter. We were embarrassed.

One F/A asked a six-year-old boy how he was.

"I am a tired little boy," he replied. We giggled.

One woman on the flight asked me to change her baby's diaper. I gave her a diaper and told her to put the dirty one in the lavatory waste container. This didn't please the passenger but I had a meal service cart in the aisle.

A woman pulled her F/A call button. I arrived and she held up her breakfast entrée for me to see. She had eaten half her omelet when she noticed something black buried inside. I took the omelet to the galley to investigate and discovered a one-inch dead cockroach cooked into the entrée. I'd heard that TIA had leased a DC-8 from Air Florida and once when an engineer checked the crew bags in the cargo hold, he came across cockroaches. This DC-8 was nicknamed the roach coach. I'd never before seen a cockroach cooked into an omelet though. How disgusting.

Two months before this in 1981, I ate a chicken crew meal when I chomped down on two pieces of something hard. I took them out of my mouth and they looked like gray glass. I didn't chip a tooth or swallow any glass but filled out an accident incident report anyway.

On this night, our passengers' final destination was Guam. The F/A's were to fly on to Clark AFB in the Philippines with an empty plane even though the passengers wanted to go to Clark. I had no idea why we couldn't take them the remainder of the way.

"Are you going to Clark AFB?" one man asked.

"Yes," I replied.

"What are you going to do on the flight?" he asked.

"Sleep and read," I replied.

"Don't you think that's a little selfish?" he said.

"You'll have to talk to your MAC representative if you'd like to go on with us," I replied. "We were told not to take any passengers to Clark."

He left in a huff, which I thought was a little rude.

We were ordered to fly empty so that's what we did.

We landed at Clark AFB and the ramp pulled up. As we waited to deplane, the crew heard a rush of water. What happened was a maintenance man who was emptying the lavatories did something incorrect and all the dirty lavatory water dumped out at one time all over him. Other workers were close by and assisted him. I cringed.

After our two-day layover in the Philippines in 1981, we boarded one hundred fifty-eight passengers to Honolulu, with a refueling stop in Guam.

In Guam, we deplaned passengers then taxied away from the terminal.

"Why?" I asked since we had never done that before.

"There's no spark resister in the truck that brings the ramp up to the airplane door," he replied. "All passengers must now take all their hand carried items off the airplane."

Our passengers gathered up all their belongings and trekked off to the terminal.

We arrived in Honolulu and the following day was scheduled to take Western flight #22 from Honolulu to San Francisco. We were scheduled to leave Honolulu at 2330 and because of the late departure time no movie would be shown and no meal offered. Western did serve all the champagne you could drink though. Also, whoever came the closest to guessing the half waypoint from Honolulu to San Francisco received a free bottle of champagne.

On January 15th, we touched down at San Francisco Airport. Home again, a very good feeling.

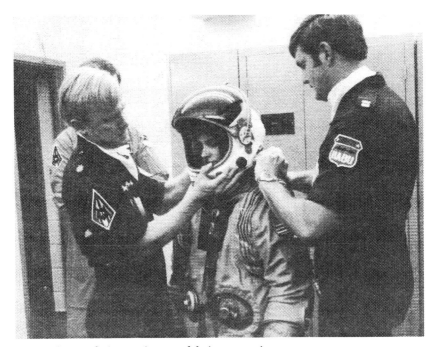

SR71 pilots outfitting me in one of their space suits.

CHAPTER 8

Alhajj & Saudi Arabia

1
NIGERIAN PILGRIMS

In November 1975, TIA was commissioned by the Nigerian Pilgrims Board to operate eighty-one round trip flights from Nigeria to Jeddah, Saudi Arabia. Eighty-seven thousand Muslims flew close enough to Mecca for the pilgrims to walk the remainder of the journey. This was called the alhajj, also known as 'the trip'. This trip to Mecca was a religious obligation that every orthodox Muslim was expected to fulfill if able according to the Koran. Only Muslims could visit Mecca. American Muslims had to prove themselves true Muslims, both in the United States and in Jeddah before they could make the journey. The literal meaning of Hajj in Arabic was "to set out toward a definite objective."

TIA was also commissioned to carry thirty- five thousand sheep to the Middle East for the Muslim holy season of Ramadan.

I left for Kano, in northern Nigeria on my twenty-fifth birthday and was thrown a surprise birthday party on the ferry flight. The crew signed a card, a cake was brought on board, and I was given a bottle of champagne. I felt special.

As we ferried into Kano from the United States, I could feel the adrenalin run through my body. We were the first TIA crew to be positioned here so no one knew what was in store for us.

The tiny airport was hot, muggy, and deserted. We claimed our red suitcases from baggage claim and headed toward the taxis. Our driver was chewing something that made his mouth, and teeth red.

"What are you chewing?" I asked.

"Kola nuts," he replied in perfect English.

Kola nuts were a bitter tasting fruit that broke up into particles that turn blood red when mixed with the juices of the mouth. The African people ate them when tired since the kola nut contained caffeine.

We reached the hotel, the Bogato, after a thirty-minute ride through the dark African countryside. Actually, it wasn't a hotel at all;

more accurately, it was many groups of round grass huts. A seven-foot African man sat in front of the hut that was assigned to my roommates and me. He was dressed in brightly colored print material, wrapped, and tucked around his body. I opened the taxi door, climbed out, and walked over to the hut. I observed that the door was the home of hundreds of bugs, spiders, and lizards. I saw the spider's intricate webs, which captured the most unusual assortment of insects. Then, out of the corner of my eye I saw something move. It was another man with a long sword in his hand. Startled, I ran back to the waiting taxi. The taxi driver assured me that both men were guards to protect the people of the village.

Protect them from what? I thought.

I bravely walked back to the hut door and opened it. Apparently, no one had opened this door in quite a while since a massive amount of critters fell like rain. The door creaked open and I felt apprehensive. I looked inside, and started laughing. I went back to the taxi thinking this had to be a joke. TIA had told me that this was a resort, and the best place to stay in Kano. The taxi driver assured me that this was where he was instructed to take us. I went back to the hut door once again, took a deep breath, and entered. It was dimly lit with bare twenty-five watt light bulbs. All I could see when I cautiously took another step was a rusty or dirty sink. I then took a few more steps on the concrete floor toward another door and saw a shower with two hand towels hanging over a rack. I peered down the narrow dark corridor and saw a toilet. I turned and then inspected the two bedrooms. Mosquito nets covered the beds, nets that were sewn down the sides.

This will be my home for the next twenty-four days? I thought.

I touched the mosquito net and lifted it up. Dust billowed up in a cloud. By this time, I was extremely concerned. I slowly pulled back the sheets and watched the bugs scatter. During my hut inspection, I listened to the disconcerting screams from other crewmembers at other huts.

Thankful that I had not only bought emergency food but also emergency medication I went to my topside that was still in the taxi and took a valium.

"Where's the check in office?" I inquired anxiously.

"It's located two miles down the road," he replied as he extended his right arm and pointed his index finger into the dark night. "There's a restaurant there if you'd like me to drop you off."

"Not tonight," I replied. "Is there a phone?"

"I don't know?" the driver replied.

The driver then proceeded to place the crew bags inside the hut. He wanted to leave, and I couldn't detain him any longer.

I'm just going to have to deal with this, I thought. I walked back to confer with my two roommates. The three of us decided we should try to communicate with our guards. I walked up to the one without the sword who was wearing a white tee shirt, dark zippered sweatshirt, and a dark stocking cap.

"Hi," I said. "What is your name?"

He said something that I couldn't understand. It started with a Ka sound and sounded something like Kumba. He smiled.

We turned to the other guard, the one with the sword and asked, "What is your name?"

"Neshi," he replied. That we understood.

Neshi was 6'6" tall and gaunt. He could be identified from afar by his long machete like sword—about five feet long—and his hat that was pointed at the top and curled up on the sides like horns. Kumba wore a knit ski cap with a pompom on the top. Both Neshi and Kumba were very courteous and smiled a lot.

I went over the situation in my mind. I was in Africa, I had no phone, the reception area was two miles away, and there were bugs in my bed. I walked over to my topside took out my Valium and popped another one into my mouth. I then reached for my insect repellent, walked over to my bed, lifted the mosquito net with one hand, and held the insect repellent in the other. I saw what looked like an earwig crawling up the side of the bed, so shot it with a quick spray of insecticide. I then sprayed a circle of repellent around my bed before changing into my pajamas. Because I was fearful of bugs crawling on me, I also wore a turtleneck sweater, knee socks, knit cap and gloves to bed. Somewhat tired but still not tired enough to climb into that bed; I downed another Valium.

About to climb into bed, I spied a big black spider at the head of the bed. With bug spray in hand, I shot it with a quick spray of insecticide. I must have been caught in its web since the vicious looking spider appeared to be coming after me. I screamed and ran, which set off a chain reaction since my roommates screamed and ran. However, once outside we realized that, there was no place to run to, so went back in.

Finally, mentally drugged from the Valium, I crawled into bed. As I moved the pillow a bit for comfort, two earwigs scurried out. Uncaring at this point, I smashed them with my gloved hand and fell asleep.

The next morning I sensed someone's presents in my room. I opened my eyes but didn't say a word. A woman in blue walked past my bed.

This was probably the maid, I thought. A man was standing at the curtain dividing my room from the other room. He looked like an African warrior. He saw that I was awake, but didn't say anything. He walked through the room also.

The woman in blue probably told him that there was a strange person in there wearing a hat, gloves, knee socks and turtleneck to bed, I thought.

I didn't say anything because I knew I had no control over the situation. After the uninvited guests left, I lifted the mosquito net and coughed from the dust that came off it.

Since it was daylight, I saw more clearly. The only other piece of furniture in the bedroom, besides the bed, was a short brown dresser. I walked to the front room. It had four red dingy stuffed pillows facing a concrete platform connected to the wall, a table, and four chairs. The floor was a stained, cracked, filthy pink. The walls were beige. Bamboo strips on the glassless windows were used as curtains. If I looked closely, I could see a whole variety of bugs running here and there.

I cautiously walked outside the hut and looked around. A group of goats were about twenty feet away. There was a small round hut made from upright twigs tied together with twine. The roof was made of straw. Some crewmembers sat outside by a large white barrel still in their pajamas and curlers. As I walked over, I could feel the heat from the round white barrel.

"I had a tough night," I said. "How were your accommodations?"

"Not good," they replied in unison.

"What do you think we can do about it?" I asked.

"I suppose we can call the union to complain," my friend Corrin said.

"You have a phone?"

"Don't you? Corrin replied.

"No."

"Then how are you going to get your wakeup calls," Corrin wondered.

"I've no idea."

"Have you heard about Chopper yet?

No, I just woke up.

It's the company bike and our only transportation in emergencies," Corrin said.

"Has anyone said when we're supposed to be ready for pickup?" I asked.

"I heard pickup is at 1400," Corrin replied.

At 1400, my roommates Kathy and Kathy and I were waiting outside dressed in our specially made navy blue polyester hajj uniform when the taxicab pulled up.

"Why weren't you by your phone?" Our senior F/A asked.

"We don't have a phone," I said.

Once at the airport, it took an hour and a half to board the Hajj pilgrims. Our representative stood at the bottom of the ramp with a whistle and a stick and got the attention of the pilgrims. He'd hit the stick on the ramp, blew his whistle, then marched the pilgrims around the plane a couple of times until they were orderly; then he marched them up the ramp in a single file. Another man stood at the side of the aircraft with a large tank on his back and a hose in his hand pointed toward our pilgrims. He sprayed this white substance and the mist would drift over to where our pilgrims were. I was told what this mist was, but found it hard to believe what I was told was true. I was told it was a disinfectant.

Another time when the pilgrims boarded in this manner through the forward exit, the aft exit was open and a ramp was in place. The pilgrims marched up the ramp, through the aircraft and started down the aft stairs while I was busy with my duties. They must have thought that this was a magic tunnel to take them to Mecca. I rushed over to the open cabin door tapped the woman in the lead on the shoulder and pointed up to the aircraft. She and the others turned and headed back in. I positioned myself in front of the open aft cabin door after that incident. I still laugh when I think about it.

Many of the pilgrims who departed from Kano were elderly people from the backwoods bush country and had never seen an airplane at close range. The men sat in the front of the aircraft and the women sat in the back. They were seated in this configuration since only married couples were allowed to sit together and our seats were three on each side of the aircraft. The women fussed since they wanted to sit with their husbands, but the men didn't seem to mind the seating arrangement. Trans International filled all 254 seats.

Many of the pilgrims TIA flew to Jeddah were very old. Trans International refused some because they appeared to be unable to walk on their own and would need constant assistance. One man was helped off the plane because of his age and I saw him placed in the back of a pickup truck where he laid down. This man didn't complain about being asked to get up and leave the airplane. I asked the Trans International representative what happened to that man on my return flight to Kano the following day.

"When I finished at the airport for the day, the man was still lying in the truck," he said.

"Do you know whose truck it was?" I asked concerned for the sweet older man.

"I only know that it's an airport employees truck," he replied.

Before boarding, the crew had placed boxed lunches on the passenger seats and coke bottles in each seat pocket. . Most of the pilgrims sat on their box lunch and opened their cokes with their teeth. When shown what the boxes contained, the pilgrims would rise and pick up their squashed boxed lunch. They ate the chicken it contained and threw the bones on the aircraft floor. Many held the boxes up for us to open and some ate the plastic around the food.

Before departure, the cabin crew did their emergency demo, which of course included how to fasten seatbelts. These pilgrims didn't fasten them though. The F/A's showed them how row by row with their demo seatbelt in their hands. I noticed that the men understood how to fasten the seatbelt after the row demo. The women didn't want to do it; therefore, each of their seatbelt had to be fastened by the F/A's. One man thought I was disconnecting the seat belts from the seats, so disconnected his, and handed it to me. I smiled.

These people were very thankful to be helped and made the sign for friendship (a clenched fist). At least that was what the English-speaking interpreter told me a clenched fist meant. There were four hundred different dialects spoken in Nigeria in 1975. Even though the interpreters were of little help with the pilgrims needs they did speak English and I was fascinated with their replies to my questions.

I noticed that some pilgrims had lines on their faces.

"Those lines were burned on when they were young to indicate the tribe they belonged to," an interpreter said. "This practice isn't as common as it used to be."

"How do these pilgrims earn enough money to afford this trip?"

"They earned money by selling craft items to tourists," he replied.

I nodded. I alone had spent two hundred dollars on crafts in Kano.

"What are the best buys in Jeddah?" I asked.

"Gold and caftans," he replied.

The women were gorgeous in their brightly colored batiks. European traders introduced the batik wax resist process into African culture. Batik material was a favorite cloth since the wearer could make a statement about the establishment with it. This statement was executed by positioning the printed portraits or their own political leaders in such a way that the wearer could sit upon them. Our Nigerian pilgrims wore numerous batik wrap around skirts (pagnes) one on top of the other. The reason the dresses (grand boubou's) were so long was that if Nigerian women showed her lower leg it meant she was interested in a man in the area.

The men's traditional robes were called grand boubou's also, but their robes were white. They also wore a white band around their heads. No matter how important the man was in the community, they dressed the same, except if they had made the journey to Mecca before. The men with the brightly colored hats the size of top hats had made the journey before.

The airport waiting area was a large dirt field with small grassy areas. Our pilgrims gathered in this area and occasionally cooked a goat over a campfire before they boarded the aircraft. In flight, I would sometimes run across a large piece of cooked meat in the overhead rack when I walked through the cabin. The women must have carried the meat under their grand boubou's since it wasn't visible upon boarding.

In 1980, a Saudi jetliner transporting pilgrims on their way to Jeddah caught fire fifty miles out of Riyadh. At least two small gas stoves had been smuggled aboard the plane and were found by inspectors after the fire. It was thought this was the cause. *Newsweek,* Fiery Death on the Runway, September 1, 1980.

Most of our pilgrims had never seen a toilet. As anyone could imagine, not knowing how to use the toilet was a problem. Even with instruction during this five-hour flight, most of our pilgrims stood on it instead. One man sat on the toilet seat and peed. This was apparent when the flight attendant showed the next passenger how to use the toilet. When a pilgrim came within two feet of me, I'd open the lavatory door, usher him or her in and start motioning to this round white object with water in it. Our pilgrims listened and some appeared concerned. After I felt I had given them sufficient instruction, I'd close the door with them inside. I'm sure I was as strange to them as they were to me.

Personally, I hadn't a clue as to why the pilgrims came to the aft of the aircraft where I was stationed by the lavatories. Many of our pilgrims didn't know how to get out of the lavatories once I closed the door on them. One woman exited the lavatory obviously distressed. I located our interpreter and found out the woman wanted that other person out of the lavatory before she would enter. The other person was her reflection.

The lavatories were outrageously disgusting. It was impossible to potty train two hundred and fifty four people on a five-hour flight. Why instruction wasn't given on the ground was beyond my comprehension. There was a trail of liquid leading from one end of the aircraft to the other. I spoke with our interpreter and he replied that the pilgrims would take a thermos of water into the bathroom to clean themselves. This water would splash all over and cause the flood. Our pilgrims walked through the cabin barefoot, and trailed the stuff back to their seats. They didn't care to wear the flip-flop sandals that ground personal had provided for them. As I watched them slosh through the soggy aisle carpeting, I noticed their feet looked like lizard skin and some had toes missing.

Jeddah, located on the Red Sea, was the official stop for the pilgrims who would travel on to Mecca. From Jeddah, it was forty miles. There were a few pilgrims who traveled by truck; but at least thirty miles had to be taken on foot. That was the Muslim law.

We were briefed it was an honor to live in the holy land, so the parents might sacrifice their children by selling them while on the pilgrimage. It was also an honor to die in Mecca or during the journey. The crewmembers were instructed that according to Muslim law Allah designates the time of demise. Crewmembers shouldn't interfere. If a passenger died on the aircraft, the crew was instructed to throw a blanket over them per Trans International's Hajj flight instruction bulletin.

TIA charged three hundred dollars for the five-hour round trip flight. All we served were boxed lunches and coke. Later we picked up the trash with a garbage bag. The planes weren't cleaned well at each stop but our pilgrims never complained and the conditions were never improved.

During one of our stays in Kano, a friend, attempted to establish better accommodations than her grass hut. She found transportation and departed with a couple of friends to locate the Wicky Game Reserve (later dubbed the Wicky Wacky). There weren't any maps and the only directions they had were general ones such as: go three miles and turn right at the post office, then go about five miles and turn left at the large tree with the white base. Since there were no road signs and few spoke English, it would be amazing if the game reserve were ever found, I thought. However, find it they did—hours later. There were rooms available so they searched for a telephone to call the others. Phones weren't easy to locate in Kano and when they found one, it had a string of people waiting to use it.

A hot water stream ran through the Wicky game reserve and there were crocodiles bathing in it, but that didn't stop the natives and the F/A's from venturing in. A native stood nearby on crocodile watch. Whenever the swimmers heard the natives yell caca wawa, everyone jumped out of the water. Something unusual was expected to live in the waters of Africa, be it smaller than could be detected or large as a crocodile.

Pleased with the accommodations the F/A's began the journey back to the Bogato's huts when the driver screeched the car to a halt and jumped out. There was a dead owl in the road. The driver was distressed. The owl was placed in the trunk of the car before the driver would continue. Somewhere in time, the owl's reputation plummeted and was associated with bad luck.

Once back at the Bogato Hotel the group requested a hotel change. This request was denied and no reason was given. The search party members were extremely disappointed.

I enjoyed bartering with the locals outside the Bogato's restaurant. Some items included silver and brass jewelry, baskets and woodcarvings. One heavy set man dressed in a long robe and batik hat sold carved items during the day. At night he would gather up his carvings, wrap himself in his blanket and sleep outside the restaurant door.

One night while seated at the restaurant a flight attendant became ill and couldn't work, so I was designated to take her trip that evening. I rode chopper (the bike) back to my hut in the dark, the full two-mile distance and changed into my uniform. That was a frightening ride, especially when a bat or something flew across my path. It was so close that I could feel its wings brush against my head.

Dressed and ready for this nights adventure I climbed into the taxi and headed out toward Kano Airport with four other F/A's and came upon a tribal celebration close to the dirt roadway. Stop, we said to the taxi driver. He stopped. I rolled down the car window and felt the hot humid air. I wasn't dreaming. A bonfire and tribal dance was underway. The Wodaabe tribe, a subgroup of the Fulani, performed a ritual. We watched and listened from the taxi. The natives wore close to nothing and had their faces and bodies painted. The men were the dancers and the women were seated. What they were celebrating was a mystery to me, possibly the birth of a child, a harvest, Ramadan or the placement of the planets. It was a close encounter of the PBS (Public Broadcasting) kind. We couldn't linger for long and once again headed off to the airport to greet our Hajj passengers.

We flew the pilgrims to Jeddah almost daily. Each time at crew pickup, someone in the limo would ask, "Why weren't you by your phone?"

"I don't have a phone," I would reply. Then we'd drive off to the airport and greet the pilgrims.

Each crew meal on the aircraft was different than anything I'd ever seen before. Since it couldn't be identified by anyone, I was reticent about eating it. I lived on rolls that were in thirteen-gallon clear plastic bags but even these had bugs in them. TIA was informed of this dilemma and sent emergency packages with canned food, cases of soda pop, medicine, and personal supplies. I did eat the curry in the hotel restaurant once. Then I was informed that this was the casserole of Kano. All the leftover meat was made into curry.

Whose leftover meat? I thought, afraid of the answer.

One evening after the hajj flight, we decided to have Neshi and Kumba in for dinner. We set the concrete table with plastic knives, forks and napkins, and poured soft drinks in paper cups. We took our leftover mystery meat dinners off the plane and set them on the table. Then we went outside to call our guests. In came Neshi and Kumba and I gestured toward the table. After a brief moment of confusion, they sat down and without touching the napkins, fork, or knife; they picked up the mystery meat with both hands and ate with gusto. As they finished one piece, they would throw the bones on the floor and attack another. Every now and then, they would look up at us and smile. We were pleased they were enjoying themselves.

Every time I arrived at the airport, our representative would ask the senior F/A who my roommates and I were. When she identified us, he would reprimand us for not being by our telephone to accept our alert for the flight. We would protest that we had no phone. Not only were we reprimanded before every flight; the representative would talk to other people about us not cooperating and being by our phone. We had to endure this throughout our stay in Kano, Nigeria and I was glad when we finally left.

Kumba, our guard, and our bike chopper in front of our hut in Kano, Nigeria.

Our passengers waiting to board our TIA flight to Jeddah, Saudi Arabia.

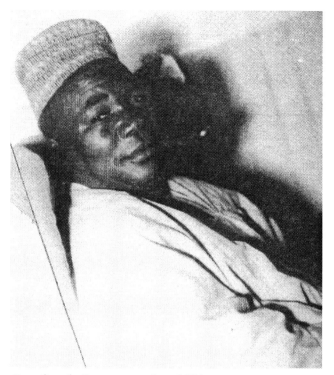

One of our haji passengers aboard TIA.

An Englishman and me visiting a village in Kano, Nigeria in 1975.

2
JEDDAH, THE TWILIGHT ZONE

A couple of years after my first 'hajj' trip to Kano, Nigeria, in 1975; I was scheduled to work another hadj flight. This time we were based in Jeddah, Saudi Arabia located on the west coast of Saudi Arabia. This trip was different from my Kano hut experience but still extremely odd.

In Jeddah, our room was about what I expected at the time. The air conditioning consisted of a large fan in the center of the ceiling. Small Persian rugs were on the floor, with a print of a stream on the wall. The curtains were falling down and the wallpaper was peeling. The area was desolate—just a few palm trees, many crooked streets with a few houses made of concrete. I had a balcony overlooking a junkyard in Jeddah, but it sure beat those huts in Kano.

I'd stare at our American TIA Representative who greeted the crew upon arrival in Jeddah dressed like an Arab, to make sure he was our representative. He wore a long white cotton dress called a thoub and a red and white cotton scarf over his head held down with the traditional black band. He had also grown a beard and sported dark mirrored sunglasses.

"Is this the twilight zone?" One of the Kathie's remarked straining to see our representative in the bright sun as he neared the aircraft.

I laughed and gathered up my belongings.

Next to our hotel I saw a man of about thirty-five years lying on his side on a Persian rug, smoking from an ornate pipe made of brass, which was six feet high.

"What are you smoking?" I asked.

"Hebe jebe," he replied. Whatever that was.

On one occasion when our airline representative greeted the flight in Jeddah before the flight back to Kano, a F/A motioned him over to show him something in the bathroom. He followed her and she opened the door and entered. She was agitated since the cleaners hadn't done what she thought was an adequate job cleaning. Our representative took off his dark mirrored glasses and peered over her shoulder.

"Look at that." The F/A said pointing to the toilet.

The representative looked at the brown matter on the toilet seat so intently his recently grown goatee brushed against her shoulder.

"It looks like poo. This is disgusting. How can you expect us to work in these conditions?" The F/A stated emphatically. "Maybe you don't believe us that this is poo?"

The representative was silent.

The F/A leaned over the toilet to get a better view. She said, "It sure looks like poo." Then she sniffed the matter and said, "It sure smells like poo." Then she put her finger in the brown matter and brought it up to her lips and said, "And it tastes like poo."

Our representative screamed and pulled the F/A out of the bathroom disgusted.

The F/A's who were watching this performance were laughing hysterically. They knew what the brown matter was. They had melted a chocolate candy bar and placed it on the toilet seat. The representative recovered from the shock and shook his head at the F/A's, unable to express his relief that this flight attendant hadn't cracked under the pressure of these unusual circumstances. We TIA flight attendants amused ourselves while away from home in creative ways.

Libby and I in Jeddah, Saudi Arabia in 1977.

3
HELLO MUDDEH, HELLO FADDUH

During time off in Kano, Nigeria in 1975, and 1977, I would visit neighboring villages. These villages looked a lot like the one the crews stayed at, except that theirs were populated with families. We'd venture over and socialize with the children. I drew a hopscotch pattern in the dirt with a stick and showed the children how to play the game. I wished I had packed trinkets, candy, and board games. People came out of their huts to see us and watched with curiosity. How strange it was going from the elegant Park Hotel in Frankfurt to the grass huts of Kano, Nigeria where the people had less stuff in their homes than we had in our suitcases.

The flight crews met at the Bogato Hotel pool and at the restaurant to catch up on the latest news and Kano adventure stories. At the pool one afternoon the crew filled in crewmembers names into Allan Sherman's song, "Hello Muddeh, Hello Fadduh."

Hello, muddeh, hello fadduh here I am at camp Bogato. Camp is very entertaining and they say we'll have some fun if we stop screaming. I went flying with Katie Albright, she developed fungus itch, you remember Josey Minner, she got curry poisoning last night after dinner. All the flight attendant's hate the insects, and the lake has enormous critters. The airlines want no sissy's so they read to us from something called Military protocol and decorum. I don't want this to scare you, but my roommate has contracted a parasite they call malaria. You remember Nancy Steward; she left yesterday looking for the hotel lobby; Take me home, oh muddeh fadduh, take me home.

Since the pool water at the Bogato was the color of moss, I chose not to dive in. Some swam anyway. Around dusk, the mosquitoes started buzzing about. They didn't concern me since I had taken my malaria pills before leaving for Africa. Then a few crewmembers become ill with fever, chills, and flu like symptoms. A local doctor diagnosed the crewmembers with malaria.

"Malaria in humans is caused by one of four protozoan species and all were transmitted by the bite of an infected female mosquito. The pills you were given only prevented you from contracting one type of malaria," the doctor said.

I wondered if I might have contracted malaria in Dakar, Senegal. I boiled water in my room for tea and other than that, I didn't eat or drink anything, so maybe a mosquito bit me and made me ill with fever. I had stayed in Dakar only fourteen hours. On the return flight, I had felt progressively worse. I swallowed a lomotil pill to settle my stomach. It didn't help. I swallowed another and it didn't help either. When we landed in New York, I caught a taxi and headed to a doctor who was versed in tropical diseases. He ordered a blood test and found I had contracted a parasite. Medication was prescribed. My crew was scheduled to layover in New York for a few days and by the time we were scheduled home; I was well enough to make the trip.

One sunny afternoon in Kano, Shep, our flight engineer, and I strolled around our village of huts and noticed a skinny elderly man about ninety years old curled up on a hill. The man was so thin his bones stuck out and his only clothing was a tattered piece of beige cloth wrapped around his waist. Although there was no verbal communication, it was apparent the man was starving. Shep had M&M's in his pocket, but the elderly man wouldn't take the candy. Shep held one up to the elderly man's lips and the man opened his mouth so he dropped the M&M's inside. Shep left the remainder beside his new friend, but as soon as he started to walk away, local people came and took the candy. The old man was too weak to protest. Everyday Shep would return and feed him until one day the old man wouldn't open his eyes. He had died. We were aware of a small doctor's office thirty minutes from Kano. We had taken a taxi there one afternoon for no other reason than to check it out. One doctor was on duty. The ill sat waiting. Those too ill to make the journey received no treatment.

When our pilgrims deplaned in Jeddah and entered the terminal, Saudi officials required every pilgrim to change an equivalent of one thousand dollars into Saudi riyals (SR's). The pilgrims were informed before departure that the Saudi riyals weren't to be exchanged back when they left Jeddah. The pilgrims had to spend the riyals in Saudi Arabia. Because of this rule, they purchased items that they might not have if they could have gotten their currency back. An older man with white hair boarded with an alarm clock the diameter of four inches. The clock hung at waist level and was tied around his neck by a rope. He was dressed in the traditional long white robe and had a stern look on his face when a photo was snapped of him. The F/A's named him "Father Time."

On another Hajj flight, on the way to Jeddah, a baby was born. The aircraft was past the point of no return approximately two and one half hours out and a F/A noticed a woman in pain. She was holding her stomach, which accentuated the size of her belly. The woman was pregnant. Pillows, blankets, and paper towels were gathered and the woman gave birth in the squat position. The woman's sister cut the umbilical cord with a razor blade and both sister and new mom walked off the aircraft upon arrival in Jeddah an hour later. How extraordinary.

4
OUAGADOUGOU AND MORE

Not only did I visit Nigeria on the continent of Africa during my employment with Trans International but also the Ivory Coast, Senegal, the Benin Republic, Niger, Upper Volta, Namibia and South Africa.

When scheduled for one trip to Africa from Oakland, California in 1976, I noticed numerous three-letter designator codes on my itinerary that were unfamiliar. I asked scheduling about this and found out they were: Dakar, Abigan, Cotonou, Dahamay, Niamey, and Ouagadougou. I would be hopscotching around Africa. I scanned the designator codes then brought out my atlas. African countries changed names so frequently I needed to purchase a current atlas.

I repeated the city name Ouagadougou three times. It sounded so exotic. In 1976, Ouagadougou was the capitol city of Upper Volta, which was declared independent from the French on August 5th, 1960. A rebellion ensued. It was during that conflict in 1976 that we ferried into Ouagadougou and ferried out again after unloading cargo.

A new constitution was written and approved in 1977.

Upon descent into Ouagadougou Airport, I saw flat land as far as the horizon. No herds of animals were present. I so looked forward to seeing herds of animals. So far, the only animals I'd seen in Africa were in Kano and they were goats and donkeys. The terrain near the Ouagadougou Airport was speckled with bushes. The airport, a two story white building with a flat roof, had an observation balcony the length of the airport. The Ouagadougou air traffic controllers had TIA park the jet aircraft far from the terminal. They probably had heard these big jets with the powerful engines had blown out windows at other African airports. This happened twice in Kano when the Nigerian Airport Authority instructed our pilots to park close to the terminal. They would instruct the pilots to push back and then the aircraft would be turned toward the runway. At this point, the pilot was told to start their engines. The four powerful jet engines of the DC-8 and the three engines on the DC -10 would send a blast of air directly toward the terminal blowing everything in its path, shaking the windows and shattering the glass. This exasperated the airport officials and made us very unpopular.

In December 1978, TIA flew the remains of Prince Sudari back to his homeland in Riyadh, Saudi Arabia. Riyadh, the capitol of Saudi Arabia was located on an arid plateau. The ruling family-House of Saudi- governs from there. The prince who was the cousin of the King of Saudi Arabia, died in a hospital in Rye, New York.

The flight included a stop in Paris to board the son of the dead Prince. The casket was placed in the cabin of the aircraft since the body had to be in the line of vision of the Royal Family throughout the entire trip. This was Islam law.

Another unusual request was made in August 1978. This request came from Air Gabon. Air Gabon was the national carrier of the Gabon Republic in Africa. They asked Trans International to help them transport laborers from Libreville, Gabon, to neighboring Cotonou in the Kingdom of Benin. The request came two weeks before the day of operation. From August 17th to 20th, five DC-10's flew between the two African countries.

TIA was also commissioned to distribute food to the starving in Ethiopia in 1984. The food was shipped into Assab, Ethiopia and then loaded onto the aircraft headed for distributaries where the starving people were located.

As was stated in a *San Jose Mercury News* article on November 11th, 1984: *"Soon after the American plane landed, it was mobbed by a dozen loaders— all barefoot and wearing green baseball caps bearing the TransAm logo. In thirty minutes, twenty tons of food was loaded."* The food was loaded at Assab after the Trans International Hercules L-100-30 touched down on the sand runway. The Trans International aircraft then promptly departed for designated areas in Ethiopia to distribute the food.

Although I was not present on most of the above-mentioned flights, it was a part of Trans Internationals schedule, so part of TIA's history and I found it to be extremely interesting.

Corrine and I in Cotonou, in the Kingdom of Benin, Africa in our TIA, Hajj uniform. The fellow behind us with his hands over his face may have had the belief that he would lose his soul if a picture were taken of him. That belief was common in Africa.

5
ARAMCO CHARTERS TO DHAHRAN

In 1981, Trans International signed a three-year contract with the Arabian American Oil Company (Aramco) and Saudi Airlines to provide cargo and passenger service from Houston to Amsterdam to Dhahran. The Dhahran area, on the east coast of Saudi Arabia on the Persian Gulf was the source of ninety-five percent of Saudi Arabia's wealth. Kuwait was located north and Oman was to the south. Actually, Dhahran wasn't a city, it was the name of the international airport, and where Aramco and the University of Petroleum and Minerals were located. Aramco was an oil company that produced manufactured, marketed, and shipped crude oil, natural gas, and petroleum. In the 1970's, Aramco constructed a master gas system in Saudi Arabia. The Saudi Kingdom purchased Aramco's assets, gaining full ownership of the company in 1980.

For these specific flights the 747 aircraft was configured for one hundred twenty oil men, one hundred and six in the main cabin, and fourteen upstairs, all first class seating. The aft of the aircraft was configured with twelve cargo pallets along with five cargo pallets in the forward lower cargo compartment. Also, four Air Medic Stretcher Carriers were set up in the forward cabin.

Since I was working a special flight (Aramco), I was allowed to stay in the main Sonesta hotel in Amsterdam, instead of the apartments across from the Bronco Saloon. The Sonesta Hotel was much quieter. It was originally a series of private residences, now joined together. One elevator took me to the fourth floor where I went down the hall to another elevator, which took me to the second floor, then down a long hall to my room. The rooms were petit and the windows had curtains to match the bedspread.

This day I was scheduled to work the Amsterdam, Dhahran, leg of the trip. The crew arrived at the airport one hour before the plane landed —the representative for TIA forgot to tell us it would be late.

Once the aircraft arrived and the crew boarded we were impressed with the first class seating. All the seats were new. The last two cabins were blocked off and when I peeked through the door, I could see large black tarps covering the cargo, which was strapped down with two inch white straps.

I climbed the spiral stairs to check out my galley. I had only nine passengers this day.

First menus were distributed, and then drinks and hors-d'oeuvres were served. Next, I placed a tablecloth down (not a linen one, but paper).

"Excuse me Miss," a passenger said. "I have a question about the menu. It says here that you're serving pissold potatoes," he said pointing to the menu.

I listened patiently then glanced at the menu. The menu did say pissold potatoes not rissole potatoes. I immediately called the senior and the menus were retrieved.

We served the hot food, then fruit, rolls and cheese. After the movie, we served a champagne breakfast, and then hot Dutch chocolate before landing in Dhahran. The flight was five and one half hours long.

One F/A was offered an eighteen karat gold chain from a passenger; two other F/A's were offered ten-dollar tips.

During our preflight briefing, the crew was informed that pearls weren't allowed in Dhahran since Dhahran sells them and doesn't want competition. I removed my pearl earrings, wrapped them in tissue, and placed them in my purse. Coca Cola wasn't allowed either; the reason being it was drunk in Israel. Whenever briefed on a country I was headed for, I had an insatiable desire to ask why.

I was the forward galley girl during Aramco very first—first class charters into Dhahran in 1981. The Saudi airport officials boarded in Dhahran, and went directly to the galley. They were interested in the liquor on board. Liquor wasn't allowed in Dhahran. I thought that the officials were planning to confiscate it. Instead, they opened some mini liquor bottles, lined them up on the galley counter, and then started chugging. I was appalled. I closed the galley curtain since the passengers were on board. The officials were still opening mini liquor bottles and drinking after the passengers had deplaned and I was collecting my things to deplane. Shortly after this incident, the rules changed.

We were now required by Trans International to place all liquor bottles, empty and full back into the liquor kits—also empty beer cans. I couldn't always fit everything back in the kits so wrapped the champagne bottles in garbage bags, got the axe from the cockpit, and smashed it. I was told to do this because the Saudis licked the tops of the empty liquor bottles. All liquor kits had to be sealed by the time the aircraft got into Saudi air space—that was one and one half hours before landing. No booze was allowed in Saudi Arabia—public whippings were common for offenses.

On arrival, the crew was ordered to put all belongings on a baggage rack. The only items we could keep with us were open bags. Since our purses weren't open, we were supposed to leave them. I opened the front flap of my purse and kept it with me. We moved on to stand in line to show passports. While standing in line, the Saudi officials sternly reprimanded my roommate and I because we were giggling. We stopped giggling. I thought that maybe the officials thought we were laughing at them, which we weren't. The female crewmembers were instructed to leave their passports with the Saudi police at the airport because we didn't have visas. The female crewmembers didn't have visas because the Saudi government wouldn't issue them in the United States because we were female. Many men stood around and stared at the crew.

Before leaving the airport, I attempted to cash a traveler's check and was told I couldn't because I didn't have a passport. I took out the forty dollars cash I had in my wallet and changed that into Saudi riyals. The exchange rate was 3.46 SR's to the U.S. dollar. The cashier handed me my money and said it was correct. I figured it out on paper. He was wrong—I was shorted two riyals which was two hundred halalah. The cashier slipped the two riyals to me without an argument.

We arrived at the Dhahran Airport in Saudi Arabia on a Thursday afternoon. In Saudi Arabia Thursday and Friday were the Saturday and Sunday of the Western world.

Our crew stayed at the recently opened Meridian Hotel in Dhahran; the only hotel in Saudi Arabia where men and women were allowed to swim in the same pool. Only one-piece bathing suits were allowed. I went to the pool for a swim and saw numerous men on the balconies around the pool. Many of these men had binoculars held up to their eyes pointing toward the pool. Although I thought this was odd behavior, I remained at the pool. Activities for women were limited in Saudi Arabia.

In the lobby of the Meridian Hotel, a Saudi man sat on a rug with a few items for sale and liquid in some small pottery cups without handles. They looked like eggcups. I asked a fellow crewmember if she knew what the liquid was.

"I don't know what it was but it tasted all right. After I drank, the Saudi man rinsed my cup in that pot full of water by his side and refilled it again," the crewmember replied pointing to the pot.

I chose not to try the drink.

This day, the crew met some oilmen from the Dhahran flight to go sight seeing. They had been to Dhahran before. We traveled by taxi to the Dhahran Yacht Club on the Persian Gulf. We passed by many sand colored buildings, streets that were badly in need of repair and flat sandy areas that stretched as far as the eye could see. It was what I expected—a great desert. We arrived at the Yacht Club when the sun was setting. The club covered an area of one square mile. The sun was setting over the Persian Gulf, which seemed strange since we were on the East coast of Saudi Arabia. It's my guess that we were in Qatar, on the peninsula facing west, which would explain the sunset. Qatar was not far from Dhahran.

We stayed only a short period and then headed for the Dhahran camp. It had a lovely golf course where the sand was oiled down so it would not blow in the wind. We stopped at the clubhouse and ate hamburgers then drove by the Western churches on the compound. Since no other religion was allowed except Islam, the churches were called special schools with special teachers.

On our return, I saw a wild one hump Arabian camel.

"It's unusual to see a single camel," our Aramco friend said. "Camels usually travel in pairs and they're not seen on the desert as often since this highway was built."

I saw my camel on the highway between Alvarcan and Dhahran. We passed by numerous shops and buildings strung with white lights for the holiday season. As we talked, a car came toward us and the people inside spoke Arabic through a megaphone.

"Do you know what they're saying?" I asked.

"They're the religious police-Mullahs- and are telling the shopkeepers to shut down their shops and pray. During the Hajj, the religious police have top authority. After the religious holiday season, the National and Military police take control. The religious police can grab someone on the street and cut their hair on the spot if they think it's too long. They can also close hotels if they don't comply with the religious aspects of the Saudi government such as separate elevators for men and women and separate swimming pools," my friend said

Since the Meridian Hotel in Dhahran where we stayed was new, the Saudi religious police hadn't put pressure on them to follow the Arabian standards.

Last month an Aramco passenger had told me about the Saudi's dating policies. "Saudi women don't date," he said. "They find a man they enjoy being with and then stay with him for about three months before they get married. Only then are they seen on the streets together. If she's seen with two men separately, she's considered a whore."

While shopping in dusty, humid Al Khobar, I attempted to locate something made in Saudi Arabia for a souvenir, only everything I found had been imported from Iran, Pakistan, Turkey, Holland, and other countries. I decided on an Arab woman's abaya-black full length dress- and full head veil – boushiya – that covers the head and face and an Arab man's – thoub – floor length cotton white robe, shumagg-scarf worn over the head held by the ogal, the black band surrounding the top of the head holding the shumagg in place.

One Saudi man attempted to hold my hand while I was window-shopping. I pushed him away and he became angry. This created a commotion and one of my Aramco friends dashed out of a shop and defended me. The Saudi men touch western woman when walking down the street and they stare.

One Friday in 1981, some crewmembers decided to witness a public execution in the town square. I chose not to join them. A person could be convicted of the death penalty in Saudi Arabia with no defender lawyer and the confession, even after torture, was accepted as evidence. The methods were the beheading of men and a firing party for the women; married women who were thought to be guilty of adultery could also be stoned. A person in Saudi Arabia could be put to death for sex crimes, drug crimes, sabotage, corruption, witchcraft, and production/distribution/consumption of alcohol, among other offences. This type of experience would probably give me nightmares for the remainder of my life.

The following was an experience that I had in Saudi Arabia concerning proper dress. I was thrilled to be in Saudi Arabia for the first time. I could hardly wait to explore the shops and converse with the locals. I was aware that the Saudis had a dress code so I wore a long loose fitting muumuu with sleeves. Libby, my roommate wore pants with a long sleeved shirt.

Once we arrived by taxi into town, Libby started to feel sharp pricks as if something bit her. Libby asked if I was also being bitten.

"No," I said.

We went on our merry way. Then the sharp pricks became more frequent and after a moment of search, I found a little wood stick in my roommate's blouse. Apparently, someone unseen flicked these sticks at her. We kept an eagle eye out for the person, but he or she was nowhere to be seen. We ducked into a shop and discussed the problem with the shopkeeper.

"Ladies don't wear pants in Saudi Arabia and the flicking of these sticks was the Saudis' way of saying, you don't conform to our customs, therefore we're going to make it miserable for you," the shopkeeper said.

He also said, "Men don't touch Muslim females in public. Only members of the same sex would hold hands, embrace, and kiss outside the confines of their homes. Muslim law is strict and the penalties harsh for disobeying it's laws."

We made a quick retreat from the shopping area and took solace back at the hotel. The more common reprimand for incorrect dress was not being served in restaurants. It was Ramadan when Muslims don't eat, drink, or smoke from sunrise to sunset. Tourists and business people weren't permitted to dine in public during the daytime either, no matter if you were male or female. Saudi Arabia was the most unusual place I've ever stayed. We were briefed not to use our left hands since it was considered dirty. Also pointing at something and crossing your legs was a no, no.

Friday, which was the Saudis' Holy Day, was the day when the Meridian Hotel served a barbecue buffet by the pool. Many of the traditional dishes from Saudi Arabia were placed on the buffet. I tasted salads, which consisted of parsley, okra, tomatoes, lettuce, green beans, and chickpeas—mixed vegetables and carrots in different sauces. The second course was eggplant and another dish that could not be identified.

The soup was a cream of rice with a slight shrimp taste. Then there was steak, chicken, crab, fish, lamb and potatoes and rice. The desserts were Baklava, and other pastries made from nuts, honey, filo dough and shredded wheat. They also served fruit salad and delicious flan with coffee. This barbecue was a one-time experience for me because the cost was 70SR's with beverage extra. That's about thirty dollars U.S. and TIA only allowed us twenty-one dollars a day for food, tips, cleaning, and transportation in 1981.

In October 1981, we flew the oilmen from Houston to Amsterdam, the first leg of the Daharan trip. It was difficult to sleep since my roommate only slept six hours a night and had smokers cough. I needed at least eight hours of sleep to be at my best. We arrived in Amsterdam at 0300 local. At eleven, I woke to the sound of the radio, which my roommate had turned on. I was definitely sleep deprived and miserable.

The crew was scheduled to commercial on Pan Am from Amsterdam to London Gatwick, to San Francisco. We stopped in London for two hours, changed planes, and next stop San Francisco. During the commercial flight back to my domicile, I plugged in my headsets, closed my eyes, and listened to John Denver sing, Take Me Home Country Road, reflecting all that had happened during the last two weeks in Saudi Arabia. We arrived in San Francisco without delays but Pan Am's baggage handlers ripped the handle off my red suitcase somewhere between Amsterdam and San Francisco. I lifted it from the bottom, which caused pressure on my spine, so placed it back on the ground, and pushed it with my foot to the Pan Am customer service office where I filled out a damaged suitcase report. Pan Am agreed to replace Big Red's handle.

I'd always gotten butterflies in my stomach and a peaceful feeling when we touched down and ended trip. It was wonderful to be home.

CHAPTER 9

KOREA, 747'S, & WHERE IS DIEGO GARCIA?

1
THE IDITAROD

It was easy to lose track of time in Anchorage, Alaska in June since the sun circled the city and never set. Three months before this trip in March 1981, we were in Anchorage where I had viewed the Iditarod festivities from my Hilton Hotel room. From my window, I had seen booths, carnival rides, dogs, and people. It was thunderous. I had attempted to change rooms since we were scheduled for a 0200 wakeup but the hotel was booked. The celebrated event three stories below commemorated the 1925 lifesaving delivery of diphtheria serum to Nome, Alaska. The one thousand one hundred mile race took the dogs and their mushier from Anchorage into Alaska's interior and ended in Nome.

That morning at 0200, we received our wakeup for a 0500 departure out of Anchorage to Osan, Korea with a fuel stop in Yokoto, Japan. We were scheduled to transport soldiers that were transferred from California military bases.

After the meal service, I pulled out my book *Africa on the Cheap*. The November before, I had planned to visit London and was reading *London On Ten Dollars a Day* while commercialing on Pan Am to Tokyo. This day I read about Africa while flying to Korea. I was surprised no one said anything to me about my choice of reading material.

On final descent into Osan, condensation droplets formed near the bulkhead by the windows. Paper towels were taped onto the overhead rack to catch the drops, but the towels were soaked and about to fall. As the plane slapped the ground, the soaked towels fell in the passengers lap. I winced.

"Excuse the landing, but this was how were taught to land when there's rain on the runway," the captain said. We landed so hard a panel fell off the aft galley ceiling and the passengers screamed. Later we were informed that a tire had blown.

In Anchorage, before departure to Seoul, Korea, I had been unable to sleep due to the noise of the Iditarod festivities. By the time we landed in Seoul, I had been awake for over thirty hours, but that landing immediately perked me up.

The main cabin door opened and a military official boarded. He asked if anyone with the rank of Colonel or above was on board since they deplane first. After the people who were stationed here deplaned, the military official said on the P.A., "Now everyone else can deboard de plane."

Rain pounded down and the passenger buses started on their way to the terminal. No other bus arrived to take the crew, so we dashed through the wind and rain. Once inside, I stopped to squeeze the water from my hair. The storm had knocked out the electricity and customs checked passports by candlelight. Wet, exhausted and miserable we stood waiting by flickering candlelight. One F/A forgot her passport, or lost it, and it delayed all of us. The head customs official said he would let her enter Korea if she would promise to stay in the hotel. She promised.

We boarded the bus for the hour ride to Osan.

"How was the landing?" the captain asked. "This was only the second time I landed the DC-8 as a captain with passengers on board."

"A bit bumpy but otherwise fine," I replied.

Usually after completing recurrent training, the F/A's and the cockpit crews were a wealth of information about what's happening with our airline.

"Last week in recurrent flight training I heard that TIA was relocating pilots to New York and only keeping a few in Oakland," the new captain stated. "They also planned to furlough seventy-five F/A's in Oakland and downgrade many seniors. I heard the upgrading of seniors was still going to take place in New York (TIA's new base in the late seventies)," the new captain added. "In fact, a friend who had been flying senior for almost ten years was downgraded and was flying junior to a New York senior who had been upgraded only two months ago." This was the price we paid to be based in California, I thought.

This new DC-8 captain mentioned a situation that happened to a

TIA cargo plane on approach to North Island Coronado, California. Apparently, a helicopter had dropped off three parachuter's over Gloritta Bay. Two of them free fell right by the cockpit window so quickly that the pilots thought they were birds, the third free fell on the wing. The parachuter then fell back and knocked a hole in the Trans International Hercules aircraft.

My parents lived in Coronado and I'd seen the Fourth of July events there. The Navy Seals might have been practicing for these festivities at that time unaware of the cargo plane's permission to land, I thought.

We were five minutes away from Seoul and I started to gather my belongings.

2
SEOUL, KOREA

The crew bus pulled up to the Seoul Hyatt Hotel. TIA bussed us to Seoul since they couldn't find us appropriate accommodations in Osan, where we landed. The last time I had stayed in Osan, we stayed in what possibly could have been a house of ill repute. Only sheets were on the beds. We all had needed to call the reception desk and request blankets. People entered and exited neighboring rooms continuously, not careful to close the doors gently. The doors would squeak open then bang closed. My earplugs didn't help that night. Squeak, Bang, Squeak, Bang all night long.

We arrived in Seoul at noon and were scheduled for a noon departure the following day. If I slept now, I probably wouldn't sleep tonight so my roommate and I decided to shop. A young man who said he was a professional golfer asked us to meet for a drink. We declined. When we arrived back at the hotel, the golfers were still in the bar. A crewmember motioned to me to join them. I ordered and handed the server the complimentary drink coupon that the Hyatt gave to everyone upon registering. Later the F/A's left for dinner.

Upon our return to the Hyatt, a waiter approached us and said the alleged golfers had signed for the drinks with a fictitious name and room number so he had to pay for the drinks out of his own pocket. We all decided to pool our money and pay the bar bill. We never caught up with those alleged golfers.

Show time in Seoul, July 3, 1981 was 1000, for our return flight to Anchorage. The crew boarded the limo to Osan, and since I wasn't exhausted, for a change, I could appreciate the beauty of Korea. We arrived at the aircraft to find the plane hadn't been refueled. Apparently, there were only two fueling trucks and the commercial aircrafts were scheduled to get them first. We were delayed three hours.

During the delay the co-pilot mentioned that we almost diverted to another airport yesterday since Osan's runway lights were in-op.,

Diverting was a problem since the pilot needed permission from Yokoto AFB in Japan, due to military regulations to change the flight plan.

"I never thought about runway lights being in-op when the terminal lights were out yesterday," I said. "I thought the runway lights would have some sort of backup system, at least ours at home do."

After takeoff, we made the customary fuel stop in Yokota, Japan. One passenger had to walk with crutches. I called forward to see if he could stay on board.

"No," the MAC official replied.

Once he boarded, after refueling, I put his crutches behind the last row of seats because the F/A's were no longer able to place anything in the closets except light bags due to 1981 FAA rulings.

We encountered another three-hour delay in Yokota.

"The VHF radio is broken," the captain said. "It was ok to fly to Yokoto without it, but it not ok to cross the ocean without it."

Because this was the second three-hour delay this day, the passenger meals defrosted. Military regulations required the meals to be frozen solid before they were cooked. Even though the F/A's informed the ground handlers that the meals had defrosted, they didn't re cater. Instead, they brought on dry ice to refreeze the meals.

At 1730, we departed with no maintenance problems, but a few passenger ones. Passengers were required to take their personal belongings off the aircraft in Yokota and couldn't remember where their seats were. The military didn't assign seats, and passengers fought for the seats with the best legroom.

This day I was number five and responsible for the emergency demonstration over the wing area. While I was demonstrating the emergency procedures, I noticed an infant was next to the window exit. Just before takeoff, I scrambled to reseat this family since infants can't be by exits. Also, smokers sat in the non-smoking section, which became apparent in-flight.

After takeoff, we removed the foil from a few chicken and beef entrees and they smelled worse then usual. The dry ice had frozen some but not all the entrees. We analyzed the situation and noted that many of these entrees had been without refrigeration for six hours. The frozen meals were probably ok but we had only enough to serve one half the passengers. If our passengers came down with food poisoning, it would be our fault since we didn't follow military rules so we decided not to serve the entrée and only served the preset with the salad, roll, and dessert. We explained the situation to the passengers and for the most part, they understood. The crew felt our representative should have dealt with the problem on the ground and re catered, instead of sticking us F/A's with a full load of ravenous passengers five miles up in the sky.

Once we arrived in Anchorage, the crew got together to celebrate the Fourth of July. We chose a cute little restaurant outside of town called Gusilo. The restaurant was festively decorated with red, white, and blue. The next day we were scheduled to work back to Osan, Korea, per our initial itinerary.

Our wakeup came at 0140 and once again, the aircraft was DC-8, 72T. In-flight to Osan I felt lethargic and could hardly see through the cabin the smoke was so thick. I went to the cockpit to inquire about this and found out two compressors were in-op. The compressors regulated the airflow in the cabin, the cabin pressurization and it clears the cabin of smoke. The cabin altitude was seven thousand feet, one thousand less than Machu Picchu in the Peruvian Andes. Normally, cabin altitude was five thousand feet. It felt unusually hot in the cabin and I asked that the cabin be cooled down a bit, but we were also low on Freon so that wasn't possible. When we landed in Osan, it was sprinkling, but I went to the bottom of the ramp anyway since the mist was refreshing. I returned to the cabin to retrieve my topside and found the military drug dog sniffing it. I patted the large dog on the head, lifted my topside, and headed down the stairs. It felt wonderful to breath fresh air.

The limo to Seoul took only an hour, which was a relief. The crew was looking forward to getting to the hotel and having something to drink and maybe some ice cream. This reminded me of an incident early in my flying career. My roommate at the time went to get ice cream and returned with a half-gallon container of fudge ripple and two eighteen year old bag boys. How bizarre. I was trapped in bed in my pajamas. It took thirty minutes to convince her that I didn't want them there. I wasn't angry though, just inconvenienced and I never roomed with her again. A couple of years later I heard this same F/A went on sick leave in Hong Kong and did not call TIA for three months. When she finally did call, she said she had lost their phone number. They fired her.

When the crew bus pulled up in front of the Hyatt Hotel in Seoul the thought of being there gave me a boost of energy so I headed out to shop. I bought eel skin products and silk beads (plastic beads covered with brightly colored silk thread). Later I called eel skin factories to make an appointment to purchase eel skin in large quantities. An agent (Mr. Kim) met me in the lobby and drove me to a factory—actually an apartment building. We took the elevator to the seventh floor and I noticed that there was no fourth floor designated. "The number four means death and is bad luck in Korea," Mr. Kim said. In this elevator, the letter F replaced the number four; elsewhere the numbers simply skip from third to fifth.

Eel skin was naturally a gray color and was dyed with shoe polish. I gathered the information and samples I needed from Mr. Kim, and he gave me his card. That card was of major importance. I was to discover most everyone in Korea was called Kim. Kim was the name of a famous Korean guerrilla leader of the early twentieth century. Koreans pride themselves on being one hundred percent Korean.

In April 1981, after a five-day layover in Seoul, Korea, we ferried the 747 aircraft into Oakland. I had my customs form in hand along with my informal entry for two hundred fifty dollars worth of eel leather purchases. This was the first time I had bought items for resale. I walked over to customs and handed the documents to a female customs official. She promptly took my informal entry and tore it up spouting that it was no good here.

"Why?" I asked.

"Because Oakland doesn't have a cashier," she replied. Then she ordered me to dump out all my resale items, count them, and price them for her. She added up the prices and they were correct but she charged me five dollars anyway. No explanation was given while the crew waited and watched. The captain was angry for the delay and I was embarrassed. Even though I had done everything correctly, I apologized to the crew.

Once home I called the Pan Am customs office. "She should have given you a numbered form," customs said. "The forms were in the Oakland customs area and necessary since without a cashier there wouldn't be a record of the bulk informal entry."

"What can I do about it?" I asked.

"You could report her and maybe cause yourself grief next time you pass through Oakland," he said, or forget about it.

I chose to forget it.

That happened in April 1981 and now it was June 1981 and I was back in Seoul, Korea buying eel leather once again in large quantities. This in mind and weak from hunger I chose a restaurant the locals frequent. The name was Kim's Kentucky Fried Chicken. I didn't see any fried chicken this day so ordered rice with an egg and vegetables and it cost 1,200 won ($1.70 U.S.). First a server brought me some Kim Chi and spicy bamboo sprouts, then a bowl of seaweed soup and later the entrée. As I finished my meal, I noticed one of the servers pour tea into a bowl and drink it. After the server finished drinking, she wiped out the bowl with a towel and placed it back on the stack with the clean dishes. An iron stomach was a definite asset for an international charter F/A.

It was a few hours before sunset. I set off to hail a green colored cab. The green ones were cheaper in Korea than the black ones, but the latter were cleaner and had air conditioning. A black cab pulled up so I decided to negotiate the price.

"1,000 won to the Seoul Hyatt," he said.

"600 won," I said.

"1,000 won," he repeated.

I started to slide out of the cab. Then he said ok, ok and I slid back in. The evening sun was eye level and I squinted.

"Excuse me," I said. "I left my sunglasses at the restaurant. I'll give you your 1,000 won price if you wait."

I entered Kim's Kentucky Fried Chicken and asked for my glasses.

"I don't have your sunglasses," he replied. "A customer picked them up."

I replied that his customer had stolen them, but the merchant insisted no, no steal—took them. I returned to the hotel and collapsed exhausted.

The following morning, items I ordered at the eel leather factory were delivered to the hotel. I met my agent, Mr. Kim, downstairs in the restaurant. I ordered Sanka and Mr. Kim ordered Sanka. When the server brought the Sanka packets, he just looked at the two orange packages next to his cup and then at me. I poured the contents into my cup and stirred it. Then he did the same. I drank some and so did he, but it was apparent he didn't care much for it. I asked him if he had ever had Sanka before.

"No," he said. Then he went on to say that he would take the other packet back to show his wife. I smiled.

It's a polite gesture in Korea to order what the client ordered, whatever that might be. The Koreans were warm and friendly once they considered you their friend. Korean society was based on Confucianism and Buddhism. Confucianism considered devotion and respect for parents, family, friends, and those in positions of authority an utmost priority. The oldest male controls the family as the supreme decision maker. Family members obey no matter how ridiculous the request may seem. They're also conservative and don't joke as Americans do and may sometimes be insulted by our humor.

On one occasion, Mr. Kim asked if I would like to see the nightlife of Korea as a benefit for a prospective client. "Yes," I said knowing his regular clients were men and he takes them out drinking and to girlie bars.

Mr. Kim took me out to dinner and we drove by the sights of Seoul, Korea. This must have been boring for him. Actually, I would have enjoyed visiting with Mr. Kim's family more than anything, but didn't think it polite to ask.

This day I went shopping for a Korean chest to fill with my purchases, which included a four-foot brass phone. The brass bed and silk beads were also packaged and taken to the post office. I juggled huge boxes and was thankful once rid of them.

I arrived back at the hotel and found a check written out for eighty dollars in my purse. No store name was on the check. Since I had bought items in about ten stores in an hour's time, I had no idea which place it was intended for, but felt sure the shopkeeper would find me. There was only one street for shopping outside our hotel and each day the F/A's walk up the street and down the other side.

This day the shopkeeper did find me, but said I owed him ninety-six dollars and started yelling at me. The customers in the shop were yelling at him and telling me not to pay and the shop owner was yelling back at them. The customers said he should have got the money when I made the purchase and that it was too late now. Overwhelmed by all the yelling, I handed the merchant the check for eighty dollars. He accepted it and I left

That evening my roommate and I went to the Sportsman's Club and then to a country music club called Sam's. We arrived back at the hotel just before the midnight curfew. Our hotel in Seoul was two hours from the South Korean Demilitarized Zone, the 38th parallel. Even though the North Koreans invaded the South in 1950, over thirty years ago the situation still wasn't settled.

On one hot summer day in 1981, while shopping on the E Tai Wan strip, a blaring sound resonated through the air, not the type of sound heard from an emergency vehicle. It came from a loud speaker on a light pole. I glanced up at the pole and then around at others who were scooting into shops along the street. A shopkeeper motioned to me to come inside. This was a military air raid drill. He closed the door and turned off the lights. The drill lasted about twenty minutes and when the siren stopped blaring, I went on with my shopping as everyone else did. This was routine for the South Koreans, scary for me.

On another occasion, my roommate, and I were in our hotel room at night when the air raid siren started blaring. Instructions on air raid drills were located in the rooms. We turned off all lights and closed the black out curtains. I peeked out and saw numerous aircraft flying around and searchlights lighting the sky. The only vehicles seen on the streets for the next hour were tanks. I had forgotten how close we were to Panmunjom's demilitarized zone.

3
PANMUNJOM

In 1948, Korea was separated into 'The Republic of Korea' in the south and 'The Democratic People's Republic,' under Communist rule in the north. In June 1950, the North Korean army attacked South Korea initiating the Korean War. This day I planned to tour Panmunjom's demilitarized zone (DMZ) where peace talks were taking place.

I had inquired at the Hyatt tour desk about this tour and they handed me my reservation. They didn't know the exact time of the tour since it differed from day to day for security reasons. The following day I went to the tour desk to check on the time of departure and was told the tour was full. I showed her my reservation slip but she said it meant nothing. I argued that this was my last day in Korea and was particularly looking forward to the tour. The woman behind the desk called a few places and found a cancellation.

"The tour cost would be twenty-three dollars," the woman said.

"The base tour only cost four dollars," I replied.

"This tour is twenty-three dollars. The bus is air-conditioned and that is the reason for the price difference. Do you want to join the tour?"

Fine, I reached inside my purse for my wallet.

"Meet at the Lotte Hotel at noon and bring your passport. There's a dress code; no blue jeans or sandals are allowed. Also, if you are going to wear that sundress you'll need to wear a jacket," she informed me.

Once I arrived at the Lotte Hotel, there were further complications. No one knew which bus I should board. I boarded a bus full of Japanese tourists. I was the only blue-eyed blonde on the bus. I turned and went back to the tour desk.

"Is that the bus I'm scheduled to be on?" I asked pointing.

"Yes," he said.

I boarded again. "Will this tour be in English?"

"It was scheduled to be in Japanese but I will speak in English also," the tour guide said as he reached for the microphone.

"The ride to the DMZ will take one and one half hours," he said into the microphone. "This is a war zone so there are certain rules that need to be followed. Don't wave to the North Koreans, or make any gestures, or touch anything in the conference room when we arrive. Smoking isn't allowed and please sign this paper saying the military isn't responsible if something happens to you," he spoke with authority and seriousness.

Our bus scooted past farms, army tanks covered with foliage and cement bunkers on our drive down Freedom highway. Our guide picked up the microphone again. "The military pays two thirds of the rent for the farms we are passing." he said. The huge signs bearing Korean letters that you see face North Korea and have information on them for the north to read. The river you see next to the road is booby-trapped and the land is dotted with land mines. This demilitarized zone is thirteen thousand feet north to south and one hundred fifty-one miles east to west across the Korean peninsula from the Han River Estuary. Two villages are inside the zone. The south village, Taesongdon, has people living in it, the north village, Kijongdong, has only loudspeakers and a couple of people who raise a flag daily and turn the lights on and off. That village is referred to as propaganda village. One thousand two hundred ninety-two yellow signs divide the north from the south," he said. "The yellow signs are in English and Korean on the south side and Korean and Chinese facing north. The war began in 1950 and a cease-fire was agreed upon in 1953, no peace treaty has been signed."

The bus entered United Nations checkpoint #1, which controlled access to the demilitarized zone (DMZ). A "Camp Kittyhawk" sign was positioned over the entrance. Standing at the entrance, their feet apart and their hands behind their backs were two United States military men. To the left was a little turquoise office with a v frame roof. Most of the tiles on the roof were painted turquoise except the top of the v frame that was painted light pink. Nobody was milling about.

After being cleared to enter we stopped for lunch. This consisted of a piece of Wonder Bread with margarine, saltine crackers, grape Kool-aid, mushroom soup, a beef patty that tasted like it was all bread and canned peas and carrots. I wondered how these men could work after eating such a meal. After lunch, we were allowed to take pictures and walk around certain areas. I clicked a picture of the small white wood building, which had a sign out front that read, 'Monastery, Home Of The Mad Monks Of The DMZ.' I spoke to a man who was stationed at Camp Kittyhawk and he clued me in to what the sign meant. "The soldiers who were stationed here lived like monks in a monastery. No women assigned or available. The merriest monk of all was the soldier due to leave next."

I laughed.

Our guide took us to where the hatchet murder of two U.S. Army officers had taken place five years before, in August 1976 at the "Bridge Of No Return." It was named the "Bridge Of No Return" since it crossed over to North Korea and those who crossed it were not welcomed back. Because of this incident, the DMZ line was moved up a few feet and the United States asked that the North's commanding officer be punished, but there was no proof that this was done. Scary.

The conference room where the North and South held their talks was the only place Americans could cross over to the Northern side. The DMZ line ran down the middle of a long table and was marked by a microphone cord. The microphones were always on and were constantly being monitored. Nothing could be touched in the hall and no motions could be made to the Northern soldiers. Red armbands identified them. The Northern soldiers stared at me and I stared back. We were forewarned that the Northern soldiers would attempt to get us to wave, smile, or make gestures toward them. If they got any reaction, they snapped a picture to be used in propaganda publications with subtitles that could be used to make the United States government look bad. Therefore, I looked stoic. I believe that the picture of Jane Fonda sitting on the North Vietnamese enemy tank smiling would be an example of how we would appear if we smiled at them.

Panmunjom was quiet, but knowing that underground and in the hills thousand of soldiers waited armed and ready made this area a tense place to be. We were told not to make any sudden movement. I thought, what if the bus backfires and someone mistakes the sound as gunfire? I was ready to hit the deck. I climbed back onto the tour bus and breathed a sigh of relief.

The next day we were bussed to Osan to depart for Travis AFB in California. We were instructed to go to the customs area upon arrival. Customs checked through our large suitcases, small topsides, packages, and purses. This procedure took an hour. One F/A had her Vitamin C taken from her since she had bought it in Korea and no medicines were allowed out of the country without a prescription.

"May I take a few before you confiscate them?" the F/A asked.

"No," he replied. "You should have taken them before you left home."

"That was seven days ago," she replied. The officials were looking for fresh fruit, vegetables and weapons along with drugs.

Before takeoff, our Trans International representative asked us if we wanted to go home directly from Travis and not crew rest there. Our individual responses needed to be telexed to Oakland before takeoff. I decided to stay in Travis since I felt tired even before takeoff. I couldn't imagine taking the limousine the one and one half hours to Oakland, then driving another hour to get home. Once a person telexed Oakland and informed them about going directly home, the crewmember could not change their decision. If they did, they would have to pay for the hotel room. If we decide to go home and ignore the telex, we would be suspended. No exceptions.

Today our passengers were soldiers. Four hundred seventeen soldiers boarded wearing their green camouflage outfits, carrying duffel bags, and equipped with water bottles, helmets, and guns.

We arrived at Travis AFB and by the time we finished at customs, the hotel bus had left. Boldly, we the exhausted F/A's hailed taxis and asked them to get payment from the hotel. In the taxi, I heard that a F/A had passed around a petition to enable us to fly on MAC flights again. MAC said it was "ok," but TIA said "No." The F/A that had started the petition was called into the office and had to apologize and so did all the F/A's who signed the petition. One F/A stated, "This isn't Russia—we can sign anything we want."

At this point, I had been flying for nine years with TIA. Each month I grossed one thousand thirty dollars. Hardly enough to live on but by 1981, my two sisters, brother, husband, brother-in-law and parents had flown for free to various countries. My husband surprised me on at least ten occasions during my career. It made me feel good to be able to give them this gift, and on some occasions TIA crewmembers even showed them around the country they were visiting.

4
DIEGO GARCIA

Diego Garcia, in the Chagos Archipelago, is located in the central Indian Ocean four and one half hours southwest of Malaysia. In December 1966, Britain had signed a bilateral agreement with the United States, which made the British Indian Ocean Territory available for defense purposes until the year 2017. Both British and American flags fly over the thirty-seven mile wide island. In March of 1971 construction of an American Naval Communication Facility along with an airstrip began. Diego Garcia was instrumental to American defense during the Yemen crisis of 1979 and the Iranian crisis of 1979-81.

When I visited in July 1980, it was an island comprised of all military men. The Navy Sea Bees that TIA brought into Diego Garcia constructed an American Naval Communications Facility along with an airstrip. These men would stay at this tiny island for as long as two years depending on their orders. Occasionally, they would fly to Singapore for leave.

The crew started boarding at 0830. There were 376 Sea Bees between the ages of eighteen and thirty-five on the DC-10. The DC-10 was divided into three cabins. The first cabin-cabin A was designated as the officer's cabin. The B and C cabins were for the enlisted men. I was in cabin C.

Very few of the men sat down once they had found their seats. They stood in the aisles and chatted. Their conversation wasn't always with the man across the aisle or a seat or two away; at times they would yell across the aircraft "Hey, Larry, did you see that one?" As the crewmembers walked through the aisles, a hand might reach out and grab the F/A on the rear. I was getting a little disillusioned with the military etiquette.

Before departure, the senior began the demonstration announcement. All the junior F/A's went to their appointed stations. The Sea Bees had come from the U.S. and had heard this announcement before. As the senior said, "Take out the emergency card located in the seat pocket in front of you," all the one hundred thirty-one men in cabin C took it out and waved it in the air. This made me smile.

"Please locate the exit closest to your seat," the senior continued.

All the men pointed to the exit closest to their seat in unison. The men then pointed to their alternate exit when the senior said to locate it. The same thing happened when we did the seat belt demonstration. You could hear all the men refasten their seat belts—one big click. I giggled.

As soon as the wheels of the aircraft left the ground, shirts, tee shirts and shoes came off. After the pilot had ascended to cruising altitude, the F/A's began to hear music. I went over to investigate. The sound was coming from a boom box. I asked the passenger to turn down the volume and he did. On the way back to the galley, two more fellows started playing their boom box music. All the music was different and annoying since each serviceman was trying to play his tape loud enough to be heard over the other tapes. I had almost made it to the galley when I tripped over wires that were crossing the aisle. One was playing rock, the other had a tape on that kept repeating, "Fuck you." I asked him to turn down the volume but he just stared at me so I pulled the plug and held the wires in my hand.

"Give that back," the serviceman demanded.

"Sorry," I said. "Could you please turn the volume down?"

"Why don't you ask the guy across the aisle to turn his volume down?" the soldier replied.

"I'll talk to him next," I said. "Actually, no electronic devises are allowed on MAC flights per MAC rules."

This caused an uproar. I tried to explain that it was against a military regulation to use any electronic device on a military aircraft and we the F/A's were trying hard to be patient. A tape was still blaring, "Fuck you," while we spoke. The Sea Bees said it didn't bother them. The F/A's stood firm and the boom boxes were switched off.

It was time to start the meal service so the F/A's went to the forward galley to get the meal carts. On my return, I saw white Kotex pads stuck on the life raft covers. At first, I took them off and handed them to the Sea Bees asking, "Is this yours?" However, the boys kept replacing them on the bulkhead so I removed them and threw them out. During the meal service, one of the boys enjoyed telling a F/A as she was serving the meals the many different ways he would like to sleep with her. The F/A, caught behind the cart, ignored him.

After the meal, one of the officers came to the aft cabin and asked how everything was going. I told him and he replied that the men were not going to see women for months since there were no women on Diego Garcia. It sounded to me like they were given the military ok to act like jerks.

"How would you feel if someone grabbed your balls?" One of the bolder F/A's said, as she looked him squarely in the eye.

He didn't answer but seemed shocked that she would say such a thing.

"Are you new F/A's or just having a bad day?" one serviceman asked.

"What do you mean?" I asked.

"Because it had taken you so long to serve the meals," he replied.

"There are 376 passengers on board today and approximately one hundred were standing in the way on the carts." I answered.

"I have served six hundred people in less time," he replied.

"Did they come to you or vice versa?" I asked.

"They came to me, and what difference does that make?" he asked.

I wanted to smack him.

The F/A's were constantly being asked questions such as, "He's sticking his wet finger in my ear. What should I do?" Vocabulary of the four-letter variety was the most popular in cabin C. Cabins A and B were orderly. When the aircraft had begun its descent, I was relieved. Only the closer these men got to Diego Garcia, the rowdier they became. Finally the pilot landed and as soon as the airplane touched ground, the servicemen yelled, "Yea" and jumped out of their seats. The senior made an announcement to please be seated until the aircraft had come to a complete stop. The majority of the Sea Bees in cabin C were already in the aisles before we arrived at the gate.

Where had the military found these men? I wondered.

Sometimes when large groups of people who knew each other from the get go were placed in an enclosed area such as an airplane they could become unruly. Not only did charter F/A's have to deal with the unruly passenger they also had to deal with the unruly passenger's friends.

When the crew deplaned, we noticed that men crowded around and stared at us.

One officer who was seated in cabin A offered to take the crew on a sightseeing tour of Diego Garcia. The island was small with one general store and one restaurant. The men ate boxed meals that consisted of hot dogs and hamburgers on a regular basis. Sometimes they were served steak or lobster. Wherever the crew went we were greeted with stares and double takes. One serviceman in a jeep kept driving back and forth looking at us. I thought that I would probably do the same thing if I was stationed on an island with all women and a truckload of men arrived. I said to a friend standing nearby, "This must be what it feels like to be famous."

Thank goodness, the servicemen we boarded in Diego Garcia for the return flight were perfect gentlemen. I believe this was the only time I flew into Diego Garcia, but I had come to realize that if I didn't write something in my journal about a trip, that trip would be forgotten.

CHAPTER 10

SOUTH AFRICA

1
ARE WE THERE YET?

I had planned a trip to South Africa in October 1981, since Bill and I were interested in going on safari, and we had never been to South Africa before. We also had non-revenue (100% no charge) tickets on World Airlines coast to coast and a ninety percent discount for unlimited travel on South African Airlines.

We handed our tickets to the gate agent and boarded one of World Airlines DC-8's headed for Newark, New Jersey.

Upon arrival in New Jersey, we dashed to catch the New York helicopter to the JFK terminal.

"We'd like two one way tickets to JFK please," I said. "We need to get to JFK by 7pm to catch our connecting flight."

"I'm sorry, the flight is full and the next one is full also," the agent replied.

We lugged our bags to the Salem limo, which left every hour to take passengers to the JFK terminal and waved frantically at it but the driver wouldn't stop. We turned, lifted our luggage, and moved toward the city bus to expedite us along. The city bus left from another area, so we hailed a taxi. The taxi driver was talkative. He told us his life story and about people who skip out without paying the cab fare and how he was beaten up a couple of times. He couldn't take us to JFK Airport for some unknown reason so instead dropped us off at a bus that went to JFK non-stop. The bus took longer than usual because of rush hour traffic and we arrived at JFK at 2000. Getting to the airport was sometimes harder than getting the flight. Our flight to South Africa had departed, so we booked the 1920 flight to South Africa the following evening.

I rung the Riviera Inn and five minutes later, we were picked up.

The following day, we departed for the airport two hours early for our sixteen-hour flight, to Johannesburg and checked our baggage. The South African Airlines gate agent put us in gold class, and we were given free headsets, slippers, and alcoholic drinks. The gold class lavatories had baby powder, cologne, face wash, and moisturizer in them.

Quite happy with this we settled into our seats. The food on this flight was delicious and included fresh fruit and block cheeses. After finishing my wine, I fell asleep and didn't wake until our descent into Ilha do Sal, Cape Verde an island off the west coast of Senegal. Russian aircraft were parked not far from our South African airplane. Military men with rifles divided the two aircraft. We refueled and a fresh crew boarded.

We were served another delicious meal followed by a movie. After the movie, I slept until my ears started popping; we had begun our descent into Johannesburg.

Once on the ground, we found that a city bus stopped at the airport every hour to take passengers the thirty-minute ride into Johannesburg for two rand per person

"Where are you from?" a passenger on the bus inquired.

"California," I replied.

"Do you need help finding a hotel?" he asked.

"No," I replied. "Were booked into the Aster on Smith Street."

"This bus goes right by the Aster," he said. "Maybe the bus driver will stop and let you off." The bus driver refused and so we hailed a cab the ten blocks back again to the Aster Hotel.

"That will be fifty rand for two nights paid in advance," the Aster hotel receptionist said. We were given a room on the street side. The traffic noise rivaled that of New York's. Bill and I listened to the zoom of traffic, then got out our earplugs and fell asleep.

The folowing morning we seated ourselves two tables away from another couple that were being served by a black waiter. Breakfast was included in the room price. Something angered the couple. He raised his right arm and whacked the waiter on the side of his head with such force the waiter fell to the ground. I was shocked. The waiter stood, went into the kitchen, and returned with something I suppose he had forgotten since the couple was now content. The waiter brought our breakfast as if nothing had happened.

"Are you ok?" I asked.

"I'm not supposed to socialize with whites, I'll be fired," the waiter said. He put the plate of food in front of me. We were no longer hungry so placed the tip on the white linen tablecloth and left.

At the desk, we arranged a three-day safari of Kruger National Park for one hundred thirty rand a person and booked a tour of a gold mine for that afternoon. With forty-five minutes before the tour left and since it would not return until 1730, we decided to eat. We ventured into a Chinese restaurant bottle of water in hand. The restaurant assured us that the water in South Africa was potable and brought us two glasses of ice water and the menu. After lunch, we left a tip, noticed how happy the waiter was to get it, and headed for the Landrost Hotel where the gold mine tour group was to meet.

The bus headed for the gold mine had ten seats and the ride took fifteen minutes through town. The area was set up like one would expect at an amusement park—very sterile. Our guide bought our tickets and gave each one of us a little yellow dot to put on our shirts to show which group we were with. We were given plastic yellow raincoats, boots, and yellow hard hats to wear. Employees of the gold mine wrapped a band around our waists that had a rather heavy battery in the back that operated a light that was placed over our shoulder. We were asked to move into a wooden elevator about six feet by six feet. It was difficult to breath behind all those people dressed in yellow plastic. The air I did breath smelled hot and sweaty. There were twenty-three of us and I started feeling claustrophobic. I pushed to the front and said, "I'd rather not go."

It's cool down there," our guide replied. "I'll take you back up if you want." Reluctantly, I went. We descended 220 meters (721 feet) to the #5 level in one hundred and twenty seconds, I counted, each agonizing second, eyes closed. Once the door slid open, I tried to forget how far underground we were, felt the cool air, and relaxed.

We were shown where the gold was found in layers between pebbles. As the miners picked at the rock they put metal spikes in the rock so that it wouldn't cave in. One area was painted white to detect cracks.

Before 1981, the miners, on their day off, put on a tribal dance show for the tourists voluntarily. They had enjoyed putting on the show. It went over so well with the tourists they were now forced to put it on. Blacks in South Africa don't have the right to say no to their boss. They could be thrown in jail if they do. I was careful to only speak to the black workers when the tour guide was not close by, since I was afraid they would be punished.

The underground tour lasted thirty minutes. Every now and then, I'd get a twinge of claustrophobia when the tunnels became narrow and we would need to squish up. When we arrived back in the wooden elevator, I looked more forward to seeing the sky above then going on the safari to Kruger Park. One hundred twenty seconds later we were ushered out of the elevator and into a large classroom.

A movie was shown about the gold mine's history and afterwards we witnessed a gold bar being poured. In the front of a room, there was a large metal oven and in it a red hot metal pot. Two people lifted the pot with long metal tongs. The tongs slanted the bucket sideways and the contents were poured into an oblong pan. It cooled almost instantly and the red-hot pail turned back to its gray metallic color. Allowed to lift the recently poured gold bar, I found it to be extremely heavy. Later we wandered around the park and then were driven back to the hotel.

The following day Bill and I were scheduled for a safari to Kruger Park.

2
KRUGER PARK

On November 3rd, 1981, at 0645, we departed for our African Safari. We were allowed only one small bag each. It was a six-hour drive to Kruger Park from Johannesburg and record temperatures of forty degrees centigrade or one hundred and four degrees Fahrenheit were reached in Johannesburg this day. It was stifling.

Once out of the city, we were in flat dry desert. Looking back over my shoulder, I could see the massive city of Johannesburg. Looking forward all I could see was flat desolate desert. Later the terrain changed to green and hilly.

Our guide, Helen, told us about the people who lived in the area we passed. "This is where the Black and Colored homesteads are located," Helen said. "Apartheid is prevalent in South Africa. The blacks are the native tribes of Africa and the colored are the Asian blacks and both are separated from the Whites."

We passed many two feet high pyramid shapes on the dirt ground. Helen told us that these were anthills and that the early settlers used to dig these out, place a log inside, and use them as ovens to cook bread.

We passed 'cream of tarter' trees. They were large and knotty and their trunks were hollow. Rain collected inside and became a source of water in the summer months. Another interesting South African tree was the sausage tree, which produced fruit that hanged down from the branches as a sausage would. The fruit of the sausage tree tasted starchy.

Twice we stopped for tea and something to eat along the way and arrived at the gate of Kruger Park at 1500. There we were given paper bags with a list of the park animals printed on them. The bags were supposed to be used for garbage but the eight passengers in the bus quickly tucked them away in their bags for souvenirs. "There is a stiff fine for littering and a twenty rand fine if you jump out of the tour bus while in the Safari area," Helen warned us.

We pulled up to our rondavel, a round hut with a grass roof. "We had only a few hours until sunset and after a quick shower and change of clothes met in front of the restaurant. That evening we saw and took pictures of eland, springbuck, impala, and many types of birds. At sunset, I returned to my rondavel too exhausted to eat dinner and fell asleep.

We awoke at 0430, forty- five minutes before we were to begin our safari. I looked outside and there was a family of bush pigs playing in the mud. In front of our hut, two springbuck were locking horns and chasing each other around. I smiled.

The bus set out at 0515. After bouncing down the dusty road for five minutes, we spied a black-backed jackal and her cubs, which played only twelve feet from us, unconcerned with our presence. We then moved on to view an enormous elephant sixty feet from the road. He looked quite content eating a bush and didn't appear to even notice us. In fact, it was difficult to imagine such a large animal moving fast so I felt a sense of false security. All of us on the tour bus flashed pictures. The elephant looked our way. We flashed more pictures. This annoyed the elephant, it bellowed, and took a couple steps toward us. As the elephant picked up speed, Helen stepped on the gas and we raced away. The elephant's legs were the size of a large tree trunk and became monstrous as it got closer and closer. Two more steps and it would have stomped on us.

"That elephant could have caught up to us if it wanted to and overturned the bus. They are extremely strong and uproot trees," Helen said. Park officials place rocks around the park trees about five feet from the trunk to keep the elephants away.

At sunset, we stopped and watched a herd of elephants in a gully on the side of the road.

Earlier in the day, we had driven by a lioness and her pride just feet from the road. They batted at each other in a tree and every now and then glanced our way. Ten more minutes down the dirt and rock road, we saw a male lion relaxing in the shade of a tree. The lion was too far away to get a good photo. One member of our group asked if he could get out of the bus to click a picture.

"Absolutely not," Helen responded. "There is a twenty rand fine if you do."

Helen spied two men climbing out of a car behind us. She went back for a closer look and remarked that they were park employees and that if they hadn't been she'd have reported them. She reiterated that these animals were wild and we were invading their territory. Later in the day, in the water, we saw the only two hippopotamus in Kruger Park. They were difficult to photograph since they kept submerging and I clicked a picture of the cranes by the water instead.

Helen drove us to where we might see the zebra and buffalo. On the way, we passed a herd of giraffe, blue wildebeest, warthogs, and kudu. About 1400 we arrived in the zebra and buffalo area. "Zebras have bad attitudes and can not be trained like horses," Helen said. "The reason the zebras bellies are distended is that they carry parasites, which may account for their nasty attitudes," she continued. We also saw a herd of long hair curved horn buffalo; the buffalo got along well with the zebras.

The sky exploded in color. That was the sign that it was time to return to the rondavals, wash up for dinner and then visit the open-air theatre. That night we moved to another group of rondavals in Kruger Park.

The following morning we started out at 0500. The sky was a magnificent blue and pink when we stepped out of our hut. The monkeys were chattering in the trees and the baboons walked the streets.

"Roll up your windows as soon as you see monkeys or baboons near the bus," Helen said. "They like to climb in and are strong. Tourists have fed these animals so when they're hungry they visit the tourists." One baboon sat on the hood of a stopped car peering in at grapes on the windowsill. Helen said it could have broken the windshield and that feeding the animals was strictly forbidden. She would report these people once back at the camp. A tree with hundreds of chattering monkeys was close but we quickly passed it to see get closer to a spotted hyena. The hyena stopped, looked at us, and showed its teeth.

At 0800, we returned to the camp for breakfast. A tree filled with yellow birds was outside the breakfast area. The males made the nests while the females sat on the branches and showed displeasure by destroying the male's work.

"The male bird sometimes needs to build up to four nests before the female is satisfied with it," Helen said. "The nest opening is at the bottom since the animals that climb trees could easily reach in and grab the eggs if the opening is on the top."

After breakfast, we stopped by a grassy area called Crocodile Lake. This was the only place we were allowed to get out of the car. A guard posted nearby with a rifle was poised ready to shot any animals that may come near. Later that day, we returned to Johannesburg and packed for our flight to Durban the next morning.

3
BEING BLACK IN SOUTH AFRICA

Before Bill and I departed for the airport, November 6th, 1981, we returned to the Aster Hotel restaurant and spoke to the waiter who'd been hit by a customer. No one was in the restaurant so it was safe for him to speak.

"What's it like to be black in South Africa?" I asked.

"I work eighteen hours a day and I'm not allowed to leave this hotel in the daylight. If I did I could be arrested by the plain-clothes police that are everywhere in Johannesburg. You see, I work in a white hotel and blacks aren't allowed even though they work there," he replied. "No family members are allowed to see me in Johannesburg. My family lives in Homesteads far away. I live in town and I'm allowed to visit my family only every few months. The white man has total control over my life," he said as he pointed to a three-inch scar along the side of his head. "The black in South Africa have no recourse, even though the white South Africans try to convince the rest of the world that they do. South Africa is made up of only a small percentage of whites that control the blacks." He abruptly stopped talking. A couple had walked into the dining room. Fearful he would be hit, we didn't say anything and walked away.

The flight to Durban lasted fifty minutes. Upon arrival, we asked a taxi driver where a nice but inexpensive hotel could be found. "The Killarney Hotel is nice and inexpensive," he replied.

We arrived at the Killarney. The twenty-six rand room price included three meals. At 0900, we boarded a city bus, paid the fare, and sat down. People stared at us and we started to feel uncomfortable. Glancing around we noticed we were on a bus with all black passengers. We knew this was a no, no in South Africa so got off at the next stop. The ride on the black bus cost the equivalent of fourteen cents US.

An Englishman saw us get off the black bus and told us the

European's bus was around the corner. He was one of the plain-clothes police officer who could have arrested us if we didn't follow South African protocol. We boarded the European's bus and the fare was the equivalent of fifty cents U.S. to travel the remainder of the way to the Indian and African markets.

The locals picked up their fruits, vegetables, and meats at the Indian Market. All kinds of dead furry animals were hanging by their heads. Surprisingly they didn't smell bad and I didn't see flies.

The African market down the road was where we purchased batiks, woodcarvings, spices, and brass items. Each time we passed a shop in the African market, the owner or worker would run out and just about drag us into his store. It was annoying.

We thought about eating somewhere besides the Killarney but an entrée cost approximately eight rand and our hotel room plus three meals cost only 26.94 rand. We returned to the hotel for the buffet. I started with six different salads, fruit, and soup before the entrée. There was also a selection of desserts and breads displayed on the buffet and coffee and tea. All of this was included in the room price. Amazing.

Breakfast and dinner was no less spectacular—it felt like we were on a cruise. The dining room was decorated with white tablecloths; white linen napkins and chandeliers hung above us. There was one waiter for each table. We tipped 1.50 rand but noticed no one else tipped.

We stayed in Durban for one more day too satiated to move on. Once, between meals, we walked to the beach. Durban looked like Santa Cruz, California, a popular hangout for young people. Along the ocean, we saw the famous Zulu-voodoo "rickshaw" puller. His headdress was almost taller then he. Voodoo man wore feathers and geometric shapes of canary yellow, blood red, coal black and winter white. He pulled a sky blue and blood red rickshaw. I asked a passerby what the charge was to snap a picture with the voodoo man. "Two rand," he replied.

I raised my camera and looked through the viewer. The Zulu-voodoo man looked straight at me. I clicked the shutter and it locked. My husband tried to fix the camera but it didn't work for the remainder of the trip. I was told I had brought the evil eye on myself. "Ozumun, ozume gozum deydi." Strange.

This day, November 1981, we flew the fifty minutes to Port Elizabeth on the only flight where food was served, and arrived at 0700. The wind blew and it was oh so cold and rainy. This aircraft was going on to Cape Town and we wished we were also. Port Elizabeth was a quiet little town with lovely beaches and parks but the weather was not conducive to either of these recreations. We made a snap decision to travel to Cape Town. My husband retrieved our luggage while I got tickets. We checked the luggage to Cape Town and re-boarded the plane. The crew thought it funny that we just got off to get on again—we did too. Bill and I were fortunate to have had unlimited travel on South African Airlines.

The treatment of people in South Africa who weren't Caucasian disturbed Bill and me. I had learned through my travels that customs and beliefs were deeply ingrained into society. I was young and a foreigner so the secret police gave me special consideration for my kindness toward dark skinned people. If I had been a local, I could have been arrested and was aware of that fact.

4
FOR WHITES ONLY

We landed in Cape Town at 0900, gathered up our belongings, and hopped on the city bus. The weather was gorgeous. So far, all South African airports had an airport bus that went into town. The buses were reliable and the cost ranged from two rand to four rand depending on the length of the journey. At the bus station in Cape Town we noticed many hotels that charged only five rand or less for a room including breakfast. We booked one where the proprietor was Dutch. We rolled our suitcases toward a taxi. He was black. Within seconds, another driver pulled up (he was white) and told us to let the other driver sleep. The black driver wasn't sleeping. I suppose we were tired since we didn't object. The driver talked all the way to the hotel usually stopping the cab to do so with the meter running the entire time. The fare was much more than it should have been. He gave us his card, which read "Cedar Radio Taxis for whites only."

The driver dropped us off at an old building that had a peeling wooden door that was falling off its hinges. We rang the bell and a man answered who had spit in his mouth that stuck to his upper and lower lips when he spoke. His old clothing looked as if it hadn't been washed in weeks. We walked through the messy house and up the stairs ignoring the barking dog. We looked at a room with two double beds and three single beds. The only sound louder then the traffic outside was the barking of his dog.

"Thank you," we said. "We had another place to look out."

"Don't come back," he muttered as drool ran down his mouth.

Off we went wheeling our bags down Norfolk Street. We tried two other hotels but they also were not quite what we wanted.

"Do you need assistance?" a passerby asked.

"We're looking for a clean hotel," I said.

"The Winchester Mansion is a nice clean hotel," the passerby mentioned. "It's down the street a couple of blocks."

We wheeled our luggage to the Winchester Mansion Hotel and checked in. It was the most expensive hotel we had stayed in this trip but this was a resort town, much like Coronado, California. It was white as cotton and had rounded windows with shutters. There was an atrium with tables set for tea, and plants everywhere. Chattering parakeets were to one side of the atrium. The rooms were quaint, everything was clean, and breakfast was included. We stayed.

We unpacked then set off for Table Mountain. Being Sunday, everything was closed as it was in all parts of South Africa on Sunday. We waited at the bus stop-but no bus. An Englishman who appeared to be timing the buses noticed us. We told him where we were going. He walked over to the next bus that arrived and changed the destination to Table Mountain. Whether or not he did this for us we'll never know. The bus driver dropped us off at the foot of Table Mountain and told us it was two miles to the top. It started to rain so we took out our windbreakers and continued our walk. A car drove by and stopped next to us.

"Are you hiking up to Table Mountain?" he asked.

"Yes," we replied.

"The top of the mountain is closed due to high winds, rain and cold temperatures."

We turned around and the view of the city was spectacular. It was a shame my camera was broken.

Once back in town we asked about restaurants where the locals go for seafood. Because of the rain, we hailed a cab the three blocks to the Carousel restaurant. Taxis were expensive in Cape Town; in fact, this ride cost almost as much as the meal. Bill had lobster and I had prawns. After dinner, we walked along the beach and watched the colorful sunset grace the sky.

The day we checked into the Winchester Mansion hotel we filled out a special request form that asked what we would like for breakfast. I mentioned that my husband liked sausages.

At 0700 room service arrived with breakfast that was included in the price of the room. She set the table by the window with a white linen tablecloth, linen napkins, silverware, salt, and pepper. She then put our first course in place and left to get our second course. Five minutes later our second course arrived, then our third, then our fourth and then our fifth. We ate fresh fruit, maltebella (oatmeal) grilled Scotch kippers, eggs and smoked haddock, grilled tomatoes and a selection of breads while drinking guava juice and hot chocolate. Since I had written that my husband loved sausages, the chef prepared six large ones for him. It was very tempting to stay another day but we also wanted to visit the German town of Windhoek.

We caught a bus for the airport and noticed that all the other passengers waiting for the flight to Namibia were soldiers with guns. Windhoek was close to the Angola border and there was some sort of situation going on.

We arrived in Windhoek at 1600 and went in search of the German castles we'd read about. Flat barren Windhoek didn't look conducive of castles. It had only one main street so we were surprised our taxi driver didn't know the three streets where we wanted to go.

A passerby offered to show the driver the way. We drove up into some hills and when our passerby guide would point to go one way, the driver would go the other. When he said stop, the driver kept on going, but we did arrive. Our passerby guide was black and the driver was white. I don't know if this had anything to do with it though.

The three castles were located in the same area and were all built by the same architect. The third was built for himself. Actually, they looked like mini castles—short towers and small bodies to the houses. People were living in them. We drove up to one and the taxi stalled. The owner of the castle looked out the window and asked what we wanted. My husband got out of the taxi and explained. The owner asked if we needed assistance then added that he was going out for the evening otherwise, he would have invited us in.

The taxi started and since the sun was setting, we decided to return to the hotel. On our return, we asked our passerby guide what it was like to be black in South Africa. He became very nervous. "A black man can't say good evening to a white girl without the possibility of being thrown in jail," he said. "White men could go out with black women but not vice versa. That was the law." He became very angry, shook his fist at us, and said he hated the white man. We changed the subject and asked him where he went to school since he expressed himself so well.

"I've gone to five years of college but am only allowed to take specific jobs no matter how much schooling I have since I am black," he replied. "I'd like to live in Philadelphia," he added.

We arrived at the hotel and ate in the dining room. I ordered Kudu pepper steak and my husband ordered Monkey Gland steak. Both were delicious. My husband stayed downstairs and drank beer with the military men and I went upstairs. I didn't feel comfortable being the only woman in the place.

At 0530, we were awakened by a knock at our door. A person outside the door handed us two cups of black coffee without a word spoken. I took them, closed the door, and wondered whom they were intended for. I decided to shower since the second course would probably arrive shortly.

The shower was down the hall and had a sign that said 'gentlemen' on it. I had my husband stand guard while I showered. There was no ladies room.

On the bathroom wall, a spider as large as my hand was spinning a web. My husband wanted to kill it but I asked him to leave it alone since it might be poisonous. I hopped in the shower and my husband marched up and down with one of my slippers following the spider. "The spider disappeared," he yelled. I dressed quickly and walked briskly back to my room.

The second course never arrived so we went to the dining room. There was a table set with juice, milk, and cereal so we helped ourselves and sat. Later we left for a day of shopping. We appeared to be the only tourists in Windhoek.

We passed by a woman weaving baskets. "How much for the basket?" I asked. Sixteen rand," she replied. We purchased two and planned to fill them with Christmas presents.

Later that day we left for Johannesburg, then New York on South African Airways. We arrived at the airport and were informed our flight was delayed five-hours. Not knowing what to do for five hours we decided to take advantage of the bath and shower facilities in the airport. The hot oil bath felt wonderful after the long day of shopping. The rooms were private and there was no charge for even a towel. It felt somewhat strange sitting in a tub at an airport with the noise of people with luggage outside.

At 1930, we went to the gate to check in. There were only ninety passengers on the 747 aircraft. A meal was served and once again, the wine was complimentary. We slept the entire way to Ilha do Sal where we deplaned for an hour.

Then another meal was served and we slept until an hour before landing in New York. Feeling well rested we decided to continue on to California.

We deplaned quickly in New York since our non-stop flight would leave in one hour. Our baskets came off the conveyer belt last, and customs was good enough to wave us through, even though we were carrying protea flowers. We hopped on the bus to the United terminal with only twelve minutes to spare. The bus waited for other passengers then made a stop at the American terminal. It was important for us to make this flight since it was the only non-stop of the day. We arrived at the United ticket counter where the agent told us to leave everything with him and to run for the plane. We ran and arrived as the door was closing, sat down and breathed a sigh of relief.

We arrived in Oakland at 1030.

"I'll get the car and you get the luggage," Bill said. He returned in two minutes. "Where did we park the car?"

I laughed. We located the car and were home by noon.

There was so much to enjoy in South Africa. Bill and I had a spectacular time and were grateful for the chance to experience this country.

CHAPTER 11

HEY! HOW COME THEY GET STEAK WHEN ALL WE GET IS CHICKEN?

1
SNIPPETS

The following snippets occurred on Trans International Airlines during my years as a flight attendant.

If I don't take this, I die.

When I began my career as a F/A we used to take medicine from passengers and place it on ice when we were requested by a passenger to keep it cold.

"If I don't need this in-flight please return it to me on descent," a passenger said handing me her medicine. Then the passenger looked at me dramatically. "If I don't take this I die."

It was a shock for me to be told that if anything happened to the medicine I was handed the owner would die. Company policy stated we were to keep medicine cold when asked. We started our descent and I went to get the medicine. It wasn't there. Perhaps another F/A had thrown it out when cleaning, I thought. None of the F/A's knew where it was. I walked over to the passenger to tell her the medicine had been misplaced.

The passenger looked up at me. "I took my medicine out of the compartment I saw you put it in," she said calmly. What a relief. I thought I was going to have heart failure. I was so relieved that I didn't inquire why she didn't tell me. In the future, I'd place medicine in a burp bag (white paper bag with a plastic lining) with ice in it and give it to the passenger.

Shall we stand?

One of the most irritating problems I've had with passengers was their standing in the aisles during the meal service for no apparent reason than to annoy us. Some passengers had circulation problems so need to stand. Those passengers we asked to stand by the lavatories during the meal service. On one occasion, a huge man stood in the aisle. It was impossible to side step around him and we knocked into him.

"I would appreciate it if you would take your seat during the meal service," I said.

"If you lose weight you could get by me," was his reply. He continued standing through the entire meal service and as soon as we finished, he sat down in his seat.

I'm not chartered

After we finished the meal service, the flight attendants ate. The crew meals were different from the passengers. Some passengers look at us eating a different meal and wanted to know why. Some apparently thought we had short changed them. I say this because of the look on their faces—they felt they chartered the plane therefore they owned it and everything on it until they get to their destination. Once I had placed a magazine I bought in the side compartment of my in-flight bag. This was my magazine. I bought it and when I went to get it, it wasn't there. I asked the other F/A if they had borrowed it. None had, so I assumed a passenger must have taken it out of my bag. I never got it back.

On another occasion a passenger wanted my crew meal after he had eaten his. He was insistent so I offered my meal to him. When I opened the food bin that contained the crew meal presets he spied sandwiches that were also in the bin. He demanded a sandwich. I gave it to him and without a smile or a thank-you he returned to his seat to eat his sandwich and hot meal, or more accurately, my sandwich and hot meal.

Make me.

It's rare that a passenger chooses to sit in seats that weren't theirs, when seats were assigned. Although one couple sat down in seats that were not theirs and when the rightful owners came along they refused to move. Only after I threatened to get the captain and have them thrown off the plane did they comply.

The hem is mightier than the hand.

An embarrassing situation happened to me on the DC-8. It was time to land so I went to my jump seat to strap in. By now, you know a jump seat is a seat on the aircraft that the F/A's pull down to sit on for take-offs and landings. Well, my jump seat didn't operate properly. It stayed down unless I pushed it up. When I started to sit, the hem of my skirt touched the jump seat, and it flipped up, landing me, stunned, on the floor. Red faced I assured everyone I was not hurt, pulled myself up and the jump-seat down to sit on it this time.

Old keys

Another embarrassing in-flight situation happened when I was bringing the captain his meal. I got out my cockpit key to unlock the door. I placed the key in the door and tried to turn it. The key wouldn't turn nor could I pull it out of the door. I was leaning over connected to the door holding the captains meal since my cockpit key was connected to a chain around my neck (our uniform did not have pockets at this time). My nose pressed up against the door, I called for help. A F/A unhooked the chain and I was free. Life with Trans International was one big "Ok, and what could possibly happen now?"

Decompression

In June of 1978, a F/A was working in the aft of the aircraft when she felt a breeze. She thought this unusual so reported it to the senior. Suddenly her barrette flew across the aircraft so she was sure something was definitely wrong. She called the captain to report it and got an oxygen bottle down from the overhead compartment. The other F/A's followed her example and checked seat belts. Seconds later the masks fell. The crew masks had hair and garbage in them since they were located at floor level. The captain quickly descended to a safe altitude. This could have been a serious problem but all the passengers were in their seats with their seatbelts fastened.

Is this a joint?

Once while in the process of picking up meal trays a passenger pointed out a rolled up joint on his tray. He asked me if he could smoke it.

"No," I replied. He picked up the joint and placed it in his pocket and I removed the meal tray.

Whose birthday?

A birthday cake was once the cause of another embarrassing situation. A birthday cake was on the galley counter. We asked the TIA representative whom the cake was for. He didn't know. He did say we were kidding the other day about his birthday. Perhaps the caterers had overheard and brought the cake. After takeoff, we thought about this and decided the representative was probably right so we ate the cake. Later the passenger who sat across from the galley mentioned to me that it was his birthday cake, but he was getting such a kick out of our concern that he didn't want to tell us. We cut him a piece of his cake and apologized. He laughed.

No soda bread for you.

During 1972, I often flew into Ireland's, Shannon Airport. The Shannon caterers gave the F/A's soda bread, cheeses, and fruit to snack on. Once a passenger came to the galley and saw us eating these items and asked for some.

"What do you think this is, a picnic?" a F/A replied. He either felt insulted or maybe he thought we were eating food that was supposed to be for him, so he wrote Trans International and told them. The F/A was fired and Shannon catering was told to stop placing soda bread and cheese on the aircraft for us.

Seat belt signs don't apply to flight attendants?

May 29th, 1981 Manchester/Miami #10930 The captain came on the PA during the meal service and announced that a hurricane was in the area therefore he was turning on the fasten seatbelt sign, but the

F/A's may finish the meal service, he said. The passengers fastened in and the F/A's continued the meal service.

Mile High Club

Ok, everyone knows what the mile high club was by now (sex in the sky). Our charters were usually packed full. If by chance someone did get an extra seat, no sane person would jeopardize it by being reseated for lewd behavior. He'd toss the gal on her booty before he'd give up that extra seat.

However, there were the bathrooms you say. Well, our bathrooms were not only small, but also stinky. You'd have to dash in there during the first thirty minutes of the flight to avoid the stench problem. In addition, you'd probably miss the liquor service.

Fire!

Something frightening happened after a meal service. Everything was going as planned when a flight attendant put a meal in the oven to cook. She sat across from the oven and opened a magazine. Within minutes, the oven flew open and flames were thrown out over the flight attendants head. Nothing flammable was in the area except the magazine. She closed the oven, and the fire went out. Trans International thought it was caused by grease catching fire in the oven and the pressure inside the oven blew the door open.

My odds

Every now and then, we had a medical problem in-flight. Perhaps on one flight in thirty, a passenger fainted or needed medical attention due to a nosebleed, nausea, or headache. These were my odds. On one occasion, a baby was born on a Trans International Airlines aircraft. We also had possible heart attacks, drug withdrawals, diabetics, and those fearful of flying who wanted to get out of the aircraft during flight. Trans International flight attendants were trained in CPR and first aid in case a doctor wasn't onboard. The most common health problem we encountered was fainting. The dizzy passenger usually forgot to ring the F/A call button for help and instead stood up and walked to the galley to faint there.

Epileptics have had seizures on our aircraft. Usually they apologize and say it's the first one they have experienced. During one of my flights out of Honolulu, a man had what looked like a seizure in his seat. I asked his wife if he had any medicine to take.

"No," she replied. The wife went on to say that her husband usually drank every day, only the day before this flight he had decided to quit.

We laid the one hundred seventy-five pound man on the floor between the seats and attempted to hold his arms still until they stopped swinging around. When we landed at Travis AFB a medical team came on board and took the passenger off on a stretcher.

For F/A use only

We had quite a few young children and babies on military flights. On one occasion, a mother and her two year old walked to the galley. The F/A jump seat was down but no one was seated on it. The mom placed her two year old on the jump seat and walked into the lavatory. The jump seat flew up and folded the baby into it. The child was terrified. A F/A quickly pulled the seat down and rescued the child who recovered after a couple of chocolate cakes and a good deal of attention. Jump seats had a placard on them that stated they were for flight attendants only.

No pillows and blankets for you

A passenger wanted a pillow and blanket but all were being used. I explained we only carried enough for the majority of passengers. I apologized for there being no more pillows and blankets and the passenger replied, "I guess I'll just have to sleep standing up."

F/A sit by exits, to exit first?

Passengers occasionally asked why F/A's sat by exits.

"We sit by exits so that the exit would be opened quickly in an emergency, and we can get everyone out," I answered.

"Oh, I thought that flight attendants sat there so they could get out first." Apparently, this passenger wasn't unaware of the extensive emergency training given F/A's.

Where are the parachutes kept?

Only my first couple of years flying did anyone ask me where we kept the parachutes. To clarify this we did not have parachutes.

A, B, C's on the right, D, E, F's on the left.

One time we were boarding passengers and I was showing one of them his seat, row 33 seat A. He refused to sit down since the letters on the right side of the aircraft for row 33 said D, E, and F. I pointed out that all the other rows on the right side of the airplane were A, B, C. He acted like I was trying to cheat him out of a better seat so refused to sit where I motioned. I then realized that I would need to move the letters A, B and C to the right side of the airplane for row 33 and put D, E and F on the left side with all the other D, E's and F's. Once I accomplished this the passenger sat where I had motioned him to sit in the first place.

On many of our charter flights, nobody's happy about where they're seated and everyone wants to move. Now that it's a law to have smoking and non-smoking sections on every aircraft, this has created another problem for the F/A's. Seat assignments were given without asking if the passenger's were smokers or non-smokers on many occasions. This was a new procedure for them as well. When the passengers boarded and the senior announced in her departure announcement where the smoking section was, some got irritated because they smoked and weren't assigned that section. It could be a zoo out there trying to switch thirty non-smokers with thirty smokers. We usually flew full. The F/A's were required to annoy thirty passengers and have them pick up all their belongings and move to another seat so that the smokers could be in the smoking section and vice versa. When we tried to switch them in the middle of the cabin where the smokers meet the non-smoker, they want a specific seat such as a window seat since they had a window seat before. We forgot who sat by the window and the other fellow refused to move so we sometimes had fistfights in the aisles.

On one occasion, a man asked me for a smoking seat. I found someone who wouldn't mind moving. The latter packed up all his carry on luggage and we walked over to the man who wanted a smoking seat. The passenger who wanted a smoking seat looked up at the passenger and me and said he wanted to sit with his wife. He had only wanted to switch seats when he wanted to smoke. I told the smoker this was impossible, thanked the other passenger for moving and he took his assigned seat once again. Enthusiasm gave me the strength to go on.

TIA or TWA?

Once after we boarded passengers and everyone was on board, the F/A's noticed one of the seats was loose from the fuselage. We deplaned everyone and after the seat was repaired, we re-boarded. When everyone was seated, we had two people standing that had tickets. No one thought they were on the wrong flight so we had to examine every passenger's ticket. We found the two extra passengers after a two and one half hour delay since many could not find their ticket. The two left our aircraft and proceeded to their TWA flight.

Flying for a charter airline was a memorable experience and different from that of a commercial flight attendant. Charter work was hard and the hours were long but the benefits made flying with a charter a positive experience.

2
WHERE DID THE GLAMOUR GO?

February 1981 we were scheduled to ferry from Travis AFB in Fairfield to Detroit since our trip had been extended. Originally, we were scheduled to go home. The flight went well until we began our descent. Then the captain began some maneuvers that they sometimes do during a ferry flight, never during a passenger flight. I suppose they don't think of the F/A's as passengers. One of these maneuvers was descending at a steep altitude. Once when we made this steep descent, I had trouble walking when I deplaned.

On one occasion, our senior F/A decided to run a relay during a ferry flight. We gathered at the over wing exits on the DC-8 and with a rolled magazine in hand, raced one by one through the open cockpit door, hit the captain on the head with the rolled up magazine and then ran back to hand the magazine to the next F/A waiting. I don't remember what this captain did to that senior for her to organize such an event. The captain dropped altitude a couple of times causing the runners knees to buckle and that ended the race. That situation was only rivaled by one of our captains who exited the cockpit during a live flight sporting sun glasses and carrying a white cane.

We deplaned in Detroit at 2200 and the Hilton (our hotel) restaurant was closed. Our contract stated all hotels where we stayed must have twenty-four hour coffee shops. I packed numerous cans of tuna fish that I called emergency food since our contract was breached on a regular basis.

Our room smelled of smoke, we had only one towel, no soap, and one drinking glass for the two of us. The light bulb wasn't in the lamp, but on the desk. We called the maid and she said she was sorry she had forgot to finish the room. It wasn't unusual for the maids to forget us F/A's.

The night before in Fairfield we had been given rooms that had the heat turned off. February wasn't high season and the hotel hadn't expected to need those rooms. Even the sheets had been damp, so I crawled into bed fully dressed. One of the nicknames the F/A's had given Trans International Airlines (TIA) had been 'Travel In Agony.' That's how I had felt sleeping on those damp cold sheets in Travis. Another nickname was 'Try It Again,' since we had numerous delays where the passengers boarded and then were told there was a mechanical problem or we missed our slot (time for takeoff) and we'd taxi back to the terminal.

After Detroit, we headed for Niagara Falls, a thirty-minute flight. We had the same captain, the same plane, and no passengers. I hadn't a clue why we didn't ferry the plane directly to Niagara Falls.

Wakeup was at 1045 to depart for Niagara Falls. It was a frosty morning -about twenty-eight degrees when we boarded the aircraft. The area around the bulkhead was as cold as a freezer. We wrapped ourselves in blankets and waited for takeoff but there was a mechanical delay. If we had power, we'd turn on the ovens in the galley to warm our hands and feet.

At 1330, the aircraft still wasn't repaired. Our representative brought us sandwiches, fruit, and milk.

"Why the delay?" I asked the engineer.

"The elevators on the tail are in-op," he said. "The elevators steer the aircraft back and forth."

At 1705, the crew was ordered to stay on the aircraft. Oakland crew scheduling didn't want to lose one minute finding us if the aircraft was repaired. I felt we were being tortured. It was six hours and twenty-five minutes since wakeup.

"If we do fly to Niagara Falls today, then on to Acapulco we'll be over our sixteen hour duty day," our senior said to our representative. There was no reply. I suppose my mouth was frozen shut since I hadn't said a word either.

At 1930, the airport officials asked the captain to move the Trans International aircraft away from the terminal since they needed our space for a Pan Am flight that was due to arrive.

"That means we won't have a heater again," the senior remarked. "We're not going to remain on this aircraft with no heat. It must be thirty degrees outside. They freeze chickens at that temperature don't they?" Again, there was no reply from our Trans International representative.

Without official permission, I gathered my belongings and headed off behind my senior flight attendant to warm up at the airport coffee shop. One hour later, our representative informed us that Oakland didn't expect the problem to be fixed tonight, so reservations were made at the Holiday Inn. Some people think, we're paid so what's the problem. The reality was, we're only paid for flight hours. We flew zero flight hours; therefore, we were paid zero for the day.

At the Holiday Inn, my telephone message light lit up. What now? I thought. Our Trans International aircraft had serious mechanical difficulties and the cockpit members took it to Canada. Why they flew it to Canada was beyond me.

"Maybe they're avoiding the draft," my roommate said.

I laughed.

The F/A's were to commercial to Buffalo and then to Bradley Field, Connecticut on U.S. Air the following day at 0830.

The next morning two of our crewmembers didn't show in the lobby at 0830. The senior flight attendant called them.

"The crew bus is here, what's the holdup?" she asked.

"We never received our wakeup call," they replied.

"The flight leaves in two hours to Buffalo. We'll go ahead and purchase tickets. You can meet us at the gate."

The two tardy crewmember's arrived at the airport five minutes before takeoff to Buffalo. We continued to Bradley Field, Connecticut and one of the tardy crewmember's bags was missing. Since they both arrived five minutes before the flight, it was strange that the other crewmember's bag wasn't missing also.

Upon arrival, we were informed of our next leg of the trip. We were to take passengers to Acapulco at 0830 the next morning, a five and one half hour flight, and then board new passengers' in Acapulco and take them to New York. We went to the Ramada Inn.

I stayed on the second floor of the Ramada Inn in Connecticut. I prefer to be anywhere but the first floor because most rapes and robberies occur on the first floor since assailants don't want to wait for an elevator or spend time running downstairs to escape. It made sense to me.

The flight attendant's missing bag was located, but only after many phone calls to U.S. Air. The airline wanted her to retrieve her luggage at the airport but it was 2300 and she insisted it be sent to the hotel. It was delivered after midnight. Wakeup was at 0630 the following day for our live (passenger) flight to Acapulco, Mexico.

On the flight to Acapulco, all the caterers had boarded were roast beef dinners. Usually the crew was catered something different, not better, just different. The captain and the co-pilot were required to eat something different per FAA regulations. If one pilot got food poisoning, the other should be ok. There was one kosher meal catered and the passenger who ordered it never identified it, so it was saved for the captain or co-pilot. The F/A's served 254 roast beef lunches on the way to Acapulco and 254 identical roast beef dinners on the flight to New York. The roast beef had a rainbow tint that looked like an oil slick. I chose to eat my canned Bumble Bee tuna later upon arrival.

Many passengers mentioned that the McDonnell Douglas DC-8 stretch 61/63 series looked like a long bus-all one cabin. It was one hundred eighty-seven feet four inches long. The pilot took off at a slight angle so not to bump the tail on the ground. If the pilot ascended at a sharp upward angle, he would bump the tail; this did occur, not often, but occasionally. There was a cylinder in the underside of the tail on the DC-8 and when the tail was bumped, the cylinder would cushion the bump so as not to damage the aircraft. After each bump, the cylinder needed to be replaced.

We had a two-hour stay at the Acapulco Airport. At first, the steamy hot air felt good as I walked into the terminal and purchased Kahlua at the duty free shop. When we boarded the returning passengers, it was stifling. In Connecticut this morning, the temperature had been twenty-eight degrees. In Acapulco it was ninety-eight.

The passengers boarded and one asked me if the plane would take off on time and I said I thought it would. As it turned out, their originating flight was delayed one hour and this passenger was upset about that and didn't want any more delays for the return flight, or he would get off the airplane and fly with someone else, so he said.

We served our oil slick roast beef dinners after departure to New York. This night we stayed at the Statler Hilton. The following day we were scheduled home on Trans World Airlines to San Francisco, California. That made me happy.

Our airline representative who had in his hand the feared telex met us at the airplane. This crew was turned around 2-6-81 and we were now to fly from New York to Philadelphia, to Bermuda, to Baltimore and then crew rest in Boston. We were scheduled to leave New York in fifteen hours. He also had a second telex that read we were leaving New York on the seventh and were scheduled to do a turnaround from Boston to Curacao, back to Boston then to New York. We'd then commercial home the next day on United to San Francisco. Our schedule had changed three times this trip. I didn't call home since it was unclear where we would be, Boston or New York or if the aircraft had a mechanical delay maybe Philadelphia, Bermuda, or Curacao. We took the flight to Bermuda and commercialed home. Two days later, I was sick with the flu.

3
THE BOEING 747 AIRCRAFT

During my preflight on the Boeing 747 aircraft headed for Osan then Yokoto in August 1981, I noticed the toilet seat was veering to one side in lavatory K. On takeoff, it fell off and crashed to the floor. The passengers turned to look at me. "That bang was a floppy toilet seat," I said with a smile. That explanation seemed to satisfy their curiosity.

Most everything was stored in the overhead compartments of this four engine 747 aircraft including cases of soft drinks, dry supplies for the meal service and bathrooms, the two foot by two foot movie cartridges and demo equipment. Getting soft drinks cases out of the overhead compartments in-flight was like weight lifting while balancing on a waterbed.

Once airborne, we pulled out the two hundred pound meal carts one by one. I stood to one side of the cart placed my hands on the front bar, pressed down to release the brakes and pulled it forward twisting at my waist. They needed to be pulled straight out across the galley while standing to the side of the cart since the carts won't turn if not pulled straight out. One of this day's meal carts brakes stuck and a thin metal strip had worked its way loose and needed to be forced back into place. I went to the cockpit to borrow the engineer's hammer, to bend back the metal strip. All TIA engineers were jet engine mechanics so carried tools. It was difficult for a 115 lb F/A to hold the cart back once it started to slide, so the metal divider between the carts get bent. These large 747's flew with the nose up so we also fought against gravity.

During the meal service, food cart #1 was brakeless. The F/A needed to place her foot under the wheel. If she let go of the cart, it would take off on its own and stop when it hit an object or an unsuspecting passenger.

Most F/A seats on this 747 faced aft and the passenger seats faced forward so the seats the crew sat on were back to back with the passenger seats. If I stood after being seated, the seat would fly up, knock into the passenger seat, and cause it to rock it back and forth. I carefully held the seat down and let it up slowly so I wouldn't give the passenger behind me whiplash.

In-flight I'd noticed the refrigerator had one wire divider hooked to one side. The other side snapped off and the engineer hadn't the parts to fix it. I cringed with my eyes closed as it tumbled to the floor of the galley. It was far more difficult to work the 747 aircraft than the DC-8.

Three of our coffee maker's shut off valves were in-op this day. They overflowed when full. Another coffee pot's light didn't work and still another's heating pad had plastic stuck to it so that left us with only a few to serve four hundred eighty-four passengers. All the galley equipment got an amazing workout on our aircrafts. Each piece was constantly being used almost twenty-four hours a day, year after year, with only rests during crew changes and mechanical delays. I didn't expect everything to run perfectly, but wished it did.

We landed in Yokoto, Japan and the passengers stayed on the aircraft while we refueled. Refueling with military passenger's onboard was a no, no but these were special circumstances. There was an air traffic controller's strike that was gumming up the system in August 1981. The air traffic controllers stated they would allow us to takeoff if we could depart in one hour. We boarded a few new passengers and told them we'd take their hats and other items later after takeoff so that we would make our slot (a slot is the time given when we're told to takeoff).

We made our slot and the engines started. We were all seated and cued up with the other airplanes on the active runway when the captain picked up the public address system.

"Even though we made our slot, the air traffic controllers have decided not to allow us to take off. This delay is due to the air traffic controller's strike in the United States."

Nearly all air traffic controllers were employed and trained by the Federal Government. They coordinated the movement of air traffic to make planes stay a safe distance apart in the air. Their main responsibility was to organize the flow of aircraft in and out of the airports.

The captain taxied back to the gate and the passengers deplaned. Since other airlines had the same problem and weren't allowed to take off, the passengers from those flights filled the hotels in the area. Our passengers slept in the terminal and the crew slept on the plane. I was taught that strikes weren't supposed to effect military flights for security reasons. The air traffic controllers were messing with the military. I'd learned early in my career that you don't mess with the military. Once I thought it wasn't necessary to sign a telex that stated I'd fly military flights during a strike since I was on a military flight at the time. I was wrong and temporarily fired.

At 2100, the air traffic controllers changed their minds and gave us clearance to take off. An announcement was made in the terminal that flight J2S4 was ready to depart to Travis AFB. We located all the disheveled passengers asleep on the floors and chairs. If there had been no delay, we'd have already landed in Travis.

We arrived at Travis AFB, California on August fifth. I'd been awake for over twenty-four hours. The next morning we drove to Oakland to sign out at crew scheduling. I was handed a pre-alert (next trip), it read: commercial to Portland, Oregon and crew rest, then work to Paris with a fuel stop in Newfoundland. I was pleased to hear that this trip would be on the DC-8 aircraft.

4
MULE MILK COUSINS

In August 1981, after I showed at Oakland crew scheduling, we boarded the limo to catch our hour and twenty minute commercial flight to Portland out of San Francisco.

The following day we boarded two hundred fifty-four loud and obnoxious French students of high school age returning to Paris.

"Please turn off your electronic game," I said to one student. "Electronic games may interfere with the cockpit communications."

He played the game anyway. I explained to the student that it was a regulation and regulations were made when there had already been a problem and in some cases people died. He didn't seem to care. I notified the captain who stopped what he was doing and spoke to the student. The game wasn't visible for the remainder of the flight.

It seemed as though everyone smoked. The aft cabin was so foggy with smoke I could hardly see. People smoked in the aisles and on the floor. Smoking was only allowed in a seat where an ashtray was provided. The senior F/A picked up the public address system and asked the students to please remain seated while smoking. The students passed the cigarette to a person who was seated and after I passed, they'd pass the cigarette back to the person in the aisle. These students weren't aware of the danger and how easily fire can get out of control. We informed the captain and he picked up the PA and spoke to the students. These students also placed chewing gum under tray tables, on the armrests and on the floor. The plane was a disaster when we landed in Paris.

I had a cousin living in Paris and called him. We met that evening and I mentioned something that had happened to me in Las Vegas that started a long conversation. In February 1981, I was on a trip that took me to Las Vegas where we laid over for seven days. The airplane stayed on the ground and waited for business, therefore we had to wait with it so that a crew would also be available. This we called, "guarding the airplane." None of us cared to gamble for seven days and hadn't money to see shows so we took many long walks.

One afternoon I thought about what my parents told me about being 'related' to Paul Anka. He was performing at Caesars Palace in Las Vegas, so I wrote him a letter. I introduced myself in the letter as his cousin and told him that I was in Las Vegas for seven days to guard an airplane. I mentioned that I was a F/A and made it sound as though I was supposed to sit on the wing of the plane with my rifle to guard it. I also said I'd always been a fan and would love to see his show.

A couple days later, his secretary called and said she had tickets for us at the eight o'clock show. Excited, I called Marilyn, our senior and we went to the hotel where Paul Anka preformed. It was a lovely night—no rain—not at all like the first days and nights we'd spent in Las Vegas. We arrived at the show early and I introduced myself to the headwaiter. He ushered us past the long line and to our front row seats. After the show, I asked Paul Anka's personal bodyguard if we could meet him. I really didn't expect the answer to be 'yes,' but thought I'd try anyway. Much to my surprise, he said 'yes' and told me the room number where a crew party was to be. I fumbled for a pen to write this down thinking that if I forgot Marilyn would never forgive me.

I joined my friends and told them what I'd done. We wandered out of the club in a daze—me clutching that little scrap of paper with the room number on it. It then occurred to me that it might be a fictitious room number so that I'd go away. It wasn't a fictitious room number though, I knew that when we were escorted to a private elevator used only for the rich and famous. I knocked on the door and a woman opened it. She introduced herself as Paul Anka's secretary. We introduced ourselves and went in.

The suite was large with a big screen TV and a few chairs set in front of it. The bar was directly ahead and was recessed somewhat with stools. Behind the bar was a spa large enough to fit six people. On my left was a bedroom with a round bed and next to it, the bathroom. We were offered hot hors oeuvres and drinks and then sat down. Paul Anka wasn't there yet. I felt a little nervous since I'd never heard the full explanation of how we were 'cousins'.

Many people involved with the music industry were there. An hour later, Paul Anka walked in and I walked over and introduced myself. For lack of anything else to say, I asked him if he would like something to drink. He said water so I got him some and sat down again feeling silly. Later my friends and I had the photographer take a picture with all of us together. We stayed for another hour and then said good-by.

Back at the hotel, I wrote a thank you note and mentioned that I'd like to send him a present. I had in mind one of the Christmas ornaments I bought in Hong Kong that were hand-embroidered. Once home I searched for the largest and best looking ornament, wrote a note, wrapped it up in gold paper, and tied it with ribbons.

A few months later, I wondered why I hadn't gotten a reply. I spoke to my husband and he said that maybe it wasn't received. Then I asked my husband if he would be insulted if someone sent him a turkey. He said he probably would be. I thought nothing of the animal when I'd wrapped it, only that it was the best I could find. I blushed to think about how Paul Anka felt when he unwrapped the hand-embroidered turkey. Perhaps I'd insulted him and that's why I never got a reply.

So here, I am telling all this to my cousin Johnny in Paris hoping that he'd know the connection between us, and he did. Johnny said that he was born in Alexandria, Egypt, and when he was a baby, his mother had jaundice and was unable to feed him. At the same time, another new mother was unable to feed her daughter for the same reason. The two mothers got together and bought a mule to milk to feed their children. Therefore, the two children who were fed by the mule were considered 'mule milk cousins'. When Johnny's 'mule milk cousin' grew up, she married Paul Anka. So this was how we were related—'mule milk cousins'.

This was our last day in Paris. I shopped at a cookware warehouse that exports to the United States and purchased eight individual French soup bowls with lids. They were heavy cast iron bowls. When we returned to the Charles de Gaulle Hotel, a message awaited us at the front desk. Johnny had come by and had wanted to go to breakfast and would call back at three o'clock.

He called at three and we decided to go to dinner at his favorite French restaurant. It was a darling little place with small tables. The bar was decorated with cowbells. Johnny sat me under a wheel that he said was good luck. Two years ago, my older sister had been in Paris and had sat in the same place so this was traditional. We arrived back at the hotel about midnight and had a 0530 wakeup to continue our trip.

The next day, after our 0530 wake-up, we ferried the aircraft to Palermo, Italy where our passengers waited. We flew them to London Gatwick to refuel and on to Charleston, South Carolina. I groaned, such a long day. I heard a man on this flight had heart problems on the flight over. He was taken off the aircraft in Winnipeg, Canada. For some reason the aircraft and passengers waited for him until he finished at the doctors.

"Why?" I asked. Not seeing the big picture.

"I don't know," was the reply. "Maybe he's the tour group leader."

This took five hours and the passengers were rioting on the aircraft. The flight crew remained with the passengers and were verbally abused.

"What kind of airline is this anyway?"

The F/A's were as upset as the passengers about the decision and were powerless to do anything.

In Palermo, we boarded two hundred fifty-four Sicilians onto DC-8 72T who were anxious to return to the United States. Each passenger boarded with bags twice the size of the space under their seats so we spent an hour explaining that all cabin baggage must fit under the seat in front of them. This was a flight full of very large Sicilians. I was positioned at the aft right jet escape for takeoff, next to the passengers, and the woman who sat next to me had the largest thighs I 'd ever seen. I glanced at her and then glanced at the jet escape wondering how difficult it would be for her to exit this aircraft in an emergency. It was important to mentally prepare for a quick and dirty (surprise) exit out of the aircraft.

The passenger who had the heart problem on the flight over to Palermo either wasn't on this flight or didn't want to be identified. We landed in Charleston, South Carolina without incident.

In Charleston, we stayed at the Mills House, a quaint hotel decorated with antiques and nick knacks that I wished I could afford. Outside the window, the clip clop of a horse driven carriage could be heard. It was a peaceful summer day in a lovely city.

Our passengers headed for Los Angeles from Charleston this day were military men and women who had just completed basic training. The rowdy bunch started celebrating their latest achievement on our flight. General Larson was aboard and jump seat 6L fell off the bulkhead (wall) close to where he was seated. I was seated on that jump seat and felt the heat of embarrassment as my arms flew up and my knees hit my chin. Currently I'd been away for sixteen days and if we really went home as planned, I'd have eight days at home. Going home always made me smile. Leaving made me smile also since each trip was so unusual. I suppose that accounts for my elementary school nickname, "Smiley."

Upon arrival at the Hyatt Hotel in Los Angeles, a stranger cut into my roommates and my conversation. We ignored him and I took my suitcase to the elevator. The stranger walked in also but I wasn't concerned since others were in the elevator. I pressed the button for the fourth floor and was the first to walk out. He got out of the elevator behind me and asked me to join him for a drink.

"No," I replied.

"Can you have dinner with me tomorrow night?" he asked.

"I'm leaving tomorrow," I replied.

"I thought your airline stayed in Los Angeles for a few days?" he said.

I thought this comment strange. I arrived at my room. He stopped and stood four feet from me. A chill ran through me, aware that the hallway was silent. I opened the door, dashed in, and locked it. I never heard from him again.

The next day I awoke early. I needed a visa for South Africa and Ed (a relative) drove me to the South African Embassy. We left the embassy with my visa stapled to my passport. Some countries won't allow you to enter if you had a visa stamped in your passport from a country they had disagreements with. Since charter F/A's fly to so many countries, it was recommended to place most visas on separate pieces of paper. I'd tear out the paper with the South African visa on it after my visit.

Ed drove me back to the hotel at 1730. Wakeup was in an hour. We were no longer commercialing home to Oakland, California. We were to work from Los Angeles to Shannon to Amsterdam. Flight 340 — 747 aircraft.

At checkout, I discovered this hotel charged fifteen cents a minute for local calls. I'd never been charged before. My charges came to four dollars and sixty cents for the two-hour call to Ed. I suppose I should have felt lucky since they could have charged me eighteen dollars which was six dollars more then the twelve dollars per diem I got from Trans International per day.

The crew bus picked us up at the Hyatt as scheduled and drove us to a Trans International DC-10 aircraft. The crew laughed. Had our airline mistaken the DC-10 for the 747 aircraft?

Our representative, confused at the change of aircraft, gave the flight paperwork to the senior then remarked, "The plane hasn't landed yet so the bags must stay on the bus but the crew can board the aircraft."

Later we learned that a Trans International 747 wasn't scheduled to arrive. We were supposed to take the DC-10 contrary to our itinerary. Had Trans International booked all seats on the 747, this could have been a problem since the 747 had a larger load factor than the DC-10. This night we had only three hundred passengers.

Our Trans International representative handed two meals to our senior and requested she taste both since he had so many complaints about catering at Los Angeles International. She tasted the meals and felt the complaints were justified. The chicken was raw and when bit, it was bloody. There was no mustard or dressing on the sandwiches either. Catering was informed and new meals were catered.

The liquor service was unusually confusing this day. We had three types of money to deal with: guilders, pounds, and U.S. dollars. No one had the correct change and since different drinks cost different amounts, it took a while to calculate. For example, a cocktail cost two U.S. dollars, which was 4.58 guilders or 1.40 pounds. I placed three empty coffee cups in front of me on the cart to place the different countries change. I received only bills so I placed the IOU's in the cups and returned later with change from other cabins.

During the liquor service, the galley F/A leaned over to fill the ice bucket and caught her pants on a metal food bin. She ripped a three-inch hole in her pants. She said she had a uniform skirt, but a roommate on the line (away from home) took it out of her suitcase and claimed it was hers. She went to the lavatory with a roll of masking tape and taped the inside of her pants to close the hole, then continued the service.

While I served coffee—I asked a man if he wanted coffee and he asked if I would like a hat. He had brought with him a hat from his company, which said, "Shaping the World of Tomorrow, Komatsu." It was a nice green felt hat. I thanked him and slipped it into my apron pocket.

We landed in Amsterdam and as the passengers deplaned, one sweet white haired woman in a flowered dress took my hand and said something in Dutch.

"Thank you," I replied.

5
DING, DING, DING

We arrived at the Sonesta Hotel after our hectic flight and the maids asked me to clean up the other crew's dishes since they had neglected to do so. The maids weren't paid to do it. Too exhausted to argue I complied.

Once more, we stayed in the apartments, which were across the street from the Bronco Saloon. Construction workers pounded from 0600 to midnight. At midnight, the Bronco Saloon was hopping. Tomorrow we leave for Manchester, England on KLM (Royal Dutch Airlines) flight #0155. I was so exhausted it was difficult to get dressed for the flight.

The KLM flight to Manchester took one hour and we were served a sandwich for which I was grateful. On the flight, I relayed a story that happened in Bath, England to my roommate.

Hungry, my husband and I had gone for pizza. The restaurant was packed with patrons. We ordered one large pizza and two drinks total cost twelve dollars. We paid with a twenty dollar U.S. travelers check. The waiter returned obviously annoyed, tossed money on the table, and left while mumbling, "What do you think this is a bank." We looked at the pile of English pounds. We should have gotten less than one pound in change. We counted eighteen English pounds plus change. After some thought, we concluded that the waiter thought we had given him a twenty-pound travelers check. We motioned him over but he wanted nothing to do with us. We followed him to explain, but he was too busy to listen. Embarrassed by his attitude we left the restaurant and returned to the hotel approximately sixty-nine dollars richer then when we entered. The following morning we left for Dublin.

My roommate laughed.

The KLM flight landed. This day in 1981, we stayed at the Piccadilly Hotel and in the past had received a free newspaper and continental breakfast. Now, all guests at the Piccadilly receive a free continental breakfast and newspaper except our airlines F/A's. "The times they are a changing," as the Bob Dylan song goes.

In September 1981, we flew a tour group (Jet Save) to Miami, Florida. During boarding, I swatted at a wasp that joined me in the upstairs galley. The passengers who boarded attempted to smash that wayward insect but it kept eluding us. It positioned itself across from my jump seat for takeoff, then disappeared in-flight.

The cockpit called me continuously during this flight. One ding sound was a passenger call button, ding, ding was the telephone, ding, ding, ding was the cockpit, and ding, ding, ding, and ding was an emergency. Almost every fifteen minutes I heard ding, ding, and ding. They demanded that I make them fresh coffee. Not from the pot. They wanted only a half-cup every fifteen minutes. This was unusual. Usually, the F/A's check the cockpit before and after the service.

After holding (flying in circles) due to thunderstorms for forty-five minutes, we received clearance to land in Miami and were greeted with a schedule change. We were to commercial to San Francisco tomorrow instead of Los Angeles. At the Coconut Grove Hotel, where we stayed, there were tinted mirrors on the ceiling above my bed, a fur bedspread, leather furniture, and brown walls. It was strange.

We arrived at the Miami Airport for our flight to San Francisco at 0730. Our senior F/A attempted to purchase tickets but the flight was booked and we weren't scheduled on it. Only one cockpit member and three F/A's were on this flights passenger list.

"Why isn't our complete crew scheduled on this flight?" our senior asked Oakland crew scheduling.

"Only four seats were available on the 0730 American flight," the scheduler replied

"Why didn't you call us at the hotel and let us know?" the senior asked.

"I thought someone had informed you," was the reply.

"Then what flight do you have us booked on?"

"We have you leaving on American Airlines at 1750 this evening."

I checked for earlier flights.

"There's a 0830 Eastern flight to Los Angeles. We could connect to PSA (Pacific Southwest Airlines) to San Francisco since it departs one hour after our arrival in Los Angeles," I said.

Oakland scheduling okayed this route and said tickets would await us in Los Angeles upon arrival. American Airlines said Eastern was a four-minute walk. We had thirty minutes to run with our suitcases to the Eastern Airline ticket counter, have tickets written up, check our bags and board the aircraft. Not discouraged we took off in the direction of Eastern. My luggage wheels broke and I didn't think I was going to arrive in time. My muscles and back ached. I stopped and sat on Big Red. A young man walked toward me.

"Excuse me," I said. "Could you please help me get to the Eastern ticket counter? I can't find a porter to take my bags."

He said he would and I caught up with the crew.

We made Eastern's flight #511Y to Los Angeles. It had been delayed thirty minutes. As I relaxed with one arm over the armrest, I felt something—it was a wad of gum stuck to the armrest. I lifted my arm and pulled off the gum. It smelled like peppermint. The F/A's closed the main cabin door for takeoff. Well, at least we made the flight, I thought.

We arrived at Los Angeles and found that PSA was located in another terminal. We trekked over to the PSA ticket counter and inquired about the tickets that awaited us. There were no tickets. We inquired about availability on the 1215 flight to San Francisco. There was no such flight. We caught the 1315 flight on PSA only now we wondered where our luggage was going.

Once we arrived in San Francisco we filled out lost baggage forms. My bag was delivered at 0100 that night and we were scheduled to depart Oakland about twenty-four hours after we arrived. I supposed TIA was short on crews since they turned me around at my home base. I ran errands and purchased sturdy wheels for my suitcase.

On 9-21-81, we worked Oakland/Seattle/Manchester on the DC-10 aircraft.

When we arrived at our TIA DC-10 at Oakland International Airport, our representative informed us that a World F/A recently was smashed and died instantly on one of World Airlines DC-10 elevators while working out of Baltimore. I spoke to maintenance and he said it was probably her fault. This angered me and I let him know what I thought after witnessing the problems with the DC-10 elevators.

Maintenance filled me in on the details of the accident. Apparently, the World F/A had been in the elevator on the DC-10 when it stopped between floors. She had opened the door from the inside to climb out. Someone pressed the up button as she was climbing out and the elevator moved, smashed, and killed her. We'd been trained that the up and down buttons don't work when the lift doors were open. It made me feel sick to my stomach.

We boarded passengers and departed. The cabin air was so dry I could hardly breath. Two lavatories were in-op—they didn't flush. Maintenance said the lavatories were fixed, but they weren't. I noticed that many of the seats had been cleaned and repaired. We recently contracted this DC-10 from Air Florida.

While I passed out tray tables in the first row of cabin C, I noticed that the armrests by the wall of the plane had been glued down. The passenger needed to lift the armrest to slip the tray table in place. Now this wasn't possible.

It would be too late for dinner by the time we landed in Manchester. I planned to make a Bumble Bee tuna fish sandwich on the aircraft. I'd packed the ingredients in my topside.

Upon arrival at the Portland Hotel in Manchester, England on September 22nd, I made a cup of tea. A plus for the Portland Hotel was that there were teapots and white china cups in the rooms. I turned on the TV and watched the first half of East of Eden, which would be continued next Monday.

We were scheduled to depart next evening for Shannon, Ireland.

Instead, of commercialing straight into Shannon, we were scheduled to commercial to Dublin then take a four-hour limo ride to Shannon. I checked and there was a more direct route but the representative for TIA refused to change the flight.

I woke early this day to take the bus to Stoke-on-Trent. I wanted to replace some of my china that had broken on a previous trip. The bus ran every four hours now, and since we were scheduled to depart this night for Shannon, I decided to wait and go another time. I took a lovely three-hour walk instead.

We departed on Aer Lingus to Dublin, Ireland on September 23rd. The flight was full and cramped. Two men seated in front of me smoked. I showed them the sign and they stopped. When I started flying in 1972 anyone could smoke in any seat on the aircraft, which made it difficult to breath without coughing.

It was oh so cold, in Dublin. It had to be less than fifty degrees in the limo all the way to Limerick. We stopped for an Irish coffee and sandwiches at a quaint hotel, which had a fake fireplace. I thought that strange for Ireland.

Upon our arrival at the Jury's Hotel in Limerick, our crew list was given to the reception desk. They had always checked this list for Irish names when I stayed there. Because my married name was McAlister, I was given the first room even before the cockpit members. The people in the hotel made me feel special.

The room was warm when I entered at 0230 but at 0300, the heat turned off and didn't come on again until morning. This was customary at the Jury's Hotel. One blanket and a thin bedspread wasn't enough to keep me warm. I donned my sweater and socks and slept well until the phone rang at 1300. Apparently, our flight was early.

We had only ninety passengers this day from Manchester to Amsterdam, and left without any delays. In Amsterdam the crew split up—half went to Frankfurt and the rest to New York on the 747 aircraft. I was off to New York fifteen hours later.

We registered and were assigned rooms in the apartments. The same I'd been in before across from the Bronco Saloon. I called someone on the hotel committee since the daytime construction paired with the nighttime Bronco Saloon music left no quiet time. The hotel committee said there was nothing they could do because the contract was almost up and the only other hotel the company would consider was one at the airport. God forbid we stay at the airport. No transportation to town and listening to the planes all night would drive us all batty.

September 24th, was my first day off in nine days. I turned on the Sonesta hotel TV and it went berserk—the sound kept going off and on at different volumes. The off button didn't work. The radio and TV were going on and off at different times. I called maintenance and left the room. When I returned at 1500, the radio and TV had been disconnected. I called maintenance again.

"That's the Christmas tree effect," the maintenance man said. "The computer in the TV console goes berserk quite often. In fact, I've fixed six today." Maintenance returned at 1800 and fixed the TV.

"I'll come back and fix the radio tomorrow," he said.

I slept poorly on September 25th, because of all the noise. It took all the energy I had to walk around the city—it's so pretty with all it's flowers and canals. I bought some fresh vegetables and cooked them in my room. I also spoke to the head porter at the Sonesta about my china that was dropped and broken on a previous trip. He said they had no insurance and there was nothing he could do. It would have taken more energy than I had to argue so didn't.

We headed for New York on September 26th, on another 'Jet Save trip'. TIA had contracted with 'Jet Save' to fly numerous charters to Europe. On 'Jet Save', trips the F/A's needed to collect vouchers for drinks and movies. We collected the vouchers after writing the drink request in the upper right hand corner, C was for cocktail, B was for beer, and W was for wine. We tore off this one-inch corner and placed them in an envelope. Before the end of the flight, we counted all of these scrapes of paper and noted what they were for on the liquor paper work.

This amounted to a lot of time spent counting corners since there were 484 passengers on this 747 and each passenger was allotted two drinks.

If we'd landed in England, there were extra custom procedures. England customs required the crew to make note of each type of miniature bottle. This meant we had to note that we had one hundred scotches remaining in the liquor kits, thirty vodkas, two hundred Canadian clubs, thirty beers, the exact count or TIA could and had been fined for being one miniature short, but we were landing in New York.

Once we arrived in New York, we waited at customs for our suitcases. One crewmember's bag was placed in with the passenger luggage and we were greeted with another schedule change.

Instead of commercialing home, we were to commercial to Bangor, Maine through Portland, Maine then work to Colorado Springs, then Travis AFB California. We'd crew rest in Travis and then on to St. Louis.

I had started to sing that Kingston Trio folk song, *MTA* (Metro Train Association) more commonly known as, *The Man Who Never Returned*, with slightly new words. Did she ever return? No, she never returned and the tale is still unheard. She'll fly forever over the oceans of everywhere. She's the charter F/A who never returned.

We landed in Maine at midnight, on September 27th, which was the time our live (passenger) flight to Travis AFB was due to depart. The TIA representative met our Delta flight, came onboard and received permission to deplane us first before the other passengers. He said he would collect our luggage and get it to our flight.

We departed only fifteen minutes late with our full load of West Pointers. Everyone was wearing green fatigues and carrying rifles. There were many highly ranked officers on board along with one two star general. We served a hot meal to Colorado Springs and a snack to Travis.

A soldier sitting in row one seat C was upset with a F/A because she giggled during the safety demonstration in the forward cabin. He was also upset with the senior because she asked him to take his equipment out of the forward closet. It was a new FAA regulation that nothing can be placed in the DC-8 closets that weren't tied down except lightweight bags with soft sides. The soldiers bag must have weighed sixty pounds. I couldn't lift it and we couldn't get the carts out of the closet to do the service.

Apparently, the problem lay with the previous crew who allowed the passenger to place the equipment in the closet from Frankfurt to Bangor. The F/A's do bend the rules a little, for example, on this flight, I allowed a soldier to put his extra bag under my seat. If this wasn't the last leg of the trip that could be a problem since the next F/A might need that space for her things.

During the flight, I read the in-flight log, which told specific information about the previous flights. It read: "Flight #306 9-24-81 DC-8 #86 JFK/SNN schedule run. Pax (passenger) hit pax in row 17E and said he had a gun. Pax in row 22C was intoxicated." I suppose everything worked out since there was no conclusion written about this incident. We landed in Colorado Springs at 0230.

At 0315, we departed Colorado Springs for the two-hour flight to Travis AFB in California. I had been awake since 0800 East Coast time—0500 West Coast time—and we landed at 0700 West coast time so I'd been awake for twenty-six hours.

We arrived in Travis on September 29th, and I only slept until 1100 since my roommate switched on the TV.

My roommate (Tara) switched off the TV when she noticed I was awake. She was disturbed by an incident that happened on her last flight and needed someone to talk to.

A Sicilian woman had boarded the aircraft carrying a large wreath of flowers. Tara suggested she remove a few flowers from the wreath since it would then fit under the seat in front of her. She also mentioned that agriculture might confiscate it on arrival in the United States. The Sicilian woman said if she couldn't have the flowers and the wreath then no one could. She dropped the wreath on the floor of the aircraft and stomped on them with all of her two hundred pounds. Tara, surprised at this behavior, didn't want to anger the Sicilian woman further, so cleaned up the mess without a word spoken and disposed of all the flowers in the trash.

"She's probably distraught about leaving her relatives," I said. "I doubt this outburst had anything to do with you personally."

"Your probably right," Tara replied.

Our luggage on Delta flight #368 that TIA claimed for us in Maine arrived at Travis AFB, California except one F/A's suitcase and I didn't get my new luggage wheels. We notified our Bangor, Maine representative.

The next day we worked to St. Louis. At checkout, I inquired about charges on my hotel bill. "You owe four dollars eighty-seven cents for phone calls," the hotel cashier stated.

"I only spoke for five minutes," I replied.

"There's a hotel surcharge of twenty five cents a minute," the cashier replied. It seemed excessive to me and I complained. I ended up losing the argument and paid the phone charge.

I worked upstairs on the 747 for this four-hour flight from Travis to St Louis on September 30th. Everyone had tens and twenties to purchase two-dollar alcoholic drinks. If I'd boarded with one hundred, one-dollar bills, I still wouldn't have had enough change for all the passengers. I wrote down their names, row numbers and amount owed, then returned with drinks throughout the flight to use up the IOU's.

We arrived in St Louis at 1830, five minutes after our commercial flight departed. Damn. The next flight to San Francisco was at 2325. We waited five hours for the four-hour flight. I called our representative about the status of my luggage wheels and was informed they were at Delta's baggage service in St. Louis. I toddled down to baggage claim and claimed them. Then I sunk down in one of the airports plastic seats and slept before the flight to San Francisco to end trip.

Currently I had 92.6 flight hours this month and had been away from my domicile for twenty-one days so had ten and one half days off before I was legal (had sufficient rest) to depart on another trip.

This was an unusually long trip.

6
JUST GIVE IT TO ME

TIA flew numerous charters from Houston, Texas to Amsterdam, to Dhahran, Saudi Arabia, in 1981, to deliver the oilmen who were assigned there. The front of the aircraft was set up like a hospital to accommodate any burnt and injured oilmen on return flights. The remainder of the aircraft was set up in first class configuration except for the aft section, which was cargo.

Our three and one half hour Pan Am flight to Houston arrived in the evening. On the flight I calculated the hours I had commercialed this month and found one third of my monthly flight hours were commercialing hours.

At 1300 on November 20, 1981 we boarded our 747 aircraft and were briefed that this flight from Houston to Amsterdam on the 747 was a first class charter. A Pan Am captain hired to trouble shoot our airline was to report to Trans International about any problems.

We encountered a thirty-minute delay since cargo needed to be boarded so I served my first class passenger's drinks. A ground service wasn't required. That's when I discovered the caterers had not stocked items in the locked liquor bins.

First, the Pan Am troubleshooter wanted a martini and I had no vermouth catered upstairs. Then his wife wanted a diet soda, which I hadn't any. I raced downstairs and grabbed a few diet sodas and filled a coffee cup with vermouth for use in-flight. Before takeoff, he asked for a *New York Times* newspaper and we only had the *Houston Post* and the *San Francisco Chronicle*. I trekked downstairs and asked if our representative would get him a *New York Times* newspaper.

"No," the representative replied.

Another passenger wanted wine before takeoff, for some reason I couldn't get the cork out. I called the check flight engineer and he held the wine bottle firmly against himself, and pulled up on the corkscrew opener. It wouldn't budge, so I found another downstairs. I finished the liquor service just in time for the captain to say, "flight attendants arm your doors."

In-flight, the Pan Am troubleshooter gave me a difficult time. He would slam his glass down and say "more wine." When I passed out mints, he stuck his hand in, grabbed a handful, and then glared at me. I returned with the mint basket after everyone else was served and he reached in again and grabbed another handful. Fifteen minutes into the flight, he asked me for a gin martini with a twist. I needed to refill the same glass since TIA hadn't unlimited glasses. The fifth time I had refilled his glass; he motioned to me, "Where's my twist?" he inquired. I looked in the glass, saw five twists of lemon from his previous drinks, said I was sorry, and would get him his twist.

During the flight another passenger wanted to try all the liquors and after I served him a few I mentioned that if he mixed drinks he may become sick.

"Just give it to me," he said in a nasty tone. Oh, I wanted to give it to him but I just smiled and returned to my duties. Later I noticed the man trouble shooting our airline seated with the man who drank the variety of liquors. It was just one of those days.

A flight attendant on this flight worked not only with the airline but also with our AFA union (The Association of Flight Attendants)

"Cindy, I heard you found the Dhahran contract," she said.

"It's in the cockpit on these Dhahran flights," I said while making a fresh pot of coffee. "A passenger told me other airlines flight attendants get more money working these Dhahran first class charters."

Our union representative went into the cockpit and brought out a folder with few pages in it.

"Is this the contract?" She asked.

"No," I replied. Then I started thumbing through it and realized it had been revised. In fact, the entire section on F/A's was missing. We the Trans International F/A's hadn't gotten extra pay for these flights. I supposed the other airlines that received extra pay had an agreement about first class charters in their contracts.

As I cleaned up the upstairs galley after the meal service a woman of approximately fifty years walked up the stairs and said, "This is the shits." I turned and looked at her then continued what I was doing afraid to ask what she meant.

"This is really the shits," she repeated.

"I'm sorry," I said.

She looked somewhat inebriated and stumbled back down the stairs. The Pan Am man approached the galley and asked me questions about my job. I explained to him the difficulties in being a F/A and what my duties were before takeoff and in the air. He told me that the Pan Am flight attendants checked the lavatories, the meals, the liquor, and the emergency equipment and changed the movies.

What could I say? I didn't expect him to give me sympathy. He asked what I did and I told him. Not only was I getting negative vibes from this man but another man in row two kept asking me to go out with him.

"No thanks," I said. He persisted, and kept moving closer and closer and finally backed me into the corner by the dry supplies. I told him I was married and didn't want a bite of his cheese or a sip of his drink when he offered them to me. I said I had work to do and he took my hand, kissed it, and then he sat down. I wanted to slap him. That was the end of round one. Later he started more of the same.

"I'd be too tired to go out." I said.

"I thought you wouldn't go out with me because you were married," he replied.

As I made coffee and managed the other passenger's requests, I told him that he didn't seem to accept my first reason so I felt I needed another. He took my hand again, kissed it, and then took his seat. Round two was over. This went on the entire flight. He gave me his name and phone number in Amsterdam and I placed it in my apron pocket to appease him.

"I'll be staying in Amsterdam for a few days and will catch the next

Trans International flight to Dhahran," he said. "Be sure to call me. I'll take you to all the best places."

I scooted past him and entered the bathroom to freshen up. I noticed my face had broken out in hives. Actually, both services went well once the aircraft got to cruising altitude except for a couple instances.

Half way through the flight, the refrigerator stopped working so the ice melted and I needed to go downstairs for more. Then the Pan Am troubleshooter wanted Port after his meal. I had none and neither did the downstairs galley. He was annoyed. Another situation that annoyed him was that we hadn't extra dishes and silver for the cheese and fruit service that I'd set up on the counter.

"Sorry," I said. "You could check with the senior flight attendant to see if this could be changed in the future." He pointed his pointer finger up in the air and waved it around intensely bothered that I hadn't produced plates and silver for him. This wasn't a fairy tale where I could click my fingers and items would appear, I thought. He traveled downstairs and spoke with the senior and I went on with my duties and controlled my desire to call him what some men would call me if I were constantly complaining.

I knew TIA felt that the passengers' were always right and if a F/A said or did anything to upset them, she or he would be fired.

By the time we landed, I wasn't feeling well. I planted the F/A grin on my face and said the usual good-bys. The man in row two still hadn't given up.

We arrived in Amsterdam at 0830. "If you're to tired to meet me in Amsterdam, why don't you meet me in Dhahran and we can go to the Dhahran swimming pool?" I thanked him, said good-by and he exited the aircraft. I didn't tell him I wasn't going on to Dhahran but back to Houston, Texas.

This day we picked up our luggage in a different terminal. Half the F/A's went to the old area, so we waited on the bus. Normally we retrieved our suitcases in the KLM (Royal Dutch Airlines) crew area.

This day our luggage was at the passenger baggage carrousel. One F/A attempted to lift her suitcase off the conveyer belt and noticed the handle had broken off.

When we reached the hotel and checked in, I went directly to my room and my roommate followed five minutes later. We talked as I unpacked, then all of a sudden my roommate turned around and said, "Where's my suitcase?" She swore she had rolled it into the room but it was nowhere to be found. I told her I thought I saw it also when I opened the door to let her in. We looked outside the door, and then called the desk to find out what crewmembers had rooms close to ours. Apparently, there was only one male crewmember close by. We thought he might have rolled her bag into his room as a joke. She called him and he said he didn't have it. She then spoke to the engineer and he said he had seen her struggle with her suitcase in the elevator. We called the reception desk and were told that a red suitcase was between a potted palm and an armchair. My roommate went down to investigate. It was her suitcase. Another case of jet lag I supposed.

I slept the entire time in Amsterdam until our wakeup at 0045 to go back to Houston on November 21st —a ten and one half hour leg. This night I worked upstairs and had six passengers. The airline representative said that two bigwigs were seated upstairs and to treat them nice.

"I treat everyone nice," I replied.

After takeoff, I completed the meal and beverage service in forty-five minutes and my six passengers fell asleep. I sat down and opened a magazine. Someone walked up the stairs and I looked up. Three men seated downstairs didn't notice or care that everyone up here was asleep, turned on lights, talked loudly, and drunk more than I had all year. The complete aircraft was set up for first class service so the passengers were allowed to roam and sit where they pleased, even upstairs. This commotion woke up all the sleeping passengers. One of the three who had graced our presents upstairs drank ten CC's (Canadian Clubs) and sevens. I was amazed that he neither acted nor looked drunk.

I started to set up for the second meal service. I had enough meals for the extra three men, so they dined upstairs. However, it got a little confusing because they kept leaving their seats and would miss a course or two, then return and ask for that course. I wondered if they ate downstairs and upstairs as well.

After the service, I went downstairs to chat with our senior F/A, the one who occasionally made monkey calls over our PA system.

"There's a man who looks like Wally Cox asking questions about our job and is particularly interested in the F/A's," Lois said.

"Wally Cox" motioned to her to come over his way. He looked secretive, walked backwards, snuck around, and acted weird. He mentioned he wanted to go out with her and persisted although she told him she was tired and wanted to sleep. She felt uncomfortable about this since she had already said she would be in Houston for three days.

"Lets sleep together," he replied.

"No thanks," our senior replied.

We arrived in Houston, gathered at customs, and placed our big red suitcases on a cart we thought was our limo drivers, and waited. This was yet another baggage handler whom we had to tip one dollar per bag to take our bags the twenty feet to the outside. Then the limo driver wouldn't place our bags into the limo unless we tipped him. I searched for another dollar. When we arrived at the Houston, Hilton. I asked the bellhop to bring my bags to the room. This was worth the tip since the rooms were far away. My room was icy cold. I switched on the heat and fell asleep.

Monday, my roommate and I exercised, shopped, and saw a movie. I'd placed my Body Design tape into my cassette player. I used to bring a pulley type exerciser that I hooked onto the doorknob. It had four ropes with handles to place on each foot and in each hand. I'd lie on the rug in front of the door and pull these ropes up and down. The doorknob would turn outside and the apparatus would squeak. I'd stopped bringing it since security would knock as I was counting motions and inquire what I was up to. "What," I would say when they knocked between counts. They thought I was moving furniture. I was embarrassed and annoyed that they disrupted my aerobics.

Tuesday's plan was the same as Monday's. My suitcase was busting at the seams with purchases. The top of the suitcase was open at an angle of three o'clock, about one foot higher then it should be to close comfortably. Each trip I tell myself I'm not going to buy so much. When I arrive home, I'm so pleased with the purchases that I over shop again.

By tomorrow my rolled suitcase items will have settled about five inches. At that point, I'd sit on Big Red, bounce a bit, and stuff the clothing that protruded out, back in, and bounced on it again to squeeze the air out. "We Are The Champions My Friend," by Queen played on the radio while I bounced. I sang along.

This night a fellow crewmember called and said our engineer set up a complimentary breakfast for all of us crewmembers before the flight tomorrow from Houston to Amsterdam. In the early seventies, in Europe, breakfast was included in the room price. The breakfast at the Frankfurt Intercontinental and Paris' Charles De Gaulle were the most spectacular. It was such a treat.

At breakfast, before the flight to Amsterdam, I sat down next to our senior.

"The Oakland supervisors called me and said that a company executive was upset. He just received a report about our crew sleeping on the aircraft during flights," she said.

"What's the name of the man who complained?" I asked.

"I don't remember his name, but he used to work for Pan Am," she said. He sat upstairs on the November 20th flight from Houston to Amsterdam."

The man who made the complaint was none other than the ex Pan Am man trouble shooting our airline. I hadn't slept on the flight. I supposed that the crew would be called into the supervisor's office to explain.

"The same passenger complained about the other leg of his trip too," our senior said.

I was amazed that the report arrived in Oakland so quickly. The Pan Am troubleshooter was on his way to Dhahran only two days ago. . . He wrote up a report that said I had to run up and down the stairs many times to get items and looked too busy. How did his report get there so quickly? I thought. Oakland must have read it and replied to it immediately for the information to get back to the F/A's on the line within two days of the flight in question. This was truly the information age.

I remembered that the Pan Am man also inquired about the sleeperette seats that were supposed to be in the upper deck of the Dhahran flights and asked my senior if she had heard anything about them.

"The seats went up in flames during a fire in the van that was carrying them—but the driver got out safely," she replied.

This remark caught me off guard and I laughed. "Somehow I missed that little bit of information," I said. "Who'd have guessed something like that would happen to our sleeperettes?"

Fifteen percent of our passengers were children on our Houston to Amsterdam leg of the flight and all passengers were seated downstairs. Three days ago, I complained that little was stocked in the 747 upper deck. This day everything was missing including the bins. Passengers enjoyed the 747's upper deck so I trekked downstairs to get items to stock the galley. Otherwise, I'd need to block off the upper deck with the rope that goes across the stairwell. That would definitely anger the passengers.

I heard another complaint from the last Houston/Amsterdam flight. A passenger was upset because the F/A's didn't take the wrap completely off the cheeses. Next time I'll cut the cheeses in half and only place half out uncovered, I thought. That way I can toss it when it becomes dried out and then place the fresh cheese out for the last five hours of the flight.

Our engineer mentioned he'd heard that the bigwigs (VIP's) could fly on TWA first class and go and come as they pleased. They chose TIA. He also said that many of these VIP's turned their TWA first class tickets in for coach tickets and kept the remainder of the money. It seemed they weren't very happy with TWA either.

After I finished the service, a passenger asked me if I made more money when I worked to Dhahran.

"No," I replied.

"The TWA flight attendants did," he said. "They made twenty to twenty-five percent more"

I had heard this before but our base pay was the same for all trips.

This flight I found a passenger asleep behind the last row of seats in the upper deck of the 747. When the seat belt sign illuminated, I asked him to take his seat and he cussed at me. Another passenger took my defense and cussed back and told him to get off his ass and into his seat. The passenger crawled out from behind the seat, fastened his seat belt and we landed in Amsterdam.

I arrived in Amsterdam too wound up to sleep therefore I read and wrote a little. The following day, Thanksgiving, we departed at 0045 to Houston.

I slept through Thanksgiving and rushed downstairs for coffee before the flight.

We arrived at the Amsterdam Airport and were briefed that we'd only thirty-six passengers this day.

The crew boarded the aircraft and heard from an incoming F/A that a man was ill on the last leg. He'd thrown up all over the galley, the curtain, and a couple of bathrooms. The ill man traveled to Houston with us but slept the entire flight.

I had only three paying passengers upstairs, and three non-revs (non paying crewmembers) this day. Cabin C (aft main cabin) was full of cargo. I was a little fearful that the plane might tip on its tail until I learned that the forward belly cargo compartment was full as well.

Eventually, we landed in Houston and all the crewmembers picked up their luggage but me. Where was my big red suitcase? Damn. All the passengers had retrieved their bags. It was clear that mine was lost.

Our representative in Houston said she would telex Amsterdam and send it on the first KLM flight to arrive at Houston at 2030. I called KLM, to confirm, but no answer. I called the cargo department also, but that was a recording. Both the Trans International numbers were ringing but no one picked up. I'd left a message for our representative but he didn't call back. Tomorrow we commercial home on Pan Am 11 from Houston to San Francisco.

Disappointed, I set off to the hotel in Houston without Big Red and found about two hundred ten-year-old soccer players were booked throughout our hotel. I walked down the hall to my room and unwillingly played dodge ball with them. They bounced the soccer balls off the walls and doors.

Since I had no clothes to change into, I chose to order room service. I ordered a grilled cheese sandwich and got a cold cheese sandwich on white bread, no butter, and no mayonnaise. It was awful. I noticed large red welts on my body that looked like mosquito bites; there were three on my face, three on my arms and a couple on my legs and back. Either I had encountered a hungry insect or these were hives again.

On November 28th, at 0900, I received my wakeup call and still no 'big red' suitcase. I called our representative.

"I'm headed for Oakland, could you ask KLM to bring my suitcase to my residence?" I asked. "Please don't go through the supervisor's office," I added, "they'd make me pick the suitcase up at crew scheduling in Oakland.

Another F/A offered to lend me a dress of hers. She was 5'9" and thin. I was 5'3" and round. I almost said, 'no thank you' but thought, what could be worse than wearing a uniform that had been worn for ten days previously? I borrowed the dress and it didn't look half bad to my surprise.

Once we arrived in San Francisco, I went into the airport bathroom, took off the dress, buttoned up my raincoat, and draped the dress over my arm. At the baggage area, I returned the dress and my roommate laughed and called me a 'flasher.' What else could I do? She lived in Santa Cruz and I lived in San Jose. I hadn't a free day to drive down and return it. I was a student at San Jose State University at the time and had work to do.

In the limo, headed for Oakland crew scheduling, the crew discussed what was happening with our airline. "I heard that in the beginning of November there was a bomb scare at one of TIA's sister companies," a crewmember said. "Nothing happened though. I also heard that on Nov. 27th, 1981, a crew commercialed to Shannon for a live (passenger) flight the next day. They arrived in Shannon, crew rested, and then headed out to the airport to return to the United States. The passengers boarded and just after takeoff, the DC-10 started leaking oil. The TIA aircraft returned to the terminal and a commercial flight was set up for them to fly home since it was a major mechanical problem. Therefore that crew commercialed to Shannon and then commercialed home again. That evening before the crew commercialed home, a woman called the captain and said he wasn't going to make it to California. She later called back and said he was going to die. Our captain had no idea who had called. Even though I had been a charter F/A for nine years, I was still amazed at what I heard.

Once home I started to worry about my lost suitcase. I wasn't the last to board the aircraft. In fact, one F/A had trouble with the handle on her suitcase (it kept falling off). It was placed on the conveyor belt about ten minutes later then the other suitcases since it took time to find twine to tie the handle on. Her bag made it. Where the hell was mine?

Two days later, I received a call from American Airlines. My bag was at San Jose Airport. I needed to retrieve it since American Airlines wouldn't deliver. They refused because they hadn't lost the suitcase. I had been away from my domicile for ten days so had five days off to recover. My favorite part of this trip was the complimentary breakfast set up for the crew in Houston. Being without my suitcase was the low point.

7
WHY DIDN'T YOU TELL US?

The crew showed at 2300 in April 1982 for a ferry flight from Oakland to Anchorage. The following day we took the same aircraft empty to Osan. It wasn't cleaned in Oakland or Anchorage. We took this dirty plane all the way to Osan, Korea. No one even bothered to dump the toilets or the trash. An empty quart bottle once filled with rum rolled out from underneath the seat in front of me. I stuffed it in the waste container in the lavatory. While in the lavatory I noticed Korean directions on the back of the toilet equipped with pictures. This was a new addition.

We showed in the lobby at 1000 this day, to work Osan, Yokota, Oakland. I rushed back to the hotel from my last minute shopping to prepare for the flight only to find it had been delayed three hours.

"What's the reason for the delay?" I asked our representative.

"This aircraft has been running late for days," he said.

"Why didn't you tell us?" I replied.

"The passengers weren't told either," he said. "They arrived at the airport at the original time. At least your not waiting at the airport like the passengers."

We departed three hours late. In-flight a passenger was worried about a friend of his since he drank two six packs of beer before this flight and had been in the bathroom for over five minutes. I knocked on the bathroom door and he said he was ok so I continued the meal service.

After the service, I attempted to unlatch the floor level hatch in the forward galley, to drop a garbage bag in. It was locked closed. Nothing and no one could unlatch that latch. It was locked closed the last time I flew on this aircraft also. Rumor was that TIA was using this garbage space for cargo. The last crew left a note saying they had to put the garbage bags in the overhead racks.

The air-conditioning was in-op this day. It was warm in the cabin.

I spoke to the engineer.

"The master trim air valve has been inoperative for seven days," he said. "There's no air coming into the trim air manifold. The remainder of the air conditioning system is functioning normally, but it's simply impossible to have individual zone control without trim air."

The ramp maintenance man deadheading aboard this day jokingly suggested bashing the valve body with a mallet in area of cabin port. The engineer joked he'd like to try this only he had to open the compartment to get at it and the compartment was stuck. They laughed.

An interesting note was posted in the engineer's discrepancy book. A F/A in the aft of the aircraft said that on the left side of the aircraft, facing forward, something fell off the outboard engine on landing-the part that sticks out like a cone, behind the wing over the engine. Aircraft engines were designed to break away from the wing since the aircraft can fly one engine short but not without the wing. The engines were bolted on using four or five bolts the size of a finger. Maybe it was one of the engine bolts that fell off, I thought.

The smoking section was erratic this day. Approximately one half of each of the five cabins was for smokers. The other half of the five cabins was for non-smokers. I had many complaints concerning the designated smoking section. Cabin A, B; C, D, and E were filled with smoke. This arrangement caused smokers to sit next to non-smokers in all the cabins instead of the usual arrangement of smokers in the aft of the aircraft and the non-smokers in the front.

This day, cabin B had lighting problems. The lights for the right side of cabin B turn off and on the lights for the left side of cabin B and vice versa. The passengers were yelling across the aisle, "Hey you, will you turn on my light?" Everyone on this flight had a good sense of humor thank goodness.

After the service, I went to the cockpit and looked at the discrepancy log. It read: St. Louis to Oakland flight # JEL3, a passenger fainted in the aisle at row forty C in front of the galley, knocked one tooth loose, chipped two teeth badly and cut lip. The passenger regained consciousness quickly.

After landing in Oakland passenger deplaned to see a dentist.

Another note I read in the discrepancy log stated on the sixth of March a passenger became nauseous and began vomiting five minutes after takeoff. The passenger informed the crew he suffers from sickle-cell trait but did not want to make an emergency landing. The crew asked for assistance from an Army Emergency Medical Technician on board.

We landed in Oakland, California and a pre-alert awaited me at crew scheduling I was to leave for Las Vegas in four days.

8
DELAYS AND DILEMMAS

Three months later, I was scheduled to catch the OC#53 flight from Oakland to Seattle, Washington. It took some time at the airport to figure out which airline OC (Air California) was. Usually we took Republic or Western to Seattle. When we arrived, another F/A took my bag to her room. I looked at the nametag on the one remaining red suitcase located by the reception desk. We exchanged. That night we left for Frankfurt.

On July 18, 1982, we worked Seattle to Frankfurt on the 747 aircraft. A honeymoon couple was on board and TIA bought them a bottle of champagne. We also had a mini red dachshund named Kazam on board. Just before we landed, the woman who owned the dachshund wrapped her up in a small blue blanket and held her. Kazam was adorable and well behaved. Better behaved than some passengers.

The following day we commercialed to Hanover, Germany then taxied to the Inter Continental Hotel. The air conditioning in our room was in-op and it was stifling. I slept with the window open and every one half hour, all night long, the clock on the city hall building across the street chimed. Hanover was a lovely city even in a sleep-deprived state. That night we left for London, Gatwick.

We joined a new cockpit crew in Hanover, and headed for London then Bangor, Maine. Before departure this stifling hot July day, we encountered numerous delays. During the preflight check of the first aid oxygen, a F/A noted that it wasn't full, so maintenance in Hanover refilled it. A thirty-minute delay was due to fueling, then something went wrong with the air coolant system and it took an hour to repair, all this time the passengers were required to sit on the aircraft to expedite the departure. It felt as if it were one hundred ten degrees Farenheight in the cabin before the F/A's were given the ok to deplane the passengers.

The delay lasted three hours before we started on our way to Bangor, Maine.

During the flight, we had no communication with the cockpit since the P.A. and the interphone were in-op. The P.A. announcements were accomplished by using the megaphone. Our senior F/A stood in the middle of the cabin by the window exits, placed the megaphone to her lips, clicked the trigger and spoke pointing it toward the aft first and then pointing it forward. It certainly got the attention of the passengers. Click, "Ladies and gentlemen," she said, keeping that F/A smile on her lips to soften the sound. Click, "Welcome aboard Trans International flight # 20827 from Hanover to London Gatwick, click. Our captain today is Captain Casanova," click.

That day we transported Americans that were part of the Friendship Force to their host country Germany. The Friendship Force was an organization started by President Carter to promote goodwill between countries. Americans stayed in foreign countries and lived in the host countries homes for five to seven days. Some of our passengers confided in me that they requested that the hosts speak English and some requested to stay with a young family. These requests weren't always honored. Other then this, our passengers spoke highly of this program. The cost to participate in the Friendship Force program was seven hundred dollars. People from foreign countries then stayed with American families in the United States. One passenger handed me a Friendship Force pin.

These passengers encountered a long delay before they departed from the United States since a wing flap was broken. They were given hotel vouchers.

We landed in Bangor and taxied to the Twin Cities to crew rest.

The following day our pickup was at 0530 to commercial on Delta #215 from Bangor to Portland, Maine at 0630 then on to New York where we had three and one fourth hours on the ground. Then we changed planes to Eastern #587 and went from New York to Greenbough, North Carolina, then on to Raleigh, North Carolina, then changed to a little prop aircraft that took us into Newberg, North Carolina.

It was a miserable stormy night and turbulent. I almost threw up and no burp bag (white paper bag with a plastic lining) was available. The small aircraft was packed full. Our knees were tucked up under our chins since our feet were positioned on our topsides that bulged out from under the seat in front of us. My purse at my side and two other people in similar circumstances on either side left no other space for my arms except wrapped around my knees. This situation reminded me of a poem I wrote that Bill called, "Confessions of a Claustrophobic."

In my dreams,
I wrote eloquently.
By morning, I would return to the normal dutiful life,
Superman to Clark Kent
In my dreams,
I could hear
The aircraft doors click, screech, thump, to close
The sound of a bank vault door closing
I could see
The shiny metal ovens,
Stuffed with chicken and beef, covered with foil
No air between them to breath and circulate
Like the overcrowded commuter trains in Japan
In my dreams
I could feel
The cold metal of the meal cart handle warm up
As I held it with both hands, and pushed down on the lever
To release the brakes
In my dreams
I could taste
The stale dry air and smoke in the cabin
Re-circulating every puff of smoke every sneeze, every breath
I could smell
The stench of the lavatories, escape the bathroom when opened
And waif under the door when closed

Each night in my dreams
My five senses were alive with color, texture, and life
Each passenger had a story to tell
Each location was filled with culture, tradition
Political and religious beliefs
This was my life adventure
The adventure
Of a charter flight attendant

After the terrifying small prop plane flight in the thunderstorm, we stayed at the Quality Inn in Newberg. The following day we limo'd to Cherry Point, North Carolina, picked up our passengers, took them to Dallas, then headed home to Oakland to end trip. Since I was still queasy after being home for twenty-four hours, I made a doctors appointment and discovered that I was one month pregnant.

CHAPTER 12

SOUTH AMERICA: FROM HERE TO MATERNITY

1
THE ROAD LESS TRAVELED

November 2, 1982, Bill, and I (five months pregnant) departed for Los Angeles on PSA (Pacific Southwest Airlines), on a cold dark night to connect with Avianca, Columbia's national airline. We were ticketed from Los Angeles/Quito/ Bogotá/Lima/Santiago/Los Angeles for one hundred eighty dollars per person roundtrip and were ready for a whirlwind adventure.

Each Tuesday a 747 was scheduled leave Los Angeles for Quito through Bogotá for the five thousand mile flight that would last nine hours. Few bought tickets to Quito our Tuesday so a smaller plane was substituted and we made an unscheduled stop in Mexico City to pick up more passengers.

We arrived exhausted in Bogotá at 1030 and had four long hours before our connecting flight to Quito. The Columbian customs officials stamped our passports, we placed our suitcases in a locker, and changed dollars into Ecuadorian secures. A departure tax out of Columbia was charged no matter if you're waiting at the airport for your connecting flight or didn't plan to be there in the first place. The local departure tax amounted to fifteen dollars per person, half the cost since we got air tourist cards in the United States.

The equator was forty-five minutes away from the city of Quito. We traveled by bus and drove through the agricultural terrain. Ecuador, known for its volcanoes and earthquakes, was slightly smaller than Nevada. On route we discussed a trip to Iquitos (Peru's Atlantic port) where tourists boarded a motorboat for a short excursion on the Amazon River, visited the Bora Indian Village, participated in a jungle walk then hoteled at the Holiday Inn. This sounded too tame; instead, we went to Leticia, the road less traveled.

Leticia, a remote city on the Amazon River located at the tip of one of Columbia's fingers sounded more adventurous. Because it was a wild and remote area tourists didn't usually fly there. We knew this before we set out.

The third of November, 1982, we boarded a small prop plane and fastened our seat belts. Once airborne, the captain came on the PA and said Leticia was closed due to repairs and we landed in Brazil's Manus Airport not far from the Leticia Airport, so they said. At least that's where they said we landed but I checked my map and Brazil's Manus Airport was far from Leticia's airport. We knew we were somewhere in Brazil since the currency was reals, and our Columbian pesos and Ecuadorian secres wouldn't work in the phones. We grabbed a cab that would take Columbian pesos and departed for the Parador Ticuna Hotel. This was the only hotel in Leticia.

The sky was cloudy and it began to rain. The cab driver turned to us and spoke in Spanish. Neither Bill nor I understood a word. All we knew was that we were bouncing on a dirt road in a rainstorm headed for Leticia. We saw no markers, nothing but foliage and water.

He stopped the cab and climbed out, rain drenched him while we waited. Our cabbie took on the appearance of a human waterfall. He popped open the trunk and pulled out a tire. We thought it was the dirt road and bad shocks that caused the cab to bounce. In reality, he had blown a tire.

Two hours later, we arrived at the Parador Ticuna Hotel on the Colombian Amazon River and checked into a large room that had an air conditioner blowing out hot air. Unpacking, I placed an item on the glass tray above the sink and it crashed down and broke. I leaned over to clean up the mess and discovered we had no toilet seat. Later we discovered that the shower only had cold water, but then who needs hot in the Amazon? I could adjust to just about anything but the lack of a toilet seat. We spoke with the owner of the hotel and were informed that A Greek man owned most of Leticia's tourist area and ever since this Greek's brother died in a small aircraft accident in Leticia he had not lived here. We discussed the toilet dilemma with the local management. Our problems unresolved we headed for the hotel restaurant and bar to try out the local delicacies.

Seated in the covered outdoor restaurant we watched the sky light up with lightening outlining all the foliage with such intense light it looked like something from a horror movie. As Bill ate the fish dish and I ate the steak— the only two items on the menu: we mentioned the lack of a toilet seat to someone who dropped by our table. The person said he was management and assured us we would get one. Tomorrow we planned to tour the Amazon River.

November 4th, 1982, our first morning in Leticia the rain poured down and there was a tap, tap, tap on our door. We opened the door. A skinny dark haired young man handed us two large black garbage bags.

"My name is Daniel Martinez, are you ready for your tour down the Amazon River?" he asked. "Put these over your heads, and tear holes for your eyes, nose and arms."

We did as instructed and headed out into the Columbian Amazon Jungle with this stranger, sloshing for five minutes through the mud to the harbor. A motorized white wooden canoe tied around a rock awaited us. Gathering the black plastic garbage bag around ourselves, we slid down the mud hill and boarded the canoe. A canopy covered a couple of seats, — the seats where the mosquitoes were flying about. This was a small canoe and when the wind blew, we got wetter and it was windy. Both sides of the Amazon River were thick with foliage, no huts, no people, and no signs of civilization. I felt small and insignificant. We slowly glided, sometimes the river was wide sometimes it became narrow, sometimes it branched out. We zigged this way then zagged that way visually seeing nothing but vegetation and water. We arrived at the Isla de los Micos or Island of the Monkeys. An American businessperson who bred and sold Capuchin monkeys to research labs in the United States lived here. Somewhat later, we learned this American businessperson was arrested and jailed for dealing in cocaine.

Daniel, our guide, took the lead with his machete and hacked the way through the jungle. Bill and I dodged the wet branches that snapped back at us. Jumping over mud puddles we trekked through the jungle, I wondered where we were going. The goulashes we wore over our shoes only came to our ankles and mud gushed in.

The Yaqua Indian Tribe lived on Monkey Island and we were introduced to the chief who wore a grass skirt and nothing else. The women wore just as little clothing as the men— grass skirts. . I was sure that we were as mysterious to them as they were to us. Daniel spoke with the Tribal Chief who stood up and went inside a hut on stilts that had a thatched palm roof. The hut was open an all sides, only a few branches held up the roof. The chief returned with a long stick, which he put in his mouth and pointed it toward a tree. Woof, the sound of air passed through the stick and a dart flew toward the tree. This blowgun was made with two pieces of wood hollowed out then wrapped with vine. The longer the stick, the more power it had. Curare, a poison, would be put on the dart when hunting small animals. After the demonstration the Yaqua Indians made us lunch.

Close by, a fat scarlet Macaw sat chained to a perch.

"What a beautiful parrot," I said. Then Daniel motioned like he was eating. I was unclear if that meant the parrot was lunch or lunch was ready.

We fed the monkeys bananas and soggy crackers out of our hands, while the chickens and chicks that must have been imitating the monkeys climbed up a couple of branches. I snapped a few pictures of the chickens in the tree since who would believe us otherwise?

We trekked back to our canoe, boarded, and headed out toward the Ticuna Indian Village. The rain had stopped and the sun shone through the foliage. The mixture of raindrops and sunlight made the spider webs glisten. Then Bill screamed and jumped up rocking the canoe. Daniel and I grabbed the sides of the canoe afraid it would tip and dump us out. A twelve-inch fish had jumped inside and landed at my husband's feet. He thought it was a piranha. It was a good size fish, but not a piranha. The Amazon River water was the lowest in November and December. The other months the jungle gets flooded and the fish hide there. Daniel and I laughed.

A two-mile walk (one mile in and one mile out) of the Columbian jungle was next on the agenda. Our quest to see this village took us across a stream. I'd thought about the possibility of leeches but nothing attached itself to us. The heat was intense. One spider with green hairy legs had placed himself on my shoulder. "Stand still," Daniel said. He brushed the spider off my shoulder and on to the ground. I eyed it briefly before it disappeared into the brush. "At least it wasn't a bird eating tarantula," he said. He pointed to a Jatoba tree who's healing properties included antibacterial agents, anti-fungal, anti-inflammatory, diuretic and tonic to name a few. "One quarter of medicines come from the rainforest," Daniel said. "These trees stored energy either as carbohydrates like sugar or hydrocarbons such as diesel fuel. One Amazonian tree can be tapped for its hydrocarbon fuel."

The Ticuna Indian Village had electricity and a school. We wandered around and then departed for yet another location called Lake Yuquacana only a five-minute walk through a swampy area. Giant water lilies covered the lake that looked like giant floating pancakes. "A small child could stand on them," Daniel remarked. The sun dropped toward the horizon, a signal that it was time to travel back to the hotel. Locals offered to take us on a nighttime crocodile hunt with flashlights but we declined.

After a much-needed shower and change of clothes, I sat in bed and watched what looked like a growing anthill on the floor near the head of my bed. I cleaned it up with a wet towel, but it reappeared. Small insects climbed in and out of my suitcase also. The hills formed in various areas of the room and shower. We still had no toilet seat so Bill pulled out his Spanish dictionary to help him communicate this and other dilemmas. We weren't concerned with expressing ourselves in detail, but simply with making sense.

The Parador Ticuna management felt the need to conserve electricity so turned it off when they felt like it day or night. To avoid sitting in the dark we left for the Anaconda Restaurant for dinner. Maybe this unexpected darkness was the call to dinner? Everyone we knew in Leticia was there—all four of them.

Tomorrow I will be thirty-two years old.

2
WHO WOULD GUESS?

November 5th, 1982, the fourth day of our journey and my thirty-second birthday we woke at dawn to fireworks and explosions. At first, we felt disoriented. Then aware that thousands of people were kidnapped and disappeared in Columbia every year we trotted over to our suitcases to hastily dress. BANG. It sounded like we were in a war zone even though the hotel officials said "No." November 5th, was National Police Day, the one day off a year for all police officers in Leticia. We decided to fly out of Leticia and go to Quito, Ecuador, by way of Bogotá hauling ourselves and our hastily packed stuff to a taxi to catch another old prop plane to Bogotá to connect to Quito and then Guayaquil.

At Bogotá Airport, every line was shoulder to shoulder. We discovered if we didn't squish up next to the people in front of us, others would cut in front. Military in uniform and first class passengers were allowed to cut in. The flights from Bogotá to Quito this day were cancelled, so we stayed the night at the Melendez Hotel. No reason was given for the cancellation into Quito. All Avianca flights to Guayaquil, Ecuador, located two hundred miles south of Quito, were cancelled the following day as well, so we chose to fly Viasa Airlines to Quito, and then caught a SAN flight to Guayaquil. SAN flew the two jet engine Caravelle airplanes, with triangle windows. It wasn't until our arrival in Guyaqual that we heard the Guagua Pichincha volcano in Quito was showing seismic activity. Who would have guessed?

We checked into the Oro Verde Hotel, a five star establishment. The hotel was close to empty and the staff so accommodating that we stayed three days. The Guagua Pichincha volcano in Quito had been showing seismic activity since June of 1982-escaping steam and minor earthquakes. Minor compared to some I experienced in California.

The maids cleaned the rooms morning and evening and offered us fresh towels, soap, mineral water, and chocolates. There was twenty-four hour room service, a pool, gym, sauna, and gambling in the casino downstairs. We felt we bet large amounts of money—100 sucres, but 100 sucres were only two dollars U.S. I don't know who the hotel thought we were but whenever we'd ask for something, it appeared. We became bold and started asking for items not on the menu. I was five months pregnant and craved yogurt.

"You want yogurt?" the waiter said confused.

I didn't think we pronounced it correctly since the waiter brought over someone else to listen to our request.

"I would like yogurt," I repeated with a smile.

"Yogurt," he said.

I wrote yogurt on a napkin. "Lots of it," I added.

He left and returned with many plastic containers of different flavored yogurt. I ate two, and then asked if they could refrigerate the remainder for me and they did. I felt rich and famous and Bill tipped them well. I had requested that he find me yogurt earlier and he couldn't find it.

We hated to leave, but the next day we set off for the Galapagos Islands aboard Tame Airlines.

3
THE GALAPAGOS ON TAME AIRLINES

November 9th, 1982 we caught a flight from Guayaquil to Baltra Island in the Galapagos aboard Tame Airlines. It had taken Bill and me six days to realize that when an airline here in South America tells you the flight time, they're including at least one hour of delay time. Flights were considered on time if they departed one hour later than posted. Ours was supposed to leave at four o'clock but at the airport, they said it was leaving at five.

The Tame Airlines' flight to Baltra Island in the Galapagos was turbulent. When the clear air turbulence subsided, meals were served. The food was unusual: purple cabbage with an egg slice that turned bright green in places, a sandwich with three slices of bread and some unknown filling that was sparse, and a cream pastry that smelled bad. It was served on a metal dish with foil covering it.

Upon arrival in Baltra, we asked a woman who worked in the airport what the mystery meat was.

"The meat is ground salami sausage," she said. Then she added that she would never eat it.

Tame Airlines was owned by the Ecuadorian military and the only airline allowed to land at Baltra Island in the Galapagos Archipelago. We survived the turbulence and the food but almost didn't survive the lime-flavored mints that were passed out before landing. This six hundred mile, one and a half hour flight, cost six hundred seventy dollars for two round trip tickets.

Baltra Airport was a shack in the desert with a bathroom that looked like it had never been cleaned and a toilet that didn't flush. The area was remote and there was only one bus to catch to go into town. The terrain changed from desert to forest as we proceeded to the other side of the island.

We were dropped off at the Solymar Hotel, a small quaint place with few rooms. It was clean, but again, no hot water. The owner gave us information about the Santa Cruz, a ship that toured the Galapagos Islands.

Bill told him that he fixed TV's and electronic items. The owner had a TV that needed repair and my husband fixed it. Because the owner was grateful, we were offered the bridal suite. It was upstairs, faced the ocean, and had a balcony with two chairs and a table. A moaning seal parked himself outside our window and slept under an upside-down canoe and huge prehistoric looking iguanas climbed up the wall at dusk to sleep under the tin roof. Off the balcony, many herons landed and sauntered over to sleep to the right of our room under pieces of timber. Everyone had his or her place.

The following day, in the open air dining area, the cook, who had served dinner the evening before, wore a traditional Indian outfit: black scarf, white embroidered blouse with puffy sleeves to the elbows and a long print shirt.

I slid across the picnic bench and knocked into a six-foot iguana asleep under the table. It didn't move, but I did, afraid my pink toes might look like something good to eat. I asked a local if he could get the iguana to move. He replied the iguanas made this area their home long before humans arrived and the locals welcomed them along with the rest of the wildlife. I sat crossed legged on the bench. The iguanas walked thru the restaurant like guests, opened their mouths, and shook their heads. These large lizards walked slowly but if you reach down with food, they snap at it. One Iguana jumped two feet in the air to catch my cracker. It amazed me that such large bulky lizards could jump that way.

After breakfast we walked to a rotting wooden pier where large fish in clear blue water swum about. This was an animal's paradise.

Later we purchased some orange wine (Vinode Naranja) made from fresh oranges and bottled in Floreana, an island in the Galapagos Archipelago south of Santa Cruz Island. We attempted to mail postcards on numerous occasions but the post office was never open. "The postal employees show up when they felt like it," a local said.

This day, November 10th, we awoke at 0600 to a fluttering sound. The hotel owner, on the beach below was feeding hundreds of bird's bread. These birds were so tiny they'd fit into the palm of your hand and had no fear of humans.

We had decided to cruise the islands and almost hired a boat and a crew of four to take us, but the wind picked up, so we thought it wiser to travel by ship. The owner of the hotel where we stayed called the captain of the Santa Cruz and mentioned we wanted to join the cruise. He wrote the captain a letter written in Spanish introducing us. At 0845, we caught a bus to the airport where the captain of the Santa Cruz was waiting to meet the incoming passengers.

We introduced ourselves and handed the captain our letter of introduction. After a short discussion about the price of the cruise, we boarded the bus to deliver us to Port Ayora where we boarded the Santa Cruz.

Our cabin M14 was air-conditioned with in-room controls. Two lights were located above each twin bed with wicker shades and we had a porthole, a shower with hot water, and a toilet. We also had two small closets, a covered compartment next to each bed and a wood desk beneath the porthole. The wood paneling around the room and brass fixtures made the cabin elegant. Constant upkeep went on throughout the ship. A room boy changed the towels twice a day and turned down the sheets in the evening. The water aboard ship was distilled and potable. We departed for Bartolome Island north west of Santa Cruz Island pleased with everything.

At 1500, an announcement came over the in room intercom; lunch was served. The buffet was similar to the airline food I served on Trans International except for the apples.

At 1600, we disembarked on tiny Bartolome Island, a volcanic island with steep pinnacles, for our two-hour walk almost straight up. Numerous people carried large black VCR's on their shoulders and had battery packs hanging from their waists as they trekked up the volcano.

The captain's cocktail hour was announced at 1800. There was a speaker in each room to inform us of the daily schedule. Pisco (a

Peruvian brandy made of white grapes) sours and vodka and orange juice were served along with little pizzas and sausages. We dined on lobster, soup, cod, potatoes, beans, and strawberries. After dinner, we were briefed about the next day's activities. We were instructed not to disturb the plants and terrain while we hiked and to make certain we didn't leave anything behind to disrupt the ecology.

Later the crew conducted an evacuation drill. Life vests were donned and we were told to go to either the port (the left hand side of the boat as you face the bow) or starboard (the right side facing the bow from the aft) side of the ship for five minutes. No one checked to see if we were in the correct place or if everyone was present. I suppose we had equal amounts of passengers on both sides and all had life vests on so we were looking good to the crew. After the drill, swimming was allowed off the ship for five minutes only, due to the hammerhead sharks in the area. Two-crew members with rifles positioned themselves on deck and watched for sharks while some people swam.

November 12th, the passengers were divided into four groups of fifteen each. Bill and I were in the Boobie group. Boobies were birds that dive into the water from great heights to get enough depth to catch fish. They pulled their wings in and dove headfirst. Boobie in Spanish means crazy.

After breakfast, we disembarked at Tagus Cove on Isabela Island where we saw the Galapagos hawk, penguins, and iguanas, blue-footed boobies, herons, sea lions, and pups. We walked for an hour over mountainous terrain then boarded the pangas (small boats) for a ride around part of Tagus Cove.

After a lunch aboard ship of meat loaf, mushroom salad, cheese, grapes and potato chips we headed out for Espinoza Point. Lunch was always a buffet and dinner was served at tables. At Espinoza Point, we walked among sea lions and marine iguanas over rocky coves. Each island was different in wild life and terrain.

On November 13th, wakeup came at 0630 and always to music piped into the rooms. There was no sleeping in. After a breakfast of scrambled eggs with onions, porridge, ham, and pineapple, we boarded the pangas to Tower Island. Tower Island was north east of Santa Cruz Island. Our ship the Santa Cruz always stayed offshore since the ship would break off the coral with the anchor. We walked along the beach and rocky shore. Here we were allowed to swim and snorkel with equipment given to us. Bill searched the caves for lobsters until he was scared away by the eels and seals. After our swim, we headed back to the Santa Cruz for a lunch of artichokes, green salad, and a purple starch that tasted like sweet potatoes, paella, and apples. Lunch this day was our first meal served while at sea. All the previous meals were served after we dropped anchor. Some became seasick.

Next, we stopped at Seymore Island where we saw surfing seals, their pups, friggets (birds) and chicks and a four-foot snake. There were no poisonous snakes in the Galapagos. We walked two hours over flat rocky terrain.

Bill chose to fish for Bacalou with the crew instead of joining me on Seymour Island. He was the only person to catch anything and that three foot brown tuna with a silver belly was served exclusively to us that evening at the captain's table. Bill sat on the captain's left and I sat to the right. I ate cream soup, beef with gravy, scalloped potatoes, onion salad, peas, and spicy tomatoes. I was craving a rich creamy chocolate dessert but it didn't materialize. Unfortunately, Bill was seasick and not able to enjoy the meal.

November 14th, the fourth day of our cruise, we visited Hood Island, which was south east of Santa Cruz Island. . It rained on Hood Island in the morning but cleared up in the afternoon for the three-hour hike. Here we witnessed sea lions, pups, boobies, and a blowhole. We walked among the wildlife but were not to touch the pups since the mother would reject them because of our human scent. The animals had no fear of us. We also snorkeled in a little cove and swam off the beach.

November 15th, our fifth day, we cruised to Santa Cruz Island after a healthy breakfast of pancakes, bananas, juice, and hot cereal. I was getting real tired of the healthy food. We disembarked at Santa Cruz Island where we visited the Darwin Museum and park. Giant tortoises were located here whose shells were the size of large boulders. Galapagos means tortoise in Spanish. These huge gentle reptiles weighed up to five hundred fifty pounds and lived one hundred and fifty years. There were three types of tortoises: saddleback, domed shape, and the intermediate species. They enjoyed being petted under their necks. They'd stretch their long necks up, look me in the eye, and smile. It was great fun.

For lunch, Bill ate the tuna fish he had caught. The chef had thoughtfully saved it for him until he felt better. At 1500 we explored Plaza Island where there were hundred of seals. They were laid out over the island as if they had too much to eat and drink.

Dinner tonight was special. All passengers were served Bill's favorite, a whole lobster with all the trimmings.

November 16th, we returned to Guayaquil, Ecuador by sea. After breakfast there was a movie on Darwin but few attended since most were sick. The same situation happened for the geology lecture in the afternoon. The captain said if he had known the sea would be so rough, he would have flown the passengers to Guayaquil. Almost everyone was violently ill. I was not.

The ship's doctor was extremely busy going from room to room. The doctor concluded that sure, the seas were rough, but the excessive vomiting of almost all the passengers was unusual. The doctor who spoke little English came to our cabin with his black bag. He sat on the desk chair next to Bill who was lying in bed and removed a syringe and glass vile. He whacked the vile on the dresser to break the top off. I jumped. I watched him place the liquid from the vile into the syringe and squirt out liquid.

"What is in that vile?" I asked. He said something in Spanish that I didn't understand and then placed the needle in my husband's arm.

"Why am I not sick?" I asked.

"Did I eat the lobster?" he asked in broken English.

"No," I replied. "I gave mine to my husband."

I discovered that 'yes' the seas were rough, but this wasn't just a case of seasickness it was also a case of food poisoning.

November 17th, there was no toast for the three of us healthy passengers at breakfast. It was rationed between the sick. There was a lecture on the animals of the Galapagos and slides were shown. We three musketeers were the only ones in the theatre. The rough sea calmed down some as we neared Guayaquil. Bill and I looked forward to the Oro Verde Hotel and room service. I craved waffles and chocolate.

At 2000, the crew dropped anchor and it sounded like a rocket taking off. Almost everyone stumbled off the ship.

Our guide Michael on Santa Cruz Island in the Galapagos.

4
THE LOCAL CHAMAS INDIANS

The luxury of the Oro Verde on November 18th, in Guayaquil, Ecuador was much appreciated. We ate waffles, chocolate and other foods we craved. Our evenings were spent at the "Sala De Bingo." I wasn't certain what numbers they called since I didn't know much Spanish, but a bingo manager stood on my right and corrected my mistakes. We won on a few occasions.

The 23rd of November we flew on a Faucett Airlines one-eleven plane to Lima, Peru "The City of Viceroys," and stayed at the Sheraton Hotel. Lima was where the Amazon River began. The weather in November was a pleasant seventy degrees.

My last visit to Lima had been in 1976. I recalled the crew had rented an Avis van and had driven to the beach. Upon leaving the beach, we had noticed we had a flat tire. This had caused us to be out after curfew. As we had driven through Lima, a military tank had turned a corner and was directly behind us. All but the driver ducked down. We were only blocks from our hotel so continued on with the large military tank gun pointed toward us. We pulled to the front of the Sheraton Lima and stopped. We silently watched the tank continue on its way patrolling the streets. Scary.

Now in 1982, Bill and I walked to Union Street to shop. We passed a Sears and entered a Thirteen Flavors ice cream parlor. It looked like a Baskin Robbins, but the owner said he had no connection with Baskin Robbins. Further down Union we came to the river Rimac and the open flea market. The locals shopped here and the prices were excellent if you bargained. The remainder of the afternoon was spent on the city bus tour, which cost seven thousand one hundred twenty soles, or thirty-six dollars U.S. The next day we departed for Cusco.

The not-to-bumpy flight to Cusco, "Land of the Incas," aboard a small six-seat prop plane lasted one and one half hours. We caught the first flight of the day. The late morning and early afternoon flights were always turbulent. Once we arrived at the Cusco Airport, locals mobbed us with requests to go to specific hotels and on tours and one man clicked a picture of me. We decided on the Samana Hotel and grabbed a taxi for the thirty minutes ride. The Samana was located in the center of town and had emerald green double doors. A two-story atrium with white pillars and more green double doors led to the guest rooms. We walked through the lobby and ascended the stairs. Bright red flowers and chairs were placed on our balcony. Our room had a toasty warm heater, double wool blankets, good lighting, and a hot water shower. The temperature was a cold sixty degrees. Coca tea was brought to our room to help us adjust to the fourteen thousand foot altitude. Coca leaves were considered magical to the local Indians. The Spanish church tried to eradicate them because they played a role in the Indian religion that was not Christianity. The leaves were chewed but not swallowed and also used for skin infections and a stimulant. Some cocaine was in these leaves but without processing with chemicals, the leaves don't make you "high."

This day we went on a private tour of the ruins and churches of pre Columbian Cusco. L. Urquizo, our guide, was a native Chamas-Indian guide. The natives of Cusco were called Chamas, not Incans and Quechua was the language of the indigenous Chamas.

We visited Saqsaywaman, a meeting place of the Chamas Indians and a mountain range. Saqsaywaman was referred to as a fortress, but Urquizo said the Chamas were not aggressive so when the Spaniards came they were greeted as friends until they tried and succeeded in taking over the area. The Spanish destroyed the limestone foundations.

Next, we visited the ruins of Pukaupukara where a watchtower and temple were located. The view was spectacular. We were at 15,000 feet, and from this altitude, one could see all of Cusco.

Tambomachay was the fresh water temple where the Chamas got their water. Urquizo told us that the information that baths were located here was false. He said the Chamas didn't take baths. Once a year perhaps, but no area was designated for these baths.

A woman nearby was sitting cross-legged on the grass and weaving a basket. I took her picture and gave her a few soles.

Urquizo drove us to the ruins of Quenqo, a ten-minute drive away. This Temple to the Gods was where sacrifices had taken place. Sometimes the lungs or hearts were removed from the people sacrificed here. Blood dripped into circles dug in the stone steps. This blood was used for the ceremony. There were many limestone caves with temples inside in Quengo. After the Spaniards destroyed the city, they ordered the Chamas Indians to rebuild it their way. Annoyed with the Spanish, the Chamas were not as neat in placing the stones.

After visiting Qenqo, we headed back to Cusco to tour the three main churches in Cusco: Saint Blaise Church, Santa Catalina, and La Cathedral. Santa Catalina was called the Indian Temple to the Sun.

The Saint Blaise Church was famous for the cedar wood carving on the sculptured altar and surrounding decorations, such as the scene of the Madonna. A leper woodcarver had a dream that the 'Virgin of Good Happenings' would heal him if he found a painting of her. He found a painting of her in a chapel in Cusco. The virgin's rosary beads became rose petals and the woodcarver rubbed them on his body and was cured of leprosy. This chapel fell. A portion of the painting of the virgin was recovered and moved to the Saint Blaise Church. The woodcarver built an altarpiece and pulpit to the virgin. He finished his work and fastened the Saint Paul statue over the pulpit, stumbled, and fell dead. His body was buried under the pulpit originally and later his skull was placed before the feet of the Saint Paul sculpture.

The Chamas Indians were used as slaves to reconstruct the churches and frescos from pictures brought from Spain. These pictures were strange to the Chamas so they changed them. Apparently, the Spanish priests didn't mind the changes since they remained on the walls of La Cathedral. Llamas were substituted for horses and since all Chamas women wore straw hats, a straw hat was placed on the Madonna's head. An interesting picture of the Last Supper was placed near one of the altars. Local fruits such as bananas and papaya, and corn were used instead of the foods we know to be in the painting of the Last Supper. Instead of a lamb, there was a guinea pig and instead of wine, the yellow beer served in Peru was substituted. A black Christ was also in the fresco. He was meant to be a copper color but smoke from La Cathedral's candles turned him black. The walls of the church were concrete. There was no marble in Cusco so to duplicate the marble interior of the European churches the Chamas painted the walls to look like marble.

The 26th of November, we drank coca tea with boiled milk in the room, and had hamburgers for breakfast. Then we shopped. The Perez Factory where they sold hand knitted sweaters and other knit items was our first stop. We also bargained for a white wool blanket and a wall hanging.

The afternoon clouded over and it began to rain. The smell of urine in Cusco made me nauseous so I returned to the hotel while Bill searched the streets for the perfect musical instrument. He collected musical instruments from around the world. The charango, a ten-string mandolin type instrument, was made from an armadillo shell and the most popular instrument in Cusco. The armadillo skin backed bandurra was the second in popularity and had twelve to sixteen strings. The local Chamas Indians believed the soul of the armadillo was kept alive when the charango and the bandurra were played. The antura and quena (small and large flutes) were made of bamboo that was hollowed out and different lengths were tied together with string. Bill bargained for and purchased all four musical instruments.

That evening we set out to see the native dancing and musicians play at the local theater in town. After the show, we ventured into a restaurant where local musicians played the charango, bandurra, antura, and quena. A stack of their cassette tapes was located on a table nearby for purchase. The music was enjoyable, light, and cheerful and we purchased a couple of cassette tapes before heading back to the Samana Hotel for the night. We looked forward to the next day, when we would travel to Machu Picchu the Incan capital of Peru.

5
ZIG ZAGGING TO MACHU PICCHU

The 27th of November, we boarded the one and only train of the day at 1700 to Machu Picchu for the four-hour ride. We purchased tourist class tickets for a closed car minus the animals brought on by the locals. The train would go forward for about ten minutes, then back for a few minutes, then forward again. It felt as if it didn't have the power to make it up the mountain. We departed Cusco at an altitude of 11,000 feet, then ascended to 12,000 feet, and then down to Machu Picchu at 8,000 feet.

A local photographer glanced at me then flipped through some photos. He handed me a picture postcard with me on it. This man had taken my picture at Cusco Airport when we arrived. I purchased the postcard. We passed by clay homes and cornfields, cows, chickens and pigs, but no llamas. The llamas were becoming extinct and few farmers used them anymore.

We passed green pastures and mountains with an occasional muddy trout stream running through. The bridges across the streams were logs trussed by stones on both shores. I saw only one paved road. It went from Cusco to Iquitos and was the ancient trail used by the Incas and Chamas when they traveled to the Amazon. Forward of us was a local man who played his antura and bandurra at the same time. "Oh Susanna" was a song we recognized.

We passed weeping willows, cactus plants, bushes with bright yellow flowers and eucalyptus trees. As we moved through the Andes Mountains we passed Kantu bushes dotted with bright red flowers, the national flower of Peru.

As we neared Machu Picchu, the foliage changed to tropical and our train ride ended. Busses took us the remiander of the way. The dirt road had only one lane so many busses ascended at the same time before the others descend. For the minute ride, there was a charge of one dollar fifty cents. The yellow buses zigzagged up the mountain as if there was some kind of emergency. The mountains looked layered and reached up to sharp peaks, clouds covered the tips. It was magical. Slivers of light lit up portions of the monstrous vertical rocks.

We checked into a charming little chalet called the Tourista that cost seventy dollars a night. Our room faced a garden and was surrounded by masses of yellow, red, and purple flowers and greenery. In the distance, the huge green mountains stood jagged against the sky in high grandeur. Our room, decorated in Spanish colonial with black iron headboards, frames, and lanterns was warm and toasty. The high wood ceiling was slanted toward the large window that faced the garden. A table and chairs with leather seats was a comfortable place to relax as we watched the clouds roll by in the post dawn hours. We sat and watched the mountains, which were crystal clear one minute, and then disappeared suddenly and completely in the clouds the next. Seconds later they reappeared. It was ethereal.

The lobby of the Tourista had a faux fireplace and a TV with Beta Max tapes but the voltage was so low it couldn't be used. Because of this low voltage problem, the lights were turned off for three hours in the afternoon and again late at night until sunrise.

It stormed in the late afternoon. A stream of water poured down from the hotel roof causing a waterfall effect. When it stopped raining, we hiked to the top of one of the mountains, over muddy paths where numerous insects were drying themselves in the sun. We were four feet from a chirping grasshopper when a hawk swooped down, grabbed it, and flew off. Workers clearing the terraces of foliage with machetes didn't bother to even look up. As I watched it soar away, I stood frozen.

We purchased a tour book and identified the different areas of the Machu Picchu ruins. We read that priests and virgins dedicated to the sun, comprised seventy-seven percent of the population in Machu Picchu. Sacrifices were common and what happened to the population was a mystery.

The following morning we finished our tour of the old mountain; then at 1300 the buses started their descent to the train station. As the bus descended the hill, a young boy stood along the roadside waved his arms madly and said, "Good-by, good-by." After every curve, the same boy appeared. He did this six times, made it to the bottom of the hill before us and waited at the door of the bus with his hand out for a tip. We laughed and tipped him. A man who had been here ten years previously said this was done then also.

Exhausted, and almost six months pregnant, I was ready to go home. We skipped going to Santiago, Chile and planned to fly to Lima then Los Angeles. My first child, Teri Cherie, was born three months later. This did not end my flying career. My travels through South America took me to Venezuela, Brazil, Peru, Ecuador, Columbia, and the islands off the northern coast Aruba, Trinidad and Curacao among others.

CHAPTER 13

YOU NAME IT, I'VE BEEN THERE

1
FIJIAN IDIOSYNCRASIES

The Fijian Archipelago located south of the equator in the South Pacific included over three hundred islands. The International Date Line was adjusted so that the entire archipelago fell into the same time zone. The two main islands of Fiji were Viti Levu and Vanua Levu.

We, the TIA crew, landed at Viti Levu at 1900 March 12th, 1978, and had reservations at the Sunlover Hotel in Nadi for our seven-day stay. I sat patiently outside the airport terminal seated on Big Red, unzipped my white plastic boots that had stuck to my nylons, and then kicked them off. The humility must be close to one hundred percent, I thought.

The hotel bus arrived an hour later and we began our journey to the Sunlover Hotel. Monkey pod trees in full bloom lit up the countryside with their bright orange flowers. We passed five hundred square foot grass huts, men, and women dressed in brightly colored skirts and a spectacular array of flowers.

A torrent rain shower began; we arrived at 2030 and escaped into the hotel with only seconds to spare. Actually, March was supposed to be a dry month, but not this day. The smell of food captured our attention and we abandoned our luggage to follow the smell of a spicy Indian dish.

"What is that marvelous aroma?" I asked.

"Curry," the waiter replied.

"Is the restaurant still open?" I inquired, noticing no one was seated.

"Yes," the restaurant closes in one half hour," he replied.

I glanced at the menu. A steak cost ten Fijian dollars, the curry cost five dollars and fish cost four dollars. I ordered the curry, which was exceptional. I asked for the recipe and learned that they used the meat and fish that was left over the night before and a special curry powder that I could purchase in the marketplace. The chef added a spice before serving that had little flavor but gave the curry a bright yellow appearance. It was 2100 and no one but crewmembers were visible. The Fijian people retired about eight thirty.

"What's there to do in the evening?" I asked.

"There's a Fijian dance group that travels to the hotels," he said.

"How about day time activities?" I asked.

"There's a highlander tour and a tour of the islands surrounding Fiji," he replied.

This day we joined the Highlanders bus tour. Upon our arrival on top of a lush mountain, black as coal mina birds graced our presence with loud cawing. Swatting at the many flies and mosquitoes I enjoyed the scenery from two thousand five hundred feet. Later the frogs took over for the mina birds with their melodious croaking. We rode through lush green valleys, rolling hills and a forest before we arrived at a lumberjack village. The circumference of some of the trees in this forest was thirty inches and many were forty-eight feet tall.

"It only takes twelve years for these 'dawa' trees to grow this high," our guide remarked. "An extract from the leaves is used as black hair dye. The leaves themselves are used to cure dysentery and the liquid inside the tree is used for influenza and joint pain. Many of the trees native to Fiji have medicinal purposes."

On our return to the hotel, we passed guava trees, papaya, pineapple, breadfruit, rock melon, and sugar cane. Our guide filled us in about some interesting idiosyncrasies of Fiji.

"The people of Fiji treat their cows as pets," he stated. "When you drive around the island you can see the locals walking their cows on ropes. Sometimes the cows get cow-napped. The owner of the cow would need to pay the cow napper's price or not get the cow back. The police don't do anything about this since they seem to not consider it a problem. The most prevalent religions in Fiji were Moslem and Hindu. "The red flags you see flying in front of homes show everyone that Hindus live there," our guide remarked.

He explained that the unemployment rate in Fiji was extremely high and even through Fiji became independent from Britain in 1970 little progress had been made. There was a law that stated no more than two foreigners may work in the same place of employment. It was difficult to get a work permit if you were a foreigner since the unemployment rate of the African and Indian natives was high.

If foreigners wanted to do business in Fiji, they were required to pay a high duty on everything they imported. The manager of the Sunlover Hotel (an Englishman) had a motorcycle he imported confiscated at the airport. The custom officials wouldn't release it until he paid four hundred Fijian dollars duty. The Englishman considered that excessive and the motorcycle was still held at customs during my entire stay in Fiji.

Each family in Fiji had four or five children. The children were required to attend school until the fourth grade. Only fifty-five percent of the children went on to high school and approximately twenty percent went on to college. There was only one college in Fiji, located in Nadi. That college prepared the students for the University in Suva, the capitol of Fiji.

The following day we decided to go the six miles into Nadi and then visit the town of Latoka. We saw groups of men gathered around passing a coconut shell with liquid in it.

"What are those men drinking?" I asked a shopkeeper.

"Yagona," he replied. Yagona (pronounced Yangona) was made from the root of the pepper tree. Sometimes it was called Kava. The root was pounded until soft then water was added. After it was mixed, the mixture was strained through a cloth.

Even though we'd eaten in Nadi and Latoka this day, we decided to visit another hotel and ended up in the buffet line for lack of anything else to do. This buffet consisted of tomatoes on one plate, cucumbers on another, lettuce on another, carrots on another, beets on another, and melon on another etc. Therefore, all I did was make my own salad. Curry was the main course and one condiment, chutney.

"What's the dessert?" I asked.

"The melon on the buffet is the dessert," the waiter replied.

I did enjoy the Fijian dance show. The dancers wore bright colors and leis around their necks and made music by beating sticks on the ground in unison. The firewalkers were the main attraction. The natives walked over hot coals and back, continuing an old religious ceremony. These dancers traveled to each of the hotels, and each show was the same. I visited all six hotels in Fiji and saw the show at three different hotels during my seven-day stay. It was the only show in town. I spent the majority of my evenings typing my journal excerpts on an old black typewriter located behind the reception desk.

During my stay, all my ink pens had disappeared. I'd leave one by my bed and then I'd leave the room. The maid cleaned the room and the pen disappeared. The same thing happened when I placed a pen and paper on the poolside table. I borrowed my roommate's pen and when I closed my eyes while lounging by the pool and then opened them, the pen was gone. It was a distinctive red pen.

That evening we went to dinner and asked to sign the bill to our room. I asked to borrow a pen. The pen that the waiter handed to me was the pen I'd borrowed from my roommate. I told the waiter I was keeping the pen since I had to return it to my roommate. He didn't seem to mind.

The crew returned to the United States on the seventh day well rested.

2
SEVEN DAYS IN TAHITI

February 1977, the crew landed at Papeete to begin a seven-day layover. Tahiti covered roughly five hundred square miles and was seventy-three miles long. The exterior of Tahiti was populated, but the interior was uninhabited. The Tahitians believed that ghosts haunted the interior. Few houses had electricity so the locals woke up at dawn and slept at dusk. The mornings were peaceful and warm. The afternoons were stifling.

After crew resting for two days, I called Bill in California and he joined me for the last four days of my layover. Bill made reservations and his arrival time was 0400.

"How am I going to pick him up at 0400?" I said to Libby, my roommate.

"You could rent a car," Libby replied.

I pulled out the phone book and called the rental agency. "I need an automatic small compact car to rent for one day," I said.

"We don't have automatics, only stick shifts," he replied.

"I don't know how to drive a stick," I said concerned.

Libby offered to teach me. We drove up and down the hilly terrain of Tahiti in my French rental car and to the airport for a trial run. The gray Renault jerked as I changed gears then came to a stop at the bottom of a hill. I grimaced, and looked at Libby, my sweaty palms grasped the wheel, white knuckles visible.

"You'll be fine," Libby said. "There's only one road to the airport."

I left for the airport alone at 0200. No street lights lighted the way and everything looked different. I pulled out of the hotel parking lot and headed in the right direction. Libby said that even if I headed in the wrong direction I would hit the airport eventually. I drove fifteen minutes in complete darkness. No one was on the road but me. Then I saw a bar across the road and a detour sign that pointed up into the hills. I stopped. Sometime during the day, workers had dug up this road. I followed the detour sign into the hills. I drove and drove and must have missed the other detour sign that would take me past the construction and down to the airport. At 0300, I stopped the car and thought about this dilemma. I started down the mountain toward the area where I had detoured. It was pitch black and silent. Maybe I should head back to the hotel, I thought. Then I decided to stop at a house, knock on the door, and ask directions even though it was now 0330. I stopped, stepped out of the car, walked up to a house, and knocked. I knocked again. No answer. I stood there for a while in the warm Tahitian night. Then, without warning a large white dog raced around the corner barking. I darted back to the car jumped in and locked the door. The dog followed. I sat for a moment to collect my thoughts while this vicious dog barked at me.

Shaken, I drove back to the roadblock and around the timber. Slowly and carefully, I drove the five-minute remainder to the airport. Bill waited outside the Papeete Airport terminal and I breathed a sigh of relief.

"Happy Valentines Day," Bill said handing me a red heart shaped box of See's chocolates.

"It's really good to see you," I replied during a hug. He drove to the hotel without incident and we remained awake to watch the sunrise.

Tahiti had the most beautiful white and black sand beaches. Inside the reef, the beaches were composed of pulverized white coral particles-white beaches. In those places where the reef was non-existent, high waves reached the shore breaking down the basalt rock, which formed Tahiti's foundation. The basalt rock being of volcanic origin was black; therefore, some of the beaches had black sand.

Sunday at sunrise (0530), the locals frequented the outdoor market in Papeete. We climbed aboard "le truck," gave the driver the equivalent of fifty cents and made ourselves comfortable on one of the two wooden benches. These trucks had no schedules or areas to cover so delivered us exactly where we wanted to go. A taxi cost the U.S. equivalent of one dollar a mile.

Chickens, ducks, and pigs were in front of the dusty open market.

We watched prospective chicken buyers fuss with the chickens' feathers and exchange money with the seller. A large Tahitian man dressed in a yellow tee shirt and orange shorts clasped both hands around a brown and white chubby chickens neck and twisted. The buyer walked away holding the dead chicken by its white scaly feet. Inside the market, there were stalls and florescent lights. Vegetables were in one area, fruits in another. Flies covered everything. We purchased a cluster of pineapples and a custard pie, which turned out to be mango pie and sat down on the curb to eat.

Every now and then, I noticed an interesting subject and clicked a picture. The older Tahitians loved to have their pictures taken. They laughed and posed for the camera. The small children ran when they saw me place my camera at eye level.

We wandered into a local grocery store off the beaten path and purchased a long thin loaf of french bread, pate, sausages, fruit juice and the largest bottle of beer I'd ever seen, 2.0 liters. All were local products and less than half the price of the tourist market.

Supplied with our emergency food we boarded the local ferry for Moorea a one hour forty-five minute ferry ride. I sat in the front of the thirty-five foot ferry, dangled my legs over the side, and watched the light blue sometimes-brown ten-inch flying fish jump out of the water and skim it for sometimes up to ten yards. They were the same shape as the stretch DC-8, but with the rudder bending down.

We docked in a remote area. This wasn't the tourist area since we decided to cruise on the ferry instead of the tourist ship. A group of locals boarded a bus that was waiting and bounced down the dirt road. Bill and I stood alone.

"Excuse me," a man said. "If you wouldn't mind going on my rounds I'll eventually go past the Bali Hai Hotel."

We climbed into the back of his truck and drove to homes with grass roofs while he delivered the week's supply of food. The foliage was thick on our journey and we ducked to avoid being slapped by the bushes. He'd honk his horn, chat for a while in French, and then leave for the next hut. We arrived at the Bali Hai Hotel in the afternoon.

The Bali Hai, and the Club Mediterranean were the only two hotels on Moorea. We went to the sports shop, borrowed fins, and goggles and snorkeled on the Leaky Tiki (a large raft with three musicians aboard). While the musicians played their music, we dived into the water and brought up all kinds of sea creatures. It wasn't necessary to venture beyond the shore to view the multicolored fish. I stared into the crystal clear water and there they were.

Back on shore Bill and I sat at the Bali Hai Restaurant, sipped our beverages, and enjoyed the view.

"Look!" Bill said pointing out over the water.

I looked and noticed our transportation back to Papeete cruise by. We should have had another hour before the one tourist boat of the day left the harbor; only my watch had stopped. We hitched a ride to Moorea's airport and bought an Air Tahiti airline ticket. Then we boarded a two prop, white and red aircraft and sat on one of the benches that sat two across. The ten passenger seat aircraft was full. I removed my large brim straw hat and placed it on my lap so as not to block the other passenger's view of the mountainous terrain. The following morning we departed Tahiti for Dallas, Fort Worth. Bill went home from Dallas and I continued my itinerary. I felt I had definitely made the most of this trip. We had a spectacular time in Tahiti.

Eight years after my initial trip to Tahiti, I was scheduled to fly into Papeete Airport once again. Only this time I was based in Los Angeles and commuted from San Francisco, California. Only fourteen F/A's were based in Oakland and they had all flown over twelve years.

The rush to the San Francisco Airport was over, and there was all of fifteen minutes before my commercial flight departed for Los Angeles. Since Los Angeles, was my new base in 1984, I paid for the hotel room, and the flight from San Francisco. The immediate problem was, will they; at PSA (Pacific Southwest Airlines) take my Continental ticket at the ticket counter? They did. Big Red was put thru the luggage carousal and there were seats available. I felt safe and secure. I arrived in Los Angeles at 1100.

Not all of us F/A's had such an easy time of it this day. One F/A hit heavy traffic coming from Santa Cruz and came close to missing the last flight to Los Angeles. Not only that, but on the shuttle bus from the PSA counter to our airline she left her purse. Thank goodness, all they took was her I.D. and money of which she had little. She still had her passport.

Another commercial airline lost one F/A's suitcase, but returned it to her before our TIA flight departed. Yet another F/A was in obvious distress and stood in front of the Los Angeles terminal. Four buttons popped off her uniform, no uniform belt, no makeup and she looked confused. As I arrived, a man noticed her distress and went to help. He was good enough to carry her suitcase to the ticket counter and since I was there, he carried mine. It was her birthday this day and the two and one half days off wasn't enough time to celebrate and prepare to leave again as well. Actually, commercialing into a flight was not allowed, although ninety-nine percent of us did.

We departed from Los Angeles to Papeete at 1400. There was only a two-hour time change and the guest (passenger) load factor wasn't full so besides worrying about the two-inch hole in my stocking the world looked wonderful. Our guests loved us as usual and repeatedly told us so. We arrived at Papeete Airport at 2000 local.

The hot Tahitian air filled the cabin upon arrival and I felt my uniform stick to my body. The collar was buttoned up tight around my neck with a scarf tied in a bow around the collar. I felt as if I was suffocating. As I started to untie the scarf and unbutton the blouse, a F/A said I'd better not since I wouldn't be in full uniform. There was a supervisor at the Papeete Airport this day and I would get an infraction. I also removed my father's Navy pilot wings from under my TIA wings and placed them in my purse since this also would be an infraction. The wings were special to my father and special to me as well.

Fiji and Tahiti were only two of the many islands in the South Pacific that I was blessed to visit. Bali was another of my favorites along with Kuala Lumpur.

Bill in Moorea.

3
MALAYSIA, KUALA LUMPUR

In the mid-seventies, we stayed at the Hilton, in Kuala Lumpur, which was supposed to be one of the better hotels. The hallway was dark and smelled of mildew and all the rooms were set back a few feet so that one couldn't see if someone lurked around the corner.

Once inside, the rooms appeared nice. The curtains were opened and closed by a switch located between the beds. Another switch turned on the light outside the room. The beds were comfortable and we had a refrigerator to cool our sodas. With four days to explore, my roommate, Eileen and I decided to take a private taxi around the city. The taxi was cheaper than the tour, only two Malaysian dollars. I sat in the front seat and learned that there was a fifty-dollar fine if I did not fasten my seat belts in the front seat of taxis and private cars in Malaysia.

We stopped at a Mosque, which was modeled after the one in Mecca, Saudi Arabia. Before I entered, a guard lent me a long black robe that covered my legs and arms. I later learned it was called an abaya. The Malaysian's were strict about all parts of a woman's body being covered before they entered a holy place, so pulled the black cloth over my head before entering. The Mosque was impressive with its tall white pillars and its large open spaces with marble floors. When we entered, chanting came over the loud speaker. A priest who stood in front of the large open space conducted the service.

In this open space, people knelt on the floor and bowed their heads sometimes in unison, sometimes not. We then trekked downstairs and found a dressing room where the Muslims washed their feet. Foot washing was required before praying. The Mosque was not ornate like churches in the western world. In fact it was quite plain, but distinctive and lovely in its simplicity.

In Malaysia, the women wore long colorful wrap around skirts and blouses. Sometimes only one piece of cloth was wrapped around the body and tied at the waist. Some of the men wore skirts also. Monkeys were everywhere and would eat out of our hands, which at first was fun, and then the monkeys became annoying.

On our second day, we traveled from Kuala Lumpur to Malacca, a three-hour bus ride along the coast. On our arrival, we ate at a Chinese restaurant. This restaurant was unique in that mice felt quite safe and scurried about. We didn't realize this until we had ordered. Little six inch gray mice scurried here and there. We discovered that if we stomped our feet the mice would run and hide. When we stopped stomping they would return so we would swallow a mouthful of food, then stomp our feet. This became a regular practice throughout the meal—eat and stomp, eat and stomp. After awhile this procedure became humorous. The restaurant itself looked clean. It had baskets and hats on one wall, a mural on another, and wicker furniture with lime green cushions. We finished our meal and headed for the streets of Malacca.

A trishaw driver who spoke English motioned to us. He peddled us all over Malacca for two U.S. dollars. The homes we past were two stories, but narrow and made from metal (now rusted). Tin grills seemed to be popular since they covered many of the windows. All foliage was overgrown and wild.

We chose to take a local bus back to the Hilton. We passed numerous little Hindu temples. Cleared brush was placed across four crooked vertical branches to house the altar where flowers and candles were displayed.

I enjoyed trekking through Kuala Lumpur and Malacca even though the mice and monkey population was out of control. Working as a charter F/A was a constant adventure. It was a time in my life that I will always cherish and one heck of an education.

Me in an abaya before entering a mosque in Kuala Lumpur, Malaysia.

4
USA ADVENTURES

My most preferred cities in the United States were Boston, New York City, Bangor, and Honolulu. My least favorite cities were the ones where we stayed near the airport, cities where the weather was icy cold, the main event of the week was a PTA meeting, and the TV cut out at 2300. I always enjoyed listening to the Star Spangle Banner when the stations signed off for the night, and by 1986, I had stayed in every state in the United States.

New York City

I had noticed that people all over the world were friendly, and New York City was no exception (except in a few incidences). The plays were fantastic and I enjoyed purchasing half price tickets at Times Square on Wednesdays and Saturdays for events that evening. The people in New York scurried around as if on an important mission. Waitress' who were aware of the time factor that ran New York City, tended to be rude. Once I sat in a restaurant, glanced at the menu and within seconds the waitress appeared and said; "I don't have all day, what do you want?" Some had the tendency to throw the menu and the silverware on the table and place the water glasses down so hard the water splashed out of them.

November 29th, 1975, after a twenty-four day stay in Kano, Nigeria we arrived in New York City thankful we'd landed in the good old USA. I could relate to those who kiss the ground upon arrival. I clicked on the TV to see what I'd missed since we had no means of communication in Kano except what little the inbound crews knew. During those twenty-four days, President Ford appointed George H.W. Bush head of the Central Intelligence Agency and Bush accepted. Francisco Franco, dictator of Spain died and Juan Carlos I became King of Spain, which changed Spain from a dictatorship to a democracy. Angola, a country on the southwest coast of Africa became independent. The Supreme Court of India overturned Indira Gandhi's guilty conviction of election tampering. Indonesia attacked the Portuguese oil rich colony of East Timor. Malcolm Fraser became Prime Minister of Australia, and Joe Clark became the youngest prime minister of Canada. Also, the Bureau of Meteorology began giving male as well as female names to cyclones and the telephone directory changed its classified section from pink to yellow. The world changed dramatically in only twenty-four days.

Tired, I switched from the news to "Saturday Night Live," with Howard Cosell before I called it a night. During a commercial break for Windex, I saw a bowl of apples sitting on the kitchen counter. Oh, how I craved an apple. It being late, I tried to control this craving. I hadn't had a piece of fresh fruit in twenty-four days. I stepped out of bed, put my uniform coat over my nightgown, and headed for Grand Central Station, which was one level down from the Hotel Commodore where we stayed. Five minutes later I was in front of a fruit stand in Grand Central Station. Someone was pulling the medal slider closed in front of a display.

"Please," I said. "May I buy an apple?"

" Sorry," he replied. "I've closed the cash register for the night."

"I can give you cash. I've been in Africa for the last twenty-four days and I'm ravenous for an apple."

He slid the metal slider open and placed the padlock on the counter. "That will be two dollars and fifty cents."

I scooted over to the apples and picked a big red one. "Thank you," I said putting the money on the counter. I picked up the apple and took a bite. I think this is the best tasting apple I have ever eaten, I thought.

The Hotel Commodore in New York City on 42nd Street was a happening place in the early seventies and full of surprises. Once while on an ice procuring quest I encountered a nude man between the ice machine and the elevators. I dashed back to my room.

"Let me in," I shouted.

"What's wrong?" my roommate asked.

"There's a nude man sleeping by the elevators," I said. We called security to report him, and then went together to investigate. We saw his chest rise and fall so he wasn't dead. Security arrived and lifted the nude man up on his feet.

"What are you doing here?" security asked.

"I have a room somewhere," he replied. His head hung down and his eyes were closed.

Security marched him back and forth in front of the elevators, to wake him. He woke and became quite indignant.

"I have a room here. Leave me alone," he sputtered.

He was either unaware that he was nude or simply didn't care. Then a woman opened her door, peered out and said, "There you are." She walked toward the nude man, grabbed his arm, and pulled him into her room. My roommate and I exchanged looks of astonishment before we headed back to our room for the night and laughed about the incident.

On another occasion, a F/A received a call from the New York Police Department after she returned to her domicile in Oakland, California. "Did you notice anything unusual about the room you stayed in?" NYPD asked.

"No," she replied.

The police informed her that there was a dead man found under the bed in the room she stayed in.

"I stayed in a room for twelve hours with a dead man under my bed?" she reiterated to the NYPD.

"Yes," NYPD replied. She was shocked.

After hearing this, I made it a habit to look under the bed, (except in the cockroach infested Philippines) in the closet and in the bathroom before settling in for the night. Soon after these incidents, the hotel committee changed our hotel to the Statler Hilton. In the seventies, the Hotel Commodore was condemned and torn down.

The hotel rooms the F/A's stayed in, at the Statler Hilton, were, hot, dark and dusty. The first time I stayed there the air conditioning was in-op and had been for a couple of days. It was stifling in the June heat.

Parched, I woke up numerous times to drink. It wasn't an improvement over the Hotel Commodore.

One problem the F/A's had with New York City was with people who scampered off with our purses and luggage. The crews watched over each other's suitcases and looked for strangers that might be suspicious. Once while seated in a restaurant, a man appeared, grabbed a woman's purse that hung over her chair and darted away. Later, a gaunt young man accosted a woman in front of me. Purse snatching appeared to be big business in the seventies.

When the Statler Hilton was booked, we stayed at the Prince George. On a layover at the Prince George Hotel, I stayed in the room while the maids cleaned and noticed that they didn't change the sheets.

"Aren't you going to change the sheets?" I asked.

"You don't change the sheets everyday at home do you?" the maid replied.

"No, but only I sleep on them," I said. The maid mumbled something, and then left. Later she came back with fresh sheets. . I wasn't the only F/A that had this conversation with housekeeping at the Prince George Hotel.

Florida

I used to think that everyone who worked in the United States spoke some English until I tried to order extra towels in Florida. Not one of the maids would admit to knowing what a towel was. I took a towel out of the bathroom and held it. "Mas por favor," I said.

"Que?" they would respond; so I'd locate the laundry and get them myself. This also happened in Los Angeles.

Boston

Boston, one of my favorite cities, was a college town with an extremely interesting cultural atmosphere. A little path marked by footprints on the sidewalk took tourists by parks and historical sights. The no sales tax policy was a definite draw as well.

Kentucky

A common practice of F/A's was to inquire at the front desk about what was happening in the area. The front desk usually had the inside scoop and were happy to fill us in on 'what to do and where to go.' Sometimes they drove us.

Once in Kentucky the fellow behind the reception desk drove my roommate and me to the points of interest in Louisville, Kentucky. Our first stop was Churchill Downs, the famous racetrack where the Kentucky Derby takes place every year in May. In 1976, tickets cost seventy- five to one hundred dollars to sit in the stands. If you waited outside before the Derby, tickets could be purchased for ten dollars to stand during the races. People went early to drink and party. The big race was the eighth. There were nine in all. The best three-year-old horses in the world congregated there for this eighth race.

We visited the Mammoth Caves, Fort Knox, and a bourbon brewery. At the bourbon brewery, vats fifty feet high filled the room. These vats were full of seventy percent corn and other grains mixed with yeast. The brew then was heated to one hundred seventy one degrees to evaporate the water and then it started looking like the bourbon you buy in stores. The darker the bourbon the longer it had aged. A federal office was located in the brewery to make sure they received the tax money due them.

Atlanta

After we commercialed to Atlanta, Georgia, one hot summer day in the early seventies, I set off for the front desk at the Sheraton Airport hotel. "What's happening in Atlanta tonight?" I asked.

"The Underground's a happening place," he replied. "It has numerous unique restaurants and shops."

Four crewmembers caught a taxi and headed for the Underground. We arrived and chose to eat at a fondue restaurant. The proprietor offered to take us sightseeing. He spoke about his exotic car collection. He was persistent and asked what car; we wanted to be picked up in tomorrow to go sightseeing.

"How about the yellow Rolls Royce?" I said.

He agreed and the next day appeared at our hotel driving a stunning yellow Rolls Royce convertible. We climbed in and set out to see the sights of Atlanta in style.

Three years later, I had another layover in Atlanta and called the restaurant to see if our friend was still the proprietor. He was, and this time sent a taxi to bring us to his restaurant. The taxi arrived with balloons floating in the back seat. Upon arrival, I noticed the restaurant had been redecorated in the atmosphere of a ship. We had a delicious dinner of fondue, meat from Australia, wine, and cheesecake. After dinner, he returned us to our hotel in another of his exotic cars. I believed it was a Morgan. We felt rich and famous.

Bangor

In Bangor, Maine, the change of seasons was awesome. One autumn day, I walked to town from the Twin Cities Motel and clicked pictures of the gorgeous landscape. The printed pictures were suitable to be enlarged and framed. I continued to click pictures until it began to rain. I hailed a taxi and returned to the Twin Cities Motel. I opened my wallet and noticed I had no money. Embarrassed I asked the taxi driver to wait until I cashed a check.

"Not to worry," he replied. "I got such a kick out of speaking to you there's no charge."

I smiled and thanked him.

Bangor was a routine fuel stop on the way to Europe so the Twin Cities Motel was full of TIA people. We'd get together for dinner in one of the rooms that had an oven and refrigerator. Eating a home cooked meal was a treat after being away from home for a week or two. This was also where we gossiped, caught up on the news, and voiced opinions. We'd spend hours sewing Christmas ornaments, teaching each other how to crochet and knit, braid hair, do makeup and sometimes cut and colored each other's hair.

However, not everything was wonderful in Bangor. Once when hitch hiking back from town with my roommate a car stopped, my roommate walked over to the car to tell the man we had decided to walk the mile and a half back to the hotel. She looked into the car and noticed he didn't have pants on, any pants. Before he had the chance to disappear down the road, my roommate managed to take down the license number and called the police. She was so upset that she planned to fly to Bangor on her days off for the trial since she thought he should be prosecuted. This didn't happen though since Trans International F/A's never know when they will be home for sure so it was impossible to set a court date.

On another layover at the Twin Cities, I had a room to myself. The crew needed to carry their luggage up the stairs since there were no elevators so I asked for a room on the first floor. This was one place I felt safe on the first floor.

Hearing pounding, I was awakened at 0300.

"What do you want?" I asked the person pounding on my door.

"Matches," a male voice replied.

"I don't smoke, I don't have any matches," I replied. "Go to the front desk and get matches."

He pounded so hard on the door that the button that locked the door popped out. This terrified me, as there were no other locks on the door. I jumped out of bed and grabbed a lamp to hit him with if he got in. My voice went up several octaves and I sounded like Minnie Mouse as I called for help. Suddenly there was silence and I went to the phone to call security. A few minutes later, someone knocked lightly on the door. I asked a few question so to make sure it was security. When I was convinced it was, I opened the door and let him in. He said he didn't see anyone in the hall or at my door. He did see a fire extinguisher that had been taken out of its bracket and was in front of my door. Marks were on the door where the man had pounded on it with the fire extinguisher. I moved to a room on a higher floor and spent the rest of the night wide-awake. I no longer felt safe in Bangor, Maine.

Chicago

I was eating an Abba Zabba taffy candy bar in Chicago, when the double bridge on the lower left side of my mouth fell out. We were scheduled to leave for Frankfurt, Germany in six hours. I reached for the phonebook to locate a dentist who was close to the O'Hare Int'l Airport where we stayed.

"I'm scheduled to fly to Europe in five hours and my lower left bridge has fallen off," I said. "I'm at the Royal Court Hotel by the airport."

"My office is only a few blocks from the Royal Court," the dentist replied. "Today's my day off, but come on in and I'll take care of it."

I chose to walk since it was only a few blocks. I headed out and discovered it was closer to four miles away. Concerned with the time and with no taxis in sight I jogged to the dentist office and arrived out of breath. The dentist checked the area and cemented the bridge back on. He charged me ten dollars and drove me back to the Royal Court Hotel. I thanked him.

I was relieved that it wasn't necessary to call Oakland and go on sick leave. There were no other crewmembers in Chicago at the time to replace me. The passengers would have been delayed since there must be a certain number of F/A's on board before takeoff. Later I found, that having no teeth on one side of your mouth wasn't an acceptable reason for sick leave.

The Royal Court Hotel in Chicago was where the bellhops gave my roommate and me a lesson in how easy it was to break into a room. We locked the door and put the chain up. He unlocked the door and reached in with a small screwdriver and removed the screws from the lock attached to the wall. From then on, I slept with my luggage wheels in front of the door to awaken me.

On another occasion at the Royal Court in Chicago, I was exposed to the swarming habits of termites. The room looked normal when my roommate and I entered, but when we turned off the lights we could feel and hear something flying about the room. We turned on the lights, but all was still and quiet. We turned off the lights and the sound of buzzing insects was apparent again.

We were confused by the mystery and decided to capture whatever it was. Ready to ambush the insects I stood by the table lamp and turned it off. My roommate stood ready with hands out close to the buzzing bugs. It worked. A few were captured. We placed them in a water glass, covered it with a tissue, and then placed a rubber band around the top. We carried them to the front desk for inspection and found them to be termites. A swarm of nocturnal termites had hatched in our room. We packed and moved to a termite free room on the other side of the hotel.

Anchorage, Alaska

Crews stayed in Anchorage, Alaska often. It was a lovely city in winter but oh so cold. Sometimes the temperature went down to thirty degrees below zero with the wind chill factor. I stuck my wet pointer finger out the door once to conduct an experiment. It felt frozen before I could pull it back in again.

During one layover in Anchorage, a crewmember called a friend who lived there. He had a motor home and invited the crew to travel around Alaska with him. At 1400, we started roaming around the countryside. We stopped at a little bar called the 'Bird House.' Hundreds of business cards were nailed to the walls of this tiny bar, the tables, the floor and under the glass bar top. We left the birdhouse at 2100 and headed for the mountains where we ran out of gas. One of the fellows agreed to walk to a gas station, while the rest of us remained in the camper. He returned with the gas after midnight. It was still light outside since the sun circled the horizon in June. We returned to the Holiday Inn at 0600. I wasn't exhausted and I attributed it to the fact that it was still light.

The crews used to store items in the baggage room of the Holiday Inn when we had multiple crossings. This was especially nice during the Christmas shopping season. Only, one Christmas in the mid seventies the employees of the Holiday Inn in Anchorage decided to do their Christmas shopping in the Holiday Inn baggage room.

"Where's my shopping bag with my Christmas presents, that I left here last week?" I asked the bellhop.

"I have no idea," the bellhop replied.

I went to the front desk and asked for my items. Someone behind the desk replied, "What do you expect leaving nice items in storage."

"Then someone stole my stuff," I said. He didn't argue with my statement. I had a list of the items I'd taken through customs so threatened to take him to small claims court if he didn't give them back. This never happened however since I'd need to fly to Anchorage for the small claims hearing and I couldn't plan any specific date to schedule since I never knew when I'd be home. I was disillusioned with the personnel at the Anchorage Holiday Inn and didn't trust any hotel with my personal items after that experience.

Hawaii

The crews stayed at the Kuhio Hotel outside the International Market Place in the early seventies. A conflict between Hawaii's natives and the State Government to allow real estate development on sacred ancient Hawaiian grounds (cemeteries) occurred in the early seventies. The Kahuna Priests didn't bless some of the hotels for this reason. The land the Kuhio was built on was never blessed and some said that the Kuhio was 'haunted'. The F/A's joked about it, but I never saw any ghosts. Later this hotel was renamed the Miramar.

One of the F/A's' favorite restaurants was the "Pieces of Eight," in downtown Honolulu. Dinner cost about eight dollars and included a salad bar with fresh pineapple and warm breads. F/A's received a free bottle of wine with their meals.

One Christmas in Honolulu a friend invited the crew for Christmas dinner. He'd prepared all the traditional fixings, turkey, dressing, salads, mashed potatoes and more. Honolulu was my second home.

Fred, a pilot and friend, owned a single engine seaplane docked at Honolulu Airport. I was co-pilot for the thirty-minute flight to Molokai from Honolulu one bright sunny afternoon. Bill was the only passenger. We began our descent onto the ocean and landed with several thumps and bumps. When we stopped and were floating, Fred started the engine and we scooted onto the shore. After a short stay, we waded out to the seaplane and departed from the water. It was quite bumpy as we gained speed and bounced across the waves before lifting up into the sky. This was the one and only time I experienced landing on water. It was a refreshingly different experience.

On another occasion in Honolulu, my roommate and I heard noises coming from the room next door. It sounded like someone was being beaten. We called the front desk. Security knocked on our door after they checked out our complaint and told us that a man and wife were next door and they couldn't interfere. Security mentioned the wife had a cut on her forehead and her husband said she'd fallen off a chair. The wife didn't say anything.

Moments later there was a tap on our door. It was our neighbor. He was annoyed since we called security and wanted us to open the door and discuss it. We wouldn't open the door and he went away.

All was quiet until we heard a noise on our balcony and went to investigate. We were on the fifth floor. To our surprise, our neighbor had one leg over our balcony railing. After latching the lock, we tore out of the room and darted into the first open room and called security. Security remained with us until we packed and headed off to our new room on the seventh floor. We heard our old neighbor checked out of the hotel.

Guam

Rarely, crews stayed at the Guam Continental Hotel. During one of my flights a serviceman gave me his name and address and said if I were ever in Guam to give him a call and he would give me a tour of the Polaris Submarine, USS Sam Houston.

I arrived at the Guam Continental and attempted to make that call. The phone system wasn't good in Guam and it took me an hour to reach him. He remembered me and I mentioned that I'd like to take him up on his offer to see the submarine. He said I could bring as many friends as I liked, but they needed to have U.S. passports. Passports were checked since the USS Sam Houston was top secret. There were fifteen crewmembers interested. I called him to ask if this were too many and there was silence. We cut the group down to ten, rented a van, and set off for Anderson AFB.

Since all ten of us couldn't fit in the narrow submarine hallways, it was necessary to tour in two groups. The length of the USS Sam Houston was four hundred ten feet and its maximum depth was in excess of four hundred feet. It carried sixteen missile tubes and one could blow up an entire city. The missiles were moved by pulleys to insure they were agile, and programmed by computer.

There were one hundred thirty-six men stationed aboard the USS Sam Houston. Most slept on cots that folded down from the wall in the hallways. Officers had six feet by six feet rooms. Later we were invited for lunch in the mess hall. While seated we heard a loud bell over a loud speaker. The door to the mess hall slid shut. There was something amiss. Two crewmembers entered through a sliding side door with black guns in their hands. They ran past us and out another sliding door. I felt like I was participating in an action adventure movie. It was a spine tingling situation. Moments later, we the visitors were informed that the ship had lost power from the ship to shore connection. It was a security precaution for all crewmembers to go to their emergency station with their weapons just in case. Our tour ended shortly thereafter. We followed the lead of our submarine tour guide and climbed the ladders back up until we emerged and once again could see the sky and breath fresh air. This was a dramatic and informative look into the life of a sailor.

I am so grateful to have had the privilege to experience these and other wonderful cities throughout the United States. Others that chartered Trans International during my fourteen years with them included:

Forty-niner fans from Oakland to Super Bowl XVI; The Irish Power Lifting Team on route to the Championship in Dallas; Trade Missions to Africa; Around the World Air Cruise; All First Class Charters by Saab Fairchild to Sweden; The 1981 Oakland Raiders champions to their football game in Dallas; four hundred seventy-five women bowlers to the Women's International Bowling Congress in Las Vegas; Over two hundred Roman Catholic Pilgrims to Lourdes, France to attend the 42nd International Eucharistic Congress; Athletes to the Goodwill Games founded by Ted Turner; Jet Save party flights and Pleasant Hawaiian Holiday flights. Flying with Trans International was the opposite of boring.

5
THE END OF AN ERA

In the summer of 1983, I heard from the Trans International ground representative that TIA lost their contract to Seoul to the Flying Tigers charter airline and lost their contract to Kadena to Northwest Orient. We also heard that TIA had no flights scheduled out of Oakland so furlough notices were sent out Sept 1st, 1983. I was three months pregnant at this time and had already put in for maternity leave. In Oakland, all F/A's except for the top fourteen would be furloughed. The furlough would include all but one hundred F/A's in New York, forty-six in Houston and all but forty-six in St. Louis. This was the beginning of the end.

In April 1984, Trans International (Transamerica) attempted to start a new competitive airline (Transinternational) and phase out the old. This was due to Transamerica Corporation's demand that Trans International employees accept a wage cut of up to sixty percent. The airline pilots association (ALPA) came to the rescue and hired Corporate Campaign, Inc. to get us a fair deal. With CCI's help the Civil Aeronautics Board denied Trans International (Transamerica) the right to start up a new airline.

A recall of sixty Oakland based F/A's became effective July 17th, 1984 and a new base in Los Angeles was opened. This was only a short-term recall to complete summer contracts. I was asked to pick up my manual, airline ID, Geneva Convention Card, and home study packet before recurrent training class on either July 10th or July 17th, 1984.

Oakland crew scheduling called F/A's from the bottom of the seniority list to take trips. I being at the top of the seniority list wasn't called for any flights. I still received a base paycheck every two weeks. This worked to my advantage since I had an eighteen-month baby girl and husband at home along with being four months pregnant with my second child. Furlough notices were sent out again on August 20th, 1984 and were effective September 11th, 1984. Furloughed F/A's were once again told to return the airline ID cards, manuals, and Geneva Convention Cards.

October 10th, 1984 I received a letter stating that my bid for my new domicile in Los Angeles was confirmed. I went on maternity leave and January 27th, 1985 my son William Robert was born.

September 30th, 1986 Trans International Airlines (Transamerica Airlines) went bankrupt.

It's difficult to express how it feels to look back on what seemed at the time, to be a day in the life of a charter flight attendant and glimpse the bigger picture. Not many could relate to the experiences except other charter flight attendants. The experiences didn't fit into normal conversations since the experiences were so unusual.

Times have changed from when charter airlines were called "non skeds," and only flew when all the seats were sold on the flight. At Trans International's peak, they had a fleet of thirty-seven aircraft. They flew to every continent and in advertising boosted of flying anyone or anything, from passengers, to polar bears, to cases of pastrami. I was extremely fortunate to be part of this organization.

Before boarding my last group of passengers headed for Moffet Field in California, I removed a burp bag from the seat pocket in front of me and began to write on it as I'd done so many times before:

"How appropriate, writing the last chapter of my journal on the back of a burp bag. It seemed my thoughts had become reality. When the crew entered the aircraft for the last time, on the galley wall, written in masking tape was; 'The End Of An Era.' This brought back many memories. I was never so happy as the times I flew the route from Travis AFB, to Hawaii, to Clark AFB in the Philippines, once a month. I had friends in all those places. I knew when I'd be home and the weather was usually nice.

I must have eaten a hundred cases of tuna fish on the line, during my fourteen years with Trans International. Eaten usually in the middle of the night alone in the bathroom while my roommate slept, so that I wouldn't awaken her. Carefully draining the oil into the toilet and flushing it away. I can't say that I've regretted any of it. Us old die-hard F/A's are now being forced to move on to new things. I am one of the lucky ones. I have a husband, daughter, and son."

"The passengers are here," a fellow crewmember just said.

"I'm off to my door to greet them."

The end of an era. My fathers navy wings are pinned under my TIA flight wings.

My family 1987.

*I wish to extend a special thank you to
my mother and Dale Aycock.
Without my mother, Patricia Fletcher Swensens'
enjoyment of my correspondence
and Dale's way with words, my memories
would have remained my memories.*

To Order additional copies, send $28.95 hard cover, or $19.95 soft cover, plus $3.00 shipping and handling to:

McAlister, Inc.
926 East Fremont Ave.
Sunnyvale, CA 94087

Or email planeanxiety@aol.com with your visa number, expiration date, and mailing address.